Economic Theory and Global Warming

In this book, Professor Uzawa modifies and extends the theoretical premises of orthodox economic theory to make them broad enough for analyzing the phenomena related to environmental disequilibrium – particularly global warming – and finding institutional arrangements and policy measures that may bring about a more optimal state in which the natural and institutional components are harmoniously blended. He constructs a theoretical framework in which three major global environmental issues may effectively be addressed. First, all global environmental phenomena exhibit externalities of one kind or another. Secondly, global environmental issues involve international and intergenerational equity and justice. Thirdly, global environmental issues concern the management of the atmosphere, the oceans, water, soil, and other natural resources and need to be addressed through a consensus of all affected countries.

Hirofumi Uzawa is Director of the Research Center of Social Overhead Capital at Doshisha University and Emeritus Professor of Economics at the University of Tokyo and Niigata University. In a teaching career spanning more than four decades, he has also taught at Stanford University, the University of California at Berkeley, the University of Chicago, Cambridge University, the University of Minnesota, and the University of Pennsylvania. Professor Uzawa is a Fellow and former President of the Econometric Society and a former President of the Japan Association for Economics and Econometrics. He is a Fellow of the American Academy of Arts and Sciences, a Foreign Associate of the U.S. National Academy of Sciences, a Foreign Honorary Member of the American Economic Association, and a Member of the Japan Academy.

Professor Uzawa has also been a Fellow at the Center for Advanced Study in the Behavioral Sciences at Stanford as well as an Overseas Fellow of Churchill College, Cambridge, and he has served for more than 30 years as Senior Advisor in the Research Institute of Capital Formation at the Development Bank of Japan.

Professor Uzawa has been one of the leading economic theorists of the past four decades. His contributions to economics cover virtually every branch of the field, ranging from the pure theory of consumer behavior to the duality theory of production and capital, general equilibrium theory, endogenous theory of technical progress, two-sector analysis of capital accumulation, optimal growth theory, and the theory of social overhead capital. In recent decades he has become particularly well known for applied research in the areas of the economics of pollution, environmental disruption, and global warming as well as the economics of education and medical care.

Professor Uzawa is the author of numerous articles in the world's leading economics journals and of more than twenty books, including *Preference, Production, and Capital: Selected Papers of Hirofumi Uzawa* (Cambridge University Press, 1988). Twelve volumes of his papers were collected and published in Japanese in 1994–5. He is the recipient of the Matsunaga Prize (1969), the Yoshino Prize (1970), and the Mainichi Prize (1974). The government of Japan designated him a Person of Cultural Merit in 1983, and the Emperor of Japan conferred the Order of Culture upon him in 1997.

Economic Theory and Global Warming

HIROFUMI UZAWA

CAMBRIDGE
UNIVERSITY PRESS

CAMBRIDGE
UNIVERSITY PRESS

University Printing House, Cambridge CB2 8BS, United Kingdom

One Liberty Plaza, 20th Floor, New York, NY 10006, USA

477 Williamstown Road, Port Melbourne, VIC 3207, Australia

314-321, 3rd Floor, Plot 3, Splendor Forum, Jasola District Centre, New Delhi - 110025, India

103 Penang Road, #05-06/07, Visioncrest Commercial, Singapore 238467

Cambridge University Press is part of the University of Cambridge.

It furthers the University's mission by disseminating knowledge in the pursuit of education, learning and research at the highest international levels of excellence.

www.cambridge.org
Information on this title: www.cambridge.org/9780521066594

First published 2003
First paperback edition 2009

A catalogue record for this publication is available from the British Library

Library of Congress Cataloging in Publication data
Uzawa, Hirofumi, 1928–
Economic theory and global warming / Hirofumi Uzawa.
p. cm.
Includes bibliographical references and index.
ISBN 0-521-82386-2
1. Air – Pollution – Economic aspects. 2. Global warming – Mathematical models.
3. Equilibrium (Economics) 4. Economics, Mathematical. I .Title.
HC79.A4U93 2003
363.738'74 – dc21 2002042901

ISBN 978-0-521-82386-9 Hardback
ISBN 978-0-521-06659-4 Paperback

Contents

List of Tables and Figures

Preface

The unremitting processes of industrialization and urbanization in the last several decades have disrupted and destabilized the global environment to a degree unprecedented in the history of mankind. Not only have global environmental issues such as global warming, acid rain, the loss of biodiversity, pollution of the oceans, and desertification become real threats to the stability of the environmental equilibrium, but they also tend to impair economic development in many developing countries and to lower the welfare of people in all future generations decisively.

The processes by which global environmental issues have arisen are interwoven with natural, historical, cultural, social, and political factors, but the predominant forces behind them are economic. Any analysis of environmental issues must involve a careful examination of the economic motives behind the activities responsible for the disruption of the natural environment, and any institutional arrangements or policy measures intended to restore environmental equilibrium must take into account the resulting economic impact on human activities.

Global environmental issues have three aspects that have not been satisfactorily addressed by orthodox economic theory until quite recently.

First, all phenomena involved with global environmental issues exhibit externalities of one kind or another. That is, as is typical with the case of global warming, what each individual decides to do is affected by the behavior of other members of the society, and vice versa.

The questions of externalities certainly are of great interest to the economist as exemplified by Cecil Pigou's classic work *The Economics of Welfare* (Pigou 1925) and Paul Samuelson's seminal paper, "The Pure Theory of Public Expenditures" (Samuelson 1954). However, externalities had been regarded as exceptional and put aside as something of an anomaly until the problems of environmental disruption became one of the focal issues in economic theory.

Secondly, global environmental issues involve international and intergenerational equity and justice. Although global environmental issues arise chiefly as the result of economic activities in developed countries, it is the people in developing countries who have to bear the burden. By the same token, the current generation may enjoy spurious benefits from the economic activities that cause environmental disruption, but it is the people in all future generations who will suffer from the consequences of the current generation's economic activities. The problems of equity and justice were among the focuses of classical economists such as Adam Smith and John Stuart Mill. However, the classical and neoclassical economists failed to construct the theoretical framework in which problems related to equity and justice can be examined satisfactorily. It was only in 1951, when Kenneth Arrow's seminal work, *Social Choice and Individual Values* was published (Arrow 1951), that the problems of equity and justice were congruently discussed.

Thirdly, global environmental issues concern the management of the atmosphere, the oceans, water, soil, and other natural resources and must therefore be addressed by the consensus of all the countries involved. Traditional economic theory primarily concerns the working of a competitive market system in which the allocation of scarce resources and the distribution of incomes are largely determined by price mechanism. The recent development of game theory, however, enables us to examine in detail the more general circumstances under which several individuals or countries are involved in conflicting activities and a set of definite rules and binding constraints are observed. Global environmental issues are precisely the problems to which the conceptual framework and analytical apparatuses of game theory may be applied effectively.

The present study is an offshoot of my attempt to modify and extend the theoretical premises of orthodox economic theory to make them broad enough to analyze the phenomena of environmental disequilibrium, particularly global warming, and to find the institutional arrangements and policy measures that will bring about the optimum state of affairs in which the natural and institutional components are blended together harmoniously to realize the idealistic stationary state, or the sustainable state if I use the terminology fashionable today, as eloquently prophesied by John Stuart Mill in his classic *Principles of Political Economy* (Mill 1848). I have particularly endeavored to construct a theoretical framework in which the three major problems relating global environmental issues just described may be answered effectively. However, the problems identified here have turned out to be much more difficult than I originally anticipated. This book, therefore, presents the results of my endeavor, albeit in a very preliminary stage, in a form that may be accessible to colleagues and students interested in environmental economics as well as in economic theory in general. Each chapter is presented in such a manner, occasionally at the risk of repetition, that it may be read without knowledge of other chapters. I wish that young economists with competent analytical skill and deep concern with the welfare of future generations will follow the lead suggested and develop a full-fledged theory of the global environment with particular reference to global warming.

Most of the work for this study was done at the Beijer Institute of Ecological Economics in the Royal Swedish Academy of Sciences. I would like to express my sincerest gratitude to Karl-Göran Mäler, Director of the Institute, and the Institute staff for the intellectual stimuli and generous hospitality they have extended to me at the Institute.

I would like to acknowledge with gratitude the valuable comments and suggestions made by several economists as well as researchers specializing in earth sciences. They are too numerous to cite here, but I would like to name a few among them: Kenneth J. Arrow, Kazumi Asako, Partha Dasgupta, Yuko Hosoda, Dale W. Jorgenson, Morio Kuninori, Mohan Munasinghe, Robert M. Solow, and Katsuhisa Uchiyama. I would also like to thank the readers of the original manuscript, who made thoughtful and detailed comments and suggestions.

Generous support, financial and otherwise, from the Japanese Ministry of Education and Science, the Japan Academy, the Development

Bank of Japan, the Asahi Glass Foundation, and the Nissan Foundation for the Advancement of Science is gratefully acknowledged.

Finally, but not the least, I would like to acknowledge with gratitude the patience and encouragement that my wife, Hiroko, and other members of my family have extended to me while I have been engaged in the study and research of economic theory in general and global warming in particular during the last 40 years.

Introduction

Global Warming: Problems and Perspectives

1. INTRODUCTION

The relations between the environment and processes of economic development have in recent years become increasingly complex. This is primarily due to the accelerated pace of economic development in many parts of the world in the last several decades, as manifested by the rapid rates at which basic statistical indicators such as gross domestic product, the volumes of industrial outputs, and the degree of urbanization have been increasing (see, e.g., World Bank 1999). This phenomenon is also closely related to the institutional arrangements, both in capitalist and former socialist countries, concerning the allocation of both privately owned and publicly managed resources.

During the last three decades, in particular, we have also seen a significant change in the nature of the social, economic, and cultural impacts on the natural environment during the processes of economic development. This is symbolically illustrated by the agendas of two international conferences convened by the United Nations – the Stockholm Conference in 1972, on the one hand, and the Rio Conference in 1992, on the other.

The Stockholm Conference was primarily concerned with the degradation of the natural environment and the ensuing health hazards caused by the processes of industrialization during the 1960s. Then the degradation of the natural environment was mainly caused by the emission of chemical substances such as sulfur oxides and nitrogen oxides that by themselves are toxic and hazardous to human health and the biological environment. In the Rio Conference, on the other hand, the main agenda focused on the degradation and destabilization of the global environment such as global warming, the loss of biodiversity, desertification, and other global environmental issues stemming from intensified industrialization and extended urbanization. These effects are primarily caused by the emission of carbon dioxide and other chemical substances that by themselves are neither harmful to the natural environment nor hazardous to human health but at the global scale cause atmospheric instability and other serious environmental disruption.

The impact of global environmental degradation is most painfully felt by developing nations because agriculture and related sectors of the economy are the most sensitive to changes in climatic and ecological conditions due to global warming. Institutional arrangements and policy measures intended to remedy environmental degradation also are most likely to have an adverse effect on developing nations or those whose income levels are low, for that matter. Traditional economic theory is not particularly well-suited to handle these problems, which are primarily concerned with distributional equity and ethics – from intergenerational and international perspectives.

The changing environmental impact of the processes of economic development has forced us to reexamine the basic premises of economic theory in general and environmental economics in particular, and to search for a theoretical framework in which the mechanisms interweaving the natural and social environments with processes of industrialization and urbanization are more closely analyzed, and their social and policy implications more explicitly brought out. We are particularly concerned with the processes of economic development sustainable with respect to the natural environment and within the market economy and the analysis of the institutional arrangements and policy measures under which the processes of sustainable development may ensue. Such institutional arrangements are generally defined in terms of property right assignments to various natural resources with specific reference to the behavioral criteria for those social institutions and organizations that manage various natural and common resources.

One of the obvious implications of the changing environmental impacts on economic processes in the last three decades is that economic incentives on the part of individual members of society are primarily replied on, and direct social control or coercion are neither effective in solving global environmental problems nor desirable from social and cultural points of view.

Abating Global Warming

Global warming evolves gradually, and the damage spreads widely – both geographically and over time. Global warming thus poses serious problems of ethics and justice from international and integenerational perspectives. Particularly serious questions have been raised by d'Arge, Schultze, and Brookshire (1982), Lind (1982a,b), Cline (1992a,b, 1993), and others about the appropriateness of standard approaches such as the theory of dynamic optimum or cost–benefits analysis. As typically stated in Cline (1992c), their argument is based primarily on the presupposition that the scientific predictions involve such a serious degree of uncertainty that any substantial action of abatement today that incurs significant costs would not be warranted. They went further by observing that, even if the scientific predictions were entirely correct, the greenhouse effect would simply be too insignificant in economic terms to warrant such preventive efforts, as emphasized by Nordhaus (1982, 1993a,b) and others.

A strong consensus, however, is now emerging among economists and government officials in many countries that control of human-generated greenhouse gases would yield a global public good. Because unilateral approaches are unlikely to be sufficient, international solutions must be sought, as emphasized by Barrett (1990) and Hoel (1991, 1992), although the likely existence of free riders may make such international agreements or conventions extremely difficult to implement, as pointed out by Hoel (1994).

As argued by Rosenzweig and Parry (1994), the benefits and costs are not uniformly distributed across nations. The developing countries, especially island nations, would suffer most primarily because the damage due to global warming tends to be most serious for agriculture, fisheries, and related industries. Still they are not the ones who emit large amounts of greenhouse gases. Regional differences in the impact of global warming are so significant that reaching an international agreement becomes almost impossible. Although regions with a cold climate might generally benefit from global warming, the Scandinavian countries, such as Sweden and Norway, would greatly suffer from a significant decrease in temperature because the warm Gulf Stream would stray away from the Scandinavian Peninsula.

The burdens of controlling greenhouse gases will be felt more severely in developing nations than developed nations, as examined in detail by Whally and Wigle (1991). Arid regions generally tend to become more arid, making an ever greater portion of land infertile desert. Generally speaking, food production in developing countries would significantly decrease with the advent of global warming, and consequently a serious food crisis during the twenty-first century would almost certainly arise.

Mendelsohm, Nordhaus, and Shaw (1994) have estimated that the damages in the United States would be slight because higher-valued crops could be substituted for the more vulnerable crops currently being cultivated. Their estimates are based on an optimistic presupposition that farmers in the United States would employ all the possible strategies to adapt to changes in climatic conditions, which is an assumption too optimistic even for the most rational and enterprising American farmers.

Contrary to the optimistic estimates of Mendelsohm et al. (1994), the estimates for the magnitude of the damages to farmers in the developing countries are pessimistic. According to Rosenzweig and Parry (1994), for example, farmers in developing nations would suffer greatly from global warming.

The Commons

The idea that the problems of externalities may best be solved within the conceptual framework of the theory of the commons was strongly criticized as the "tragedy of the commons" as originally put forth by Lloyd (1833) and elaborated by Hardin (1968). The "tragedy of the commons" dispute was followed by numerous contributions to the search for those institutional arrangements whereby the "tragedy of the commons" might effectively be avoided. Among them, there are two influential papers, each of an entirely opposite view: Scott Gordon's study of the commons in the marine fishing industry (Gordon 1954) and Ronald Coase's classic paper (Coase 1960).

The institutions of the commons have been much criticized by some economists such as Demsetz (1967), Furubotn and Pejovich (1972), and Godwin and Shepard (1979) among others. A typical statement is the following one made by Demsetz (1967, pp. 354–5):

> Suppose that land is communally owned. Every person has the right to hunt, till, or mine the land. This form of ownership fails to concentrate the cost associated with any person's exercise of his communal right on that person. If a person seeks to maximize the value of his communal "right," he will tend to overhunt and overwork the land because some of the costs of his doing so are borne by others. The stock of game and the richness of the soil will be diminished too quickly.

It is difficult to find the commons described by Demsetz. The commons of the barbarian age might have matched his conception, if we use the terminology of another Chicago economist, Thorstein Veblen (1899), but it is extremely difficult to find such commons in modern times. Any commons would have a set of rules governing the way members might use the common property resources to ensure that they would be sustained for a long time, as documented in detail by McCay and Acheson (1987) and Berkes (1989).

Contrary to the arguments presented by Demsetz and others, more reasonable and sane views were forcefully put forward by Sen (1973), Dasgupta (1982b), Cornes and Sandler (1983), Leggett (1990), Uzawa (1992b), Barrett (1994), and others.

However, Demsetz's criticism is valid regarding the earth's atmosphere – the largest commons all the people on the earth share. As Barrett (1994) has pointed out, the theoretical arguments for supposing that international cooperation for the stabilization of the earth's atmosphere will not develop are compelling, but they can hardly be complete. Cooperation occasionally take place, as the successful case of the *Montreal Protocol on Substances That Deplete the Ozone Layer, 1987* illustrates.

Coase's Theorem

Coase (1960) argued that the institutions of private property rights would induce an efficient allocation of scarce resources. Coase's theorem, however, was derived under the presupposition that the wealth effect is zero and that there are no transaction costs. Coase's arguments are based on the proposition that, if the conditions of private ownership were to prevail, the result would be the same whether polluters had to compensate the victims of pollution for the damage suffered or the victims had to pay to the polluters to induce them to stop the operation or to clean the polluted air, soil, or water. We understand that Coase's theorem was intended to point out the unethical and unrealistic basis of neoclassical economic theory, but it actually was often understood differently, as in Demsetz (1967).

Coase's presuppositions that the wealth effect is zero and that there are no transaction costs are critically related to the theoretical framework of neoclassical economic theory. They in particular preclude the existence of social overhead capital. The earth's atmosphere is one of the more crucial components of social overhead capital, and the analysis of global warming begins with the recognition that social overhead capital generally precludes private ownership arrangements, but not necessarily. When the rights to utilize social overhead capital itself or the services derived from it are assigned to individual members of the society, the central issue is how to realize the pattern of allocation and the resultant distribution of welfare in a way that will be acceptable in terms of the prevailing sense of equity and social justice.

As pointed out by Bromley (1995), when wealth effects exist, the initial assignment of property rights is crucial in determining the welfare distribution of outcome, as is precisely the case with global warming. The world faces a genuine choice to be made among alternative future climates, as argued, for example, by Rosenberg et al. (1989).

Regarding the principle to judge the distribution of welfare among individual members of a society under the presence of public goods in the Samuelsonian sense or of social overhead capital in general, an important role is played by the concept of the Lindahl solution, which was originally introduced by Lindahl in his classic paper (Lindahl 1919). The Lindahl solution is realized when the amount of public goods or social overhead capital actually provided by a society is precisely equal to the amount that each member of the society wishes to have under the budgetary constraints each member is subject to.

Many contributions have since been made to reinforce the proposition that the concept of the Lindahl solution concretely formulates the sense of equity and social justice prevailing in society. It has turned out, however, in the case of the market for tradable emission permits, that the Lindahl solution has a tendency to reinforce rather than to mitigate the inequality in the initial distribution of welfare among individual members of the society. Because the concept of the Lindahl solution is defined so esoterically as to abscure this basic property of the Lindahl solution, only a few thoughtful economists have noticed it and made oral comments about it. Indeed, this observation will be one of the major conclusions in Chapter 3, where the function of markets for tradable emission permits will be examined in detail.

Policy Instruments for Global Warming

As argued by Bertram (1992), the institutional and policy arrangements to curtail the emission of greenhouse gases may be categorized into three types: direct quantitative emission restrictions, carbon taxes, and tradable emission permits.

Direct quantitative emission restrictions are not only ineffective in abating the processes of global warming but also tend to obstruct the freedom of individuals only to enlarge the domain of bureaucratic control. The primary policy instruments now are environmental taxes, such as carbon taxes, and markets for tradable emission permits or some other form of pricing scheme by which market institutions in a broader sense may effectively bring in to play the role of allocative mechanisms. With respect to global warming and other global environmental issues, these problems were extensively examined by Markusen (1975a,b), Warr (1983), Bergstrom, Blume, and Varian (1986), and Copeland and Taylor (1986), among others.

Several policy instruments have been proposed by Grubb and Schenius (1992), Hoel (1991), Pearce (1991), Victor (1991), Rose and Stevens (1993), and Weyant (1993) to combat the greenhouse effect, and theoretical analyses have been developed by Poterba (1991) of carbon taxes and by Tietenberg (1985, 1992), Barrett (1990), Barrett et al. (1992), and Bertram (1992) of tradable emission permits. Hoel (1991) and Pearce (1991) have proposed levying a uniform carbon tax and then distributing targeted reimbursements. However, the underlying assumption is that there is an international agency that can be relied on to do this efficiently.

As argued by Grubb (1989), of all the instruments examined, the system of tradable emission permits may be the most promising. It is flexible in operation and efficient in abating global warming. Bertram, Stephens, and Wallace (1989) argued that a global system to regulate greenhouse gas emissions over timespans of several decades should start from a strong presumption in favor of the long-term property right of the world population to inhabit a sustainable global ecosystem.

As pointed out by Bertram (1992), the concept of tradable emission permits emerged from a theoretical debate over the economics of externalities (Dales 1968 and Baumol and Oates 1988). Bertram et al. (1989) argued that a world-wide system of tradable mission permits could be an effective way of advancing the interests of developing countries in harmony with the global community's interest in protecting the atmosphere. This view was expounded on and reinforced by Grubb (1989, 1990), Hoel (1991), and others.

The main advantages of the institution of markets for tradable emission permits are their ability to achieve environmental aims with a minimal bureaucratic apparatus. The central problem with most such schemes is determining the initial allotment of tradable emission permits. The costs of alternative permit allocations have tentatively been calculated by Larsen and Shah (1992, 1994) and others.

The reliance on market institutions and private incentives, however, may occasionally bring about unstable and socially unjust outcomes in the distribution of income, both nominal and real. The consequences are particularly undesirable for the economic health of developing nations, occasionally resulting in a decisive widening of the gaps between developed and developing nations.

2. GLOBAL WARMING

In the last 20 years or so, we have been warned continuously by geophysicists and meteorologists of numerous symptoms indicating that the atmospheric equilibrium is being disturbed on a global scale. The phenomenon of global warming is such a symptom – apparently one of the most serious – and will have enormous implications for virtually every aspect of human life on earth, affecting not only current but all future generations.

The Industrial Revolution ushered in a new phase in the history of mankind. Scientific inquiries have stimulated the development of new technologies, which, in turn, have been utilized effectively by avid entrepreneurs for large-scale production of goods and services – ostensibly to enrich the lives of people. In spite of many breakdowns in the process of economic development, the living standard of the average person – at least one not residing in a despotic country – seems now to have reached an unprecedentedly high level. However, advanced technologies and their large-scale applications, if not properly managed, tend to inflict intense and irrevocable damage to natural environments.

The new technologies brought in by the Industrial Revolution are characterized by the massive consumption of fossil fuels – particularly coal and oil. Recently, several scientific studies have demonstrated that excess burning of fossil fuels disturbs the atmospheric equilibrium and brings about a global warming of the earth's surface.

Increase in Global Average Surface Air Temperature

The extent of global warming may best be indicated by the global average surface air temperature, which has continuously risen during the approximately 200 years since the Industrial Revolution with an accelerated rate of increase in the last three decades.

The temperature on the earth's surface is rather difficult to identify. It varies a great deal between the regions. The seasonal variations are large and so are the yearly changes. However, the historical data show an evident long-term trend for an increase in global temperature. Among the many studies made concerning the mechanism by which the global average surface air temperature changes, we may cite a few: Hansen et al. (1981), Fraser, Elliott, and Waterman (1986), Hansen and Lebedeff (1987, 1988), and Conway et al. (1988).

The global average surface air temperature has increased 0.3°–0.6°C in the last hundred years. The early studies by Hansen and Lebedeff (1987, 1988) indicate that the rate of increase in the global average surface air temperature has increased from −0.5°C in 1880 to 0.2°C in 1980 on the 5-year moving average basis. According to the second report issued by the Intergovernmental Panel on Climate Change (IPCC 1996a,b), the global average surface air temperature will most likely increase by 1.0–3.5°C during the period from 1990 to 2100. The third IPPC Report predicts a much higher increase of 1.4–5.8°C during the same period (IPCC 2001a,d). This is a disturbing phenomenon if we note that the global average surface air temperature had risen only 0.7°C during the nearly 10,000 years since the end of the last Ice Age to the time of the Industrial Revolution. As suggested by Dickinson (1986), the actual warming equilibrium would be an increase in magnitude comparable to the increase the earth has experienced in the 10,000 years since the last Ice Age.

An increase in the global average surface air temperature of such magnitude will bring about alarming changes in rainfall patterns and other climatic conditions, resulting in serious ecological disequilibrium. An immediate impact of global warming is a rise in sea level. Gornitz, Lebedeff, and Hansen (1982) have reported that the sea level has risen about 10 cm because of the increase in surface air temperature from 1880 to 1980. The first IPCC report predicts that the sea level could rise about 20 cm (10–32 cm) by 2030 and about 45 cm (33–75 cm) by 2070 (IPCC 1991a). The second IPCC Report predicts that the sea level will rise 13–94 cm during the period from 1990 to 2100 (IPCC 1996a), and the third IPPC Report predicts a slightly lower increase of 9–88 cm during the same period (IPCC 2001a). A sea level rise on the order of 20–60 cm would have an almost catastrophic impact on human life because the majority of human settlements are located either near the seashore or by rivers. It is estimated that more than half a billion people would be directly affected by such an increase in the sea level.

The strength and frequency of hurricanes and typhoons would also intensify, and the distribution of rainfall would become more unstable. Climatic changes accompanied by global warming would place a particular hardship on farmers and fishermen because the choice of crops and the mode of cultivation have been adjusted to suit climatic and soil conditions slowly over many years and the availability of fish is delicately correlated with the natural environment. Tropical or subtropical climatic conditions would spread farther to the north (or the south for those in the Southern Hemisphere), thus disseminating the danger of tropical diseases and insects.

Atmospheric Concentrations of Greenhouse Gases

The principal cause for global warming is the atmospheric concentration of radiative forcing agents, which keep infrared radiation from the earth's surface and warm the surface air temperature. The radiative forcing agents, often referred to as greenhouse gases, are water vapor, carbon dioxide (CO_2), methane (CH_4), nitrous oxide (N_2O), and chlorofluorocarbons (CFCs), among others (Keeling 1968, 1983; Keeling et al. 1976; Woodwell and Houghton 1977; Dyson and Marland 1979; Khalil and Rasmussen 1983; Ramanathan et al. 1985; Pearman and Hyson 1986; Lerner, Matthews, and Fung 1988; World Resources Institute 1991, 1996; and IPCC 1991a,b, 1992a,b, 1996, 2000, 2001a,b,d,; among others).

A particularly important role is played by carbon dioxide. If carbon dioxide did not exist in the atmosphere, the global average surface air temperature would be −18°C, thus making life on earth virtually impossible. On the other hand, an excess concentration of atmospheric carbon dioxide would warm the globe significantly. It is estimated that the planet Venus, which has a high atmospheric concentration of carbon dioxide, has a surface temperature of about 470°C (see Keeling 1968, 1983; Komhyr et al. 1985; Neftel et al. 1985; From and Keeling 1986; Rotty 1987; World Resources Institute 1996, and others).

The atmospheric concentration of carbon dioxide has increased from the level of 280 parts per million (ppm) just prior to the Industrial Revolution to the current level of 360 ppm, as estimated by Neftel (1985), Fraser et al. (1986), and From and Keeling (1986). More reliable measurements have been made at Mauna Loa and the South Pole since 1958. Keeling et al. (1976), Komhyr et al. (1985), and Conway et al. (1988), among others, report findings that the atmospheric concentration of carbon dioxide increased from 315 ppm in 1959 to 335 ppm in 1978. From 1880 to 1958, it increased at the annual rate of 0.3–0.5 ppm, and from 1958 to 1988, it increased at the annual rate of 1.3 ppm, which is a significant increase over a 30-year period. If the current trend were to persist, carbon dioxide would reach the level of 540–970 ppm by 2100, which would represent a 90–250 percent increase compared with the preindustrial level of 280 ppm.

The extent to which the atmospheric concentration of carbon dioxide contributes to the increase in global temperature has been extensively analyzed. Hansen et al. (1981) estimated that an increase of 0.2°C is due to the atmospheric concentration of carbon dioxide from 1880 to 1980, whereas Ramanathan et al. (1985) calculated an increase of 0.52°C during the same period. According to Dickinson (1986), the atmospheric concentration of carbon dioxide will reach a level twice as high as the preindustrial level of 280 ppm, and the resulting equilibrium warming will be 2.5°–4.5°C. These findings have been reinforced by the recent studies published in the series of the IPCC Reports (IPCC 1991a,b, 1992, 1996a,b, 2000, 2001a,b,d).

The atmospheric concentration of carbon dioxide is largely anthropogenic, mostly resulting from the combustion of fossil fuels. The depletion of tropical rain forests has also become another major source of the atmospheric concentration of carbon dioxide in the last three decades, which is now estimated to be responsible for one-third of that emitted by the combustion of fossil fuels.

Global Carbon Cycle

To understand the mechanisms by which the anthropogenic emissions of carbon dioxide disturb the atmospheric equilibrium, it would be helpful to draw a crude picture of the global carbon cycle, as suggested by Woodwell and Houghton (1977), Hampicke (1979), and Keeling (1983). There are three major reservoirs of carbon on the earth's surface, each roughly of the same capacity: the atmosphere, the surface ocean (to a depth of 75 m), and the terrestrial biosphere, respectively containing 700, 700, and 800 GtC (GtC refers to gigatons of carbon = 10^9 tons of carbon). Terrestrial plants in detritus contain a much larger quantity of carbon on the order of 3,000 GtC.

The exchange of carbon between the atmosphere and the surface ocean is approximately in equilibrium, amounting to 90–100 GtC annually. The mechanisms by which atmospheric carbon dioxide is absorbed into the oceans are complicated. They depend partly on the extent to which the surface waters of the oceans are saturated by carbon dioxide and partly on the extent to which excess carbon dioxide is accumulated in the atmosphere. The findings reported by Takahashi et al. (1980) and Keeling (1968, 1983) suggest that the rate of ocean uptake is closely related to the excess quantity of atmospheric carbon dioxide over the stable, preindustrial level of 280 ppm.

The terrestrial biosphere plays an important role in the global carbon cycle and absorbs atmospheric carbon dioxide through the process of photosynthesis, amounting to about 60 GtC annually. Roughly the same amount of carbon is returned to the atmosphere through the processes of decomposition and respiration. Thus, the exchange of carbon between the atmosphere and the terrestrial biosphere is also in equilibrium.

The stability of the global carbon cycle began to be disturbed by the massive consumption of fossil fuels – particularly of coal and oil – that characterized the new technologies brought about by the Industrial Revolution. The combustion of fossil fuels now emits 6 GtC of carbon dioxide annually. This has an important implication for the stability of the global carbon cycle. Although the cycle on the earth's surface takes place within a period of 10 to 100 years, fossil fuels are made of plants and animals that used to live on the earth's surface some several hundred million years ago and they are now being extracted at an extremely high pace. According to the estimates made by Rotty (1987) and others, the combustion of fossil fuels emits roughly 5.6–6.0 GtC of carbon dioxide into the atmosphere annually. The most detailed data on global CO_2 emissions are available from Oak Ridge National Laboratory, as shown in Table 1. The largest contribution is made by the United States (22.5%), followed by China (13.0%), the Russian Federation (5.9%), Japan (4.7%), and India (4.4%). These five countries contribute half of the carbon dioxide emitted into the atmosphere.

Table 1. *Global CO_2 Emissions from Fossil Fuel Burning, Cement Manufacturing, and Gas Flaring: 1998*

	Emissions (Million Tons of Carbon)	**Share (%)**
United States	1,487	22.5
China	858	13.0
Russian Federation	392	5.9
Japan	309	4.7
India	290	4.4
Germany	239	3.6
United Kingdom	148	2.2
Canada	128	1.9
Italy	113	1.7
Australia	90	1.4
New Zealand	8	0.1
Other EU countries	351	5.3
The rest of the world	2,195	33.2
Total	6,608	100.0

Source: Oak Ridge National Laboratory.

Table 2. *Emissions of Gases in 1998*

				(Million Tons of CO_2 Equivalent)	
	CH_4	N_2O	HFC	PFC	SF6
Australia	117.5	27.8	—	1.4	0.0
Canada	89.5	64.9	0.9	6.0	1.5
France	54.3	84.2	3.4	1.6	2.3
Germany	73.2	49.5	3.6	1.6	5.7
Italy	41.4	38.6	1.6	0.1	0.4
Japan	27.3	22.3	19.0	12.4	12.8
Netherlands	22.4	22.2	6.9	2.2	1.5
New Zealand	33.4	12.1	0.4	0.1	0.0
Poland	49.0	16.0	—	—	—
Russian Federation	—	—	5.9	30.3	
Spain	43.6	43.8	8.5	0.1	0.2
Ukraine	135.6	4.9	—	—	—
United Kingdom	55.4	56.0	20.2	0.1	1.3
United States	663.4	437.7	93.1	18.0	36.7

Sources: UNFCCC, Ministry of Environment of Japan.

Note, however, that the quantity of carbon dioxide emitted by the combustion of fossil fuels per unit of Gross Domestic Product varies a great deal among the countries. The Japanese figure is roughly half that of the United States, suggesting a rather significant degree of substitutability for energy use. Table 2 shows total emissions of greenhouse gases in 1998.

The stability of the global carbon cycle has also been disturbed by the massive depletion of land forests – particularly of tropical rain forests in the last three decades. Total acreage of land forests is estimated at about 4 billion hectares, including open and closed forests and woodlands. According to the estimate made by the World Resources Institute, the acreage of tropical rain forests annually lost is now 160 million to 240 million hectares (World Resources Institute 1991, 1996), which is a magnitude much higher than the previous estimate of 110 million hectares made by the Food and Agriculture Organization for 1980.

According to estimates made by Houghton et al. (1987) and Detweiler and Hall (1988), 0.4–2.6 GtC of carbon dioxide are released into the atmosphere because of changes in the pattern of land use, and about 95 percent of this amount is regarded as being the result of deforestation of tropical rain forests. More than one-third of the increase in the atmospheric level of carbon dioxide is due to the depletion of land forests.

Atmospheric Concentrations of Greenhouse Gases

Carbon dioxide is estimated to be responsible for 64 percent of the greenhouse effect, whereas methane accounts for 19 percent, nitrous oxide for 6 percent, and CFCs for 10 percent.

Methane is estimated to be responsible for about 15 percent of the anthropogenic increase in global temperature, which is a magnitude second only to that of carbon dioxide. The atmospheric concentration of methane has more than doubled since the Industrial Revolution began, and it is currently increasing at an annual rate of 1 percent. Methane remains in the atmosphere for a relatively short time (10 years). However, it has a greenhouse effect 25 times more powerful than that of carbon dioxide, and a higher temperature implies a larger quantity of methane released into the atmosphere because land plants in detritus decay faster at a higher temperature.

The mechanisms by which methane is released into the atmosphere are not exactly known. However, the major sources of the anthropogenic increase in atmospheric methane are identified as irrigated rice fields, animal husbandry, biomass burning, landfills and sewage facilities, and fossil fuel production. According to the estimates made by Cicerone and Oremland (1988), Crutzen, Aselmann, and Seiler (1986), and Lerner, Matthews, and Fung (1988), the annual rate of methane emission is 0.6 Gt, of which irrigated rice fields are responsible for about 25 percent, domestic animals for 15 percent, biomass burning for 15 percent, landfills for 10 percent, and fossil fuel production for 15 percent.

Nitrous oxide is now estimated to be responsible for about 6 percent of the increase in the atmospheric temperature. The atmospheric concentration of nitrous oxide has increased from the preindustrial level of 270 parts per billion (ppb) to the current 310 ppb. However, most of the increase in atmospheric nitrous oxide has occurred in the last

50 years, as estimated by Pearman and Hyson (1986) and Khalil and Rasmussen (1983). In addition, it has a greenhouse effect 230 times more powerful than carbon dioxide. The major sources of nitrous oxide emissions are in the soil. A particularly important role is played by nitrogenous fertilizers and biomass burning. Nitrous oxide is also emitted by the combustion of fossil fuels, and changes in the pattern of land use contribute to the atmospheric emission of nitrous oxide.

Chlorofluorocarbons are the greenhouse gases that are solely anthropogenic. They were released into the atmosphere for the first time during the twentieth century. The most common CFCs are CFC-12 and CFC-11, which had atmospheric concentrations of 392 and 226 ppt, respectively, in 1986. Although the atmospheric levels of CFCs are low, their greenhouse effects are estimated as 20,000 times more powerful than those of carbon dioxide, which is currently responsible for 24 percent of global warming. Chlorofluorocarbons tend to remain in the atmosphere for a long time, almost permanently, and are responsible for the depletion of stratospheric ozone. In view of the eminent danger to which CFCs have exposed us, an international agreement was reached in 1987. *The Montreal Protocol to Control Substances That Deplete the Ozone Layer* stipulates a substantial reduction, and the eventual abolishment, of the production and use of CFCs. Even if the Montreal Protocol is successfully implemented, we have to face the atmospheric concentrations of CFCs that have been accumulated in the past and still remain in the atmosphere.

3. GLOBAL WARMING AND ECONOMIC THEORY

The phenomenon of global warming is basically anthropogenic and is primarily due to the massive consumption of fossil fuels and secondly to the depletion of tropical rain forests. The predominant forces behind these human activities are economic, and any policy or institutional measures to arrest the process of atmospheric disequilibrium effectively will have to take into account the economic, social, and political implications.

Two distinct features in the phenomenon of global warming exist that traditional economic theory is hardly equipped to deal with. First, global warming is caused by unstable concentrations of carbon dioxide and other greenhouse gases in the atmosphere. The atmosphere plays the role of social overhead capital that is neither privately appropriated nor subject to transactions in the market. Traditional economic theory has been almost exclusively concerned with those scarce resources that are privately appropriated and whose ownership rights are transacted on the market.

The second feature concerns the equity problem between different generations and between different countries. Those who emit most of the carbon dioxide are those who benefit most from the combustion of fossil fuels, whereas those who suffer most from global warming are those who benefit least from the emission of carbon dioxide.

By the same token, while the current generation enjoys a rather high living standard from the combustion of fossil fuels, future generations will have to suffer from global warming and other problems related to the atmospheric concentrations of carbon dioxide and other greenhouse gases. Again, traditional economic theory has shied away from problems involving equity and justice, restricting its realm to the efficiency aspect, but notable exceptions are found in the works by Arrow (1951, 1973, 1983), Rawls (1971), Sen (1973), Solow (1974a), Atkinson (1975), Sen and Williams (1982), Howarth and Norgaard (1990, 1992, 1995), Howarth and Monahan (1992), and Dasgupta (1993), among others.

Thus, the problem of global warming offers us a unique opportunity to reexamine theoretical premises of traditional economic theory and to search for a theoretical framework that will enable us to analyze the dynamic and equity problems involving environmental disruption. Such a framework is provided by the theories of optimum economic growth and social overhead capital, both of which have been developed in the last three decades. In particular, the dynamic theory of environmental economics, as developed by Karl-Göran Mäler (1974) and William Nordhaus (1980, 1982), gives us the basic framework that can be used to analyze the economic and political circumstances under which global warming and other environmental problems occur and to find the policy measures and institutional arrangements to arrest them effectively. Mäler's and Nordhaus's theory, in which the concept of imputed price plays a central role, concerns finding the pattern of intertemporal allocation of scarce resources where the optimum balance between environmental quality and economic growth is attained.

The concept of imputation was originally introduced by Carl Menger (1871) in his attempt to construct modern economic theory, and since then it has served as one of the basic concepts in price theory.

Menger was first concerned with the problem of imputing the subjective utility value to various types of consumption goods that have contributed to generate such a value. Under the assumption of cardinal utility, the imputed price of each consumption good becomes equal to its marginal utility. The consumer optimum then is attained if, and only if, the imputed price of each consumption good is proportional to the market price.

Menger's theory then proceeds to extend the concept of imputed price to productive activities. The imputed price of a factor of production is equal to the marginal value product of that factor of production, and the producer optimum is attained if, and only if, the imputed price of each factor of production is equal to the market price.

Menger's theory of imputation, however, is static, for it does not take the time element into explicit consideration. Contributions to the theory of optimum economic growth – particularly those of Ramsey (1928), Uzawa (1964), Srinivasan (1965), Koopmans (1965), Cass (1965), and others – have extended the concept of imputed price to the dynamic situation in which one inherits accumulating impacts from past human activities and tries to choose the current economic activities with the interest of all future generations explicitly taken into account. The phenomenon of global warming is precisely the kind of dynamic problem to which the modern theory of imputation is aptly applied, as effectively explored by Mäler (1974) and Nordhaus (1980, 1982).

The first major work on incorporating the environment into economic theory was done by Alan Kneese and his associates at Resources for the Future in the early 1960s (Kneese, Ayres, and d'Arge 1968). They succeeded in constructing an analytical framework in which the flow and circulation of all natural resources and materials in processes of economic activities are fully accounted for and the interactions with economic activities are effectively analyzed. Their theoretical construct is a generalization of the Arrow–Debreu model of general equilibrium to one in which the natural environment is integrated into standard economic theory (Arrow and Debreu 1954). The Kneese model of environmental equilibrium, however, is largely confined to the static circumstances with the dynamic implications only tangentially noted because a systematic theory of economic dynamics was not yet fully developed then.

Beginning in the middle 1960s, various attempts have been made to develop full-fledged dynamic analysis for both decentralized and centralized economies. Karl-Göran Mäler was the first to apply the techniques of optimum economic growth theory to formulate a systematic, dynamic model in which the environment is an integral component of processes of economic development. Mäler then analyzed the patterns of intertemporal economic activities that are dynamically optimum in terms of the intertemporal preference ordering induced by a Ramsey–Koopmans–Cass utility integral where effects of environmental degradation upon the schedules of marginal utilities and marginal products of private factors of production are fully taken into account. Numerous studies since have been made to apply Mäler's theory of optimum environmental quality to more specific cases such as forestry resources, subterranean water, coastal wetlands, and fisheries commons, as is discussed in detail by Clark and Munro (1975) and Clark (1990).

The empirical studies have been extensively developed by several economists, particularly by Jorgenson and Wilcoxon (1990a,b; 1992; 1993), Hogan and Jorgenson (1991), Manne and Richels (1992), and Manne, Mendelsohm, and Richels (1995).

Concerning the inherent difficulties in reaching a consensus among nations on issues related to the global environment, one may be reminded of the Impossibility theorem as formulated by Kenneth Arrow in his classic work *Social Choice and Individual Values* (Arrow 1951, 1983). Arrow addresses the problem of how social choice may consistently be made in a democratic society. His theory is set in an inspiring model of formal logic, clarifying the logical and social implications of two basic modes of social choice: voting, typically used to make political decisions, and the market mechanism, traditionally used to make economic decisions. Arrow's conclusions are summarized as the pessimistic Impossibility theorem, which precludes the processes of consistent social choice, except for the cases of dictatorship and convention. Arrow's *Social Choice and Individual Values* opened an entirely new dimension and vista, bringing to the fore the traditional concern of economists with the issues of justice and equity and initiating a new and important branch in economic theory.

As was emphasized earlier, a distinct feature of the atmosphere is that it is neither privately appropriated nor subject to transactions on the market. Thus, the atmosphere may be regarded as a component of social overhead capital, and some of more relevant propositions in the theory of social overhead capital may be applied to examine institutional arrangements for the stabilization of the atmospheric composition.

The concept of social overhead capital was originally introduced by Uzawa (1974a, b), in which the mechanisms by which social overhead capital interacts with the working of market institutions are explicitly brought out and the effects social overhead capital exerts on the distribution of real income are briefly analyzed. The concept of social overhead capital has since been extended to include the natural environment, social infrastructure, and institutional capital to explicitly analyze the phenomena of externalities, both static and dynamic, and to examine the implications for the dynamically optimum structure of intertemporal allocation of scarce resources (Uzawa 1974c; 1975; 1982; 1991; 1992a,b; 1998).

The dynamic analysis of global warming to be described here is based on some of the recent studies in the theory of social overhead capital and the theory of optimum dynamics. The simplest version of our analysis was first introduced in Uzawa (1991, 1993), where the primary concern was with the problems related to global warming in the Pacific Rim region, and the accumulation of private capital and changes in the size of population have not explicitly been brought into the analysis. In the following chapters, we take into account, albeit tangentially, the implications of the accumulation of private capital and changing population for the process of dynamic imputation, and at the same time we try to extend our analysis to cover the world as a whole even though the basic tenor of the conclusions remains intact.

One of the intrinsic difficulties involved with global warming is that the marginal private loss each country suffers from curtailing its atmospheric emission of carbon dioxide and other greenhouse gases is significantly greater than its own marginal welfare loss due to global warming, although the marginal social costs due to global warming that are borne either by other countries or by future generations are of a much larger magnitude. Global warming thus is a phenomenon to which the conceptual framework and analytical apparatuses of game theory may appropriately be applied. In Chapter 7, we regard global warming as a cooperative game and examine the conditions under which the core of the global warming game is nonempty, as originally proved in Uzawa (1999).

1

Global Warming and Carbon Taxes

1. INTRODUCTION

The atmospheric concentration of greenhouse gases, particularly of carbon dioxide, has been increasing since the Industrial Revolution, and this has been occurring at an accelerated rate in the last three decades. As described in detail in the Introduction, it is estimated that, if the emission of carbon dioxide and other greenhouse gases and the disruption of tropical rain forests were to continue at the present pace, global average air surface temperature toward the end of the twenty-first century would be 3–6°C higher than the level prevailing before the Industrial Revolution, resulting in drastic changes in climatic conditions and accompanying disruption of the biological and ecological environments. In view of the significant impacts such climatic changes would exert upon human life, a large number of policy measures and institutional arrangements have been proposed to stabilize atmospheric concentrations of greenhouse gases effectively.

Among them, the institutional arrangements of carbon taxes and markets for tradable emission permits have attracted widespread attention – particularly among economists such as Ingham, Maw, and Ulph (1974), Baumol and Oates (1988), Grubb and Sibenius (1992), Whally and Wigle (1991), Hoel (1991, 1992), Pearce (1991), and Rose and Stevens (1993). Theoretical analyses have been developed, for example, by Bergstrom, Blume, and Varian (1986), Copeland and Taylor (1986, 1995), Poterba (1991), and Uzawa (1991, 1992a, 1993, 1995) of carbon taxes and by Tietenberg (1985, 1992), Barrett (1990), Grubb (1990), Barrett et al. (1992), Bertram (1992), and Larsen and Shah (1992, 1994) of tradable emission permits.

In this chapter and Chapters 2 and 3, we address the theoretical analysis of implications for an allocative mechanism of carbon taxes and the market for tradable emission permits. Our analysis is strictly confined to the realm of static analysis, leaving a full dynamic analysis for later chapters.

In this chapter, we are particularly concerned with the proportional carbon tax schemes under which the tax rate is made proportional either to the level of the national income in the countries where greenhouse gases are emitted or to the sum of the national incomes of all countries in the world. Welfare implications of these institutional arrangements will be examined in detail in Chapter 2.

2. THE MODEL OF GLOBAL WARMING IN THE STATIC CONTEXT

We postulate that each greenhouse gas is so measured as to equate the greenhouse effect with the activity of carbon dioxide (CO_2). Hence, in our model, carbon dioxide is the only chemical agent that has a greenhouse effect. In the static context with which this and Chapters 2 and 3 are concerned, we postulate that the welfare effect of global warming is measured in relation to the total quantity of CO_2 emitted annually into the atmosphere, where the dependency upon the stock of CO_2 accumulated in the atmosphere is not explicitly brought out. This may be regarded as a valid hypothesis because we are concerned with the problem of global warming from the short-run point of view, where the stock of CO_2 accumulations in the atmosphere remains constant.

We consider the world economy to consist of a finite number of individual countries that share the earth's atmosphere as a common environment. Each country is generically denoted by $\nu = 1, \ldots, n$.

The behavioral characteristics of individual countries are expressed in the aggregate by two representative economic agents: the consumers, who are concerned with the choice of economic activities related to consumption, on the one hand, and the producers, who are in charge of the choice of technologies and levels of productive activities on the other.

Specifications for Utility Functions

We assume that the economic welfare of each country ν is expressed by a preference ordering that is represented by the utility function

$$u^\nu = u^\nu(c^\nu, a),$$

where $c^\nu = (c_j^\nu)$ is the vector of goods consumed in country ν; j generically refers to consumption goods ($j = 1, \ldots, J$), and a is the total quantity of CO_2 annually introduced into the atmosphere measured in tons of the carbon content of CO_2 emitted into the atmosphere; that is,

$$a = \sum_\nu a^\nu,$$

where a^ν is the amount of CO_2 emitted into the atmosphere by country ν in relation to its productive activities.

The phenomenon of global warming is expressed by the postulate that the welfare level of each country is influenced by the aggregate of CO_2 emissions of all countries in the world. If a country is relatively small, then its CO_2 emissions may have only a negligible effect on global warming. However, it would be greatly influenced by the CO_2 emissions of large countries such as the United States or Japan.

For each country ν, we assume that the utility function $u^\nu(c^\nu, a)$ satisfies the following neoclassical conditions:

(U1) $u^\nu(c^\nu, a)$ is defined, positive, continuous, and continuously twice-differentiable for all $(c^\nu, a) \geqq (0, 0)$.

(U2) Marginal utilities are positive for the consumption of private goods c^ν, but CO_2 emissions a have a negative marginal utility:

$$u_{c^\nu}^\nu(c^\nu, a) > 0, \quad u_a^\nu(c^\nu, a) < 0, \quad \text{for all } (c^\nu, a) \geqq (0, 0).$$

(U3) Marginal rates of substitution between any pair of consumption goods are diminishing, or, more specifically, $u^\nu(c^\nu, a)$ is strictly quasi-concave with respect to c^ν for any given $a \geqq 0$.

(U4) $u^\nu(c^\nu, a)$ is homogeneous of order 1 with respect to c^ν; that is,

$$u^\nu(tc^\nu, a) = tu^\nu(c^\nu, a), \quad \text{for all } t \geqq 0, \quad c^\nu \geqq 0.$$

We also assume that utility functions $u^\nu(c^\nu, a)$ are strongly separable with respect to c^ν and a; that is,

$$u^\nu(c^\nu, a) = \varphi(a)u^\nu(c^\nu). \tag{1}$$

The concept of separability of utility functions was analyzed in detail by Leontief (1947), Strotz (1957), Gorman (1959), and Houthakker (1960), among others. The concept of separability being used here corresponds to that of strong separability, as introduced in Goldman and Uzawa (1964).

The function $\varphi(a)$ expresses the extent to which people are adversely affected by global warming. It may be referred to as the *impact index* of global warming.

The large number of attempts that have been made to measure the value of environmental quality – particularly by McKenzie (1983), Randall and Stoll (1983), Bishop and Woodward (1995) – also have pertinent implications for the measurement of the impact index of global warming.

In this chapter as well as in the following chapters, except for Chapters 2 and 7, we assume that the impact index of global warming $\varphi(a)$ is identical for all countries involved. We assume that the impact index function $\varphi(a)$ satisfies the following conditions:

$$\varphi(a) > 0, \quad \varphi'(a) < 0, \quad \varphi''(a) < 0 \quad \text{for all } 0 < a < \hat{a},$$

where $\hat{a}$ is the critical level of CO_2 emissions. The critical level of CO_2 emissions $\hat{a}$ is the level of the annual rate of CO_2 emissions that, if CO_2 emissions were continued at a level higher than $\hat{a}$ for a long period, would produce drastic changes in climatic conditions and inflict irrevocable damage on the global environment.

With regard to global warming, the impact index function $\varphi(a)$ of the following form is often postulated, as in Uzawa (1991, 1992a):

$$\varphi(a) = (\hat{a} - a)^\beta, \quad 0 < a < \hat{a}, \tag{2}$$

where $\hat{a}$ is the critical level of CO_2 emissions, and β is the sensitivity parameter, $0 < \beta < 1$.

The relative rate of the marginal change in the impact index due to the marginal increase in the atmospheric emission of CO_2 is defined by

$$\tau(a) = -\frac{\varphi'(a)}{\varphi(a)},$$

which will play a crucial role in our analysis of global warming. It may be referred to as the *impact coefficient* of global warming. It is easily seen that the impact coefficient function $\tau(a)$ satisfies the following conditions:

$$\tau(a) > 0, \quad \tau'(a) - [\tau(a)]^2 > 0.$$

With respect to the impact index function $\varphi(a)$ of the form (2), the impact coefficient $\tau(a)$ is given by

$$\tau(a) = -\frac{\beta}{\hat{a} - a}.$$

The neoclassical conditions (U1–4) for the utility function $u^\nu(c^\nu, a)$ of each country ν are rephrased for the utility function $u^\nu(c^\nu)$ as the following conditions:

(U1′) $u^\nu(c^\nu)$ is defined, positive, continuous, and continuously twice-differentiable, respectively for all $c^\nu \geqq 0$.

(U2′) Marginal utilities are positive for the consumption of private goods $c^\nu = (c_j^\nu)$:

$$u_{c^\nu}^\nu(c^\nu) > 0, \quad \text{for all } c^\nu \geqq 0.$$

(U3′) $u^\nu(c^\nu)$ is strictly quasi-concave with respect to $c^\nu \geqq 0$; that is, for any pair of vectors of consumption, c_0^ν, c_1^ν, such that $c_0^\nu \neq c_1^\nu$,

$$u^\nu((1-t)c_0^\nu + tc_1^\nu) < (1-t)u^\nu(c_0^\nu) + tu^\nu(c_1^\nu), \quad \text{for all } 0 < t < 1.$$

(U4′) $u^\nu(c^\nu)$ is homogeneous of order 1 with respect to c^ν:

$$u^\nu(tc^\nu) = tu^\nu(c^\nu), \quad \text{for all } t \geqq 0, c^\nu \geqq 0.$$

We will frequently make use of the Euler identity:

$$u^\nu(c^\nu) = u_{c^\nu}^\nu(c^\nu)c^\nu, \quad \text{for all } c^\nu \geqq 0.$$

NOTE. In the analysis of global warming that will be developed in this book – except for Chapters 2, 5, and 7 – a central role will be played by the impact coefficient function $\tau^\nu(a)$, not by the impact index function $\varphi^\nu(a)$; thus, one may want to work on the premises, that the impact coefficient functions $\tau^\nu(a)$ rather than the impact index functions $\varphi^\nu(a)$ are identical for all countries involved. However, if one assumes that the impact coefficient functions $\tau^\nu(a)$ are identical for all countries involved, then an impact index function $\varphi(a)$ and a set of positive numbers $\beta^\nu > 0$ exist such that

$$\varphi^\nu(a) = \beta^\nu \varphi(a), \quad \text{for all } a > 0 \quad (\nu = 1, \ldots, n).$$

Hence, working with different impact index functions $\varphi^\nu(a)$ with an identical impact coefficient function $\tau(a)$ gives one only a spurious feeling of generality. We might as well assume from the beginning that the impact index function is the same for all countries involved.

The Consumer Optimum

Suppose the world markets for produced goods are perfectly competitive and prices of goods are denoted by an J-dimensional vector $p = (p_1, \ldots, p_J)$. Considering the possibility of zero prices for some goods, one assumes price vectors p to be nonzero, nonnegative: $p \geq 0$; that is, $p_j \geqq 0$ for all j, and $p_j > 0$ for at least one j.

Suppose national income of country ν in units of world prices is given by y^ν. Then, the consumers in country ν would choose the vector of consumption c^ν that maximizes country ν's utility function

$$u^\nu(c^\nu, a) = \varphi(a) u^\nu(c^\nu)$$

subject to the budget constraints

$$pc^\nu = y^\nu, \; c^\nu \geqq 0.$$

The optimum vector of consumption c^ν is characterized by the following marginality conditions:

$$\varphi(a) u^\nu_{c^\nu}(c^\nu) = \lambda^\nu p,$$

where λ^ν is the Lagrangian unknown associated with the budgetary constraint. The Lagrangian unknown λ^ν is nothing but the marginal utility of income y^ν.

Specifications for Production Possibility Sets

The conditions concerning the production of goods in each country ν are specified by the production possibility set T^ν that summarizes the technological possibilities and organizational arrangements for country ν; the endowments of factors of production available in country ν are given.

We assume that there are a finite number of factors of production that are essentially needed in the production of goods. They are generically denoted by $\ell\,(\ell = 1, \ldots, L)$. Without loss of generality, we may assume that the factors of production needed in productive activities are the same for all countries involved.

The endowments of factors of production available in each country ν are expressed by an L-dimensional vector $K^\nu = (K_1^\nu, \ldots, K_L^\nu)$. We assume that each country ν is endowed with a positive quantity of at least one factor of production:

$$K^\nu \geq 0; \text{ that is, } K_j^\nu \geqq 0, \text{ for all } j, \text{ and } K_j^\nu > 0, \quad \text{for at least one } j.$$

In each country ν, the minimum quantities of factors of production required to produce goods by the vector of production $x^\nu = (x_1^\nu, \ldots, x_L^\nu)$ with CO_2 emissions at the level a^ν are specified by an L-dimensional vector-valued function:

$$f^\nu(x^\nu, a^\nu) = \left(f_1^\nu(x^\nu, a^\nu), \ldots, f_L^\nu(x^\nu, a^\nu)\right).$$

We assume that marginal rates of substitution between the production of goods and the emission of CO_2 are smooth and diminishing, that there are always trade-offs between the production of goods and the emission of CO_2, and that the conditions of constant returns to scale prevail. That is, we assume

(T1) $f^\nu(x^\nu, a^\nu)$ are defined, positive, continuous, and continuously twice-differentiable for all $(x^\nu, a^\nu) \geqq 0$;

(T2) $f_{x^\nu}^\nu(x^\nu, a^\nu) > 0,\ f_{a^\nu}^\nu(x^\nu, a^\nu) \leqq 0, \quad$ for all $(x^\nu, a^\nu) \geqq 0$;

(T3) $f^\nu(x^\nu, a^\nu)$ are strictly quasi-convex with respect to (x^ν, a^ν) for all $(x^\nu, a^\nu) \geqq 0$;

(T4) $f^\nu(x^\nu, a^\nu)$ are homogeneous of order 1 with respect to (x^ν, a^ν); that is,

$$f^\nu(tx^\nu, ta^\nu) = tf^\nu(x^\nu, a^\nu), \quad \text{for all } t \geqq 0,\ (x^\nu, a^\nu) \geqq 0.$$

From the constant returns-to-scale conditions (T4), we have the Euler identity

$$f^\nu(x^\nu, a^\nu) = f_{x^\nu}^\nu(x^\nu, a^\nu)x^\nu + f_{a^\nu}^\nu(x^\nu, a^\nu)a^\nu, \quad \text{for all } (x^\nu, a^\nu) \geqq 0.$$

The production possibility set of each country ν, T^ν, is composed of all combinations (x^ν, a^ν) of vectors of production x^ν and CO_2 emissions a^ν that are possibly produced with the organizational arrangements and technological conditions in country ν and the given endowments of factors of production K^ν of country ν. Hence, it may be expressed as

$$T^\nu = \{(x^\nu, a^\nu): (x^\nu, a^\nu) \geqq 0,\ f^\nu(x^\nu, a^\nu) \leqq K^\nu\}.$$

Postulates (T1–3) imply that the production possibility set T^ν is a closed, convex set of $J+1$-dimensional vectors (x^ν, a^ν).

The Producer Optimum

As in the case of the consumer optimum, prices of goods on the world market are denoted by a price vector $p = (p_1, \ldots, p_J)$. Suppose that the carbon taxes at the rate of θ^ν are levied on the emission of CO_2 in country ν. Carbon tax rate θ^ν is assumed to be nonnegative: $\theta^\nu \geqq 0$; thus the case of the laissez faire regime $(\theta^\nu = 0)$ is not excluded.

Then the producers in country ν would choose those combinations (x^ν, a^ν) of vectors of production x^ν and CO_2 emissions a^ν that maximize net profits

$$px^\nu - \theta^\nu a^\nu$$

over $(x^\nu, a^\nu) \in T^\nu$.

Conditions (T1–3) postulated above ensure that, for any combination of price vector p and carbon tax rate θ^ν, the optimum combination (x^ν, a^ν) of vector of production x^ν and CO_2 emissions a^ν always exists and is uniquely determined. We may denote them by the functional form

$$x^\nu = x^\nu(p, \theta^\nu), \quad a^\nu = a^\nu(p, \theta^\nu).$$

The optimum production plan $(x^\nu(p, \theta^\nu), a^\nu(p, \theta^\nu))$ may be characterized by the following conditions:

(i) $(x^\nu(p, \theta^\nu),\ a^\nu(p, \theta^\nu)) \in T^\nu$

(ii) $px^\nu(p, \theta^\nu) - \theta^\nu a^\nu(p, \theta^\nu) > px^\nu - \theta^\nu a^\nu,$

for all $(x^\nu, a^\nu) \in T^\nu$, $(x^\nu, a^\nu) \neq (x^\nu(p, \theta^\nu), a^\nu(p, \theta^\nu))$.

To see how the optimum levels of production and CO_2 emissions are determined, let us denote the vector of imputed rental prices of factors of production by $r^\nu = (r^\nu_\ell)$, $[r^\nu_\ell \geqq 0]$. Then the optimum conditions are

$$p \leqq r^\nu f^\nu_{a^\nu}(x^\nu, a^\nu) \qquad (\text{mod. } x^\nu) \tag{3}$$

$$\theta^\nu \geqq r^\nu[-f^\nu_{a^\nu}(x^\nu, a^\nu)] \qquad (\text{mod. } a^\nu) \tag{4}$$

$$f^\nu(x^\nu, a^\nu) \leqq K^\nu \qquad (\text{mod. } r^\nu). \tag{5}$$

The first condition (3) means that

$$p_j = \sum_\ell r^\nu_\ell f^\nu_{jx^\nu_\ell}(x^\nu, a^\nu) \quad (\text{with equality when } x^\nu_j > 0),$$

which expresses the familiar principle that the choice of production technologies and levels of production are so adjusted as to equate marginal factor costs with output prices.

The second condition (4) similarly means that CO_2 emissions are so controlled that the marginal loss due to the marginal increase in CO_2 emissions is equal to carbon tax rate θ^ν when $a^\nu > 0$ and is not larger than θ^ν when $a^\nu = 0$.

The third condition (5) means that the employment of factors of production does not exceed the endowments, and the conditions of full employment are satisfied whenever rental price r^ν_ℓ is positive.

In what follows, for the sake of expository brevity, marginality conditions are often assumed to be satisfied by equality.

We have assumed that the technologies are subject to constant returns to scale (T4), and thus, in view of the Euler identity, conditions (3), (4), and (5) imply that

$$\begin{aligned} px^\nu - \theta^\nu a^\nu &= r^\nu[f^\nu_{x^\nu}(x^\nu, a^\nu)x^\nu + f^\nu_{a^\nu}(x^\nu, a^\nu)a^\nu] \\ &= r^\nu f^\nu(x^\nu, a^\nu) = r^\nu K^\nu. \end{aligned}$$

That is, the net evaluation of output is equal to the sum of the rental payments to all factors of production.

Suppose all factors of production are owned by individual members of the country ν. Then, national income y^ν of country ν is equal to the sum of the rental payments $r^\nu K^\nu = \sum_\ell r^\nu_\ell K^\nu_\ell$ and the tax payments $\theta^\nu a^\nu$ made by the producers for the emission of CO_2 in country ν;

that is,

$$y^\nu = r^\nu K^\nu + \theta^\nu a^\nu = (px^\nu - \theta^\nu a^\nu) + \theta^\nu a^\nu = px^\nu.$$

Hence, national income y^ν of country ν is equal to the value of outputs in units of market prices px^ν, thus conforming with the standard practice in national income accounting.

The producer optimum is similarly characterized when a perfectly competitive world market for tradable emission permits exists. Suppose prices on the market are given by the pair of $p = (p_j)$ and q. Then the vector (x^ν, a^ν) that maximizes net profits

$$px^\nu - qa^\nu, \quad (x^\nu, a^\nu) \in T^\nu$$

is uniquely determined and continuously twice-differentiable in (p, q); we may also denote them by the functional form

$$x^\nu = x^\nu(p, q), \quad a^\nu = a^\nu(p, q).$$

The optimum production plan $(x^\nu(p, q), a^\nu(p, q))$ may also be characterized by the following conditions:

(i) $(x^\nu(p, q), a^\nu(p, q)) \in T^\nu$

(ii) $px^\nu(p, q) - qa^\nu(p, q) > px^\nu - qa^\nu,$
for all $(x^\nu, a^\nu) \in T^\nu$, $(x^\nu, a^\nu) \neq (x^\nu(p, q), a^\nu(p, q))$.

Activity Analysis and Technological Possibility Sets

The specifications of technological possibility sets introduced earlier in this section contain certain ambiguities when more than one factor of production is involved. The quantities of factors of production required to produce goods by the vector $x^\nu = (x_1^\nu, \ldots, x_L^\nu)$ with the CO_2 emission at the level a^ν are determined by the choice of technologies and levels of production activities; thus, the quantities of factors of production required for (x^ν, a^ν) are mutually dependent, and the minimum quantity required for each type of factors of production may generally not be uniquely defined independently of the employment of other factors of production.

To explicitly examine the relationships between the choice of technologies and the quantity of CO_2 emissions, we may carry out the discussion better within the framework of the theory of activity analysis. Let us denote the vector of activity levels by $\xi^\nu = (\xi_s^\nu), \xi_s^\nu \geqq 0$, where ξ_s^ν stands for the level of activity s. We assume that activities $\{s\}$ comprise all possible production activities carried out by the producers in country ν.

The vector of produced quantities of goods, the quantity of CO_2 emissions, and the quantities of factors of production required when production activities are carried out at $\xi^\nu = (\xi_s^\nu)$ are, respectively, represented by the functional form

$$x^\nu(\xi^\nu) = \left(x_j^\nu(\xi^\nu)\right),\ a^\nu(\xi^\nu),\ K^\nu(\xi^\nu) = \left(K_\ell^\nu(\xi^\nu)\right).$$

We assume that functions $x^\nu(\xi^\nu), a^\nu(\xi^\nu), K^\nu(\xi^\nu)$ satisfy the following conditions:

(T1′) Substitution between outputs and various factors of production are smooth; that is, $x^\nu(\xi^\nu), a^\nu(\xi^\nu), K^\nu(\xi^\nu)$ are defined, continuous, and continuously twice-differentiable for all $\xi^\nu \geqq 0$.

(T2′) Marginal rates of substitution are diminishing; that is, $x^\nu(\xi^\nu)$ is strictly quasi-concave with respect to $\xi^\nu \geqq 0$, whereas $a^\nu(\xi^\nu)$ and $K^\nu(\xi^\nu)$ are strictly quasi-convex with respect to $\xi^\nu \geqq 0$.

(T3′) Constant returns to scale prevail; that is, $x^\nu(\xi^\nu), a^\nu(\xi^\nu), K^\nu(\xi^\nu)$ are homogeneous of order 1 with respect to $\xi^\nu \geqq 0$.

The production possibility set T^ν of country ν may now be defined by

$$T^\nu = \{(x^\nu, a^\nu) \colon 0 \leqq x^\nu \leqq x^\nu(\xi^\nu), a^\nu \geqq a^\nu(\xi^\nu), K^\nu(\xi^\nu) \leqq K^\nu, \xi^\nu \geqq 0\}.$$

The production possibility set T^ν thus defined is a nonempty set of $J+1$-dimensional vectors (x^ν, a^ν) that describes the technologically possible combinations of the vectors $x^\nu = (x_j^\nu)$ specifying the aggregate quantities x_j^ν of goods produced in country ν and the amount a^ν of CO_2 emitted into the atmosphere in country ν. Postulates (T1′–3′) imply that the production possibility set T^ν is a closed, convex set in the space of $J+1$-dimensional vectors (x^ν, a^ν).

The Producer Optimum

Suppose prices on a perfectly competitive market are given by price vector $p = (p_j)$, and carbon taxes at the rate θ^ν are levied. Then the producers in country ν would choose those vectors of activity levels $\xi^\nu = (\xi_s^\nu)$ and combinations (x^ν, a^ν) of production vector x^ν and CO_2 emissions a^ν that maximize net profits

$$px^\nu - \theta^\nu a^\nu$$

over $(x^\nu, a^\nu) \in T^\nu$.

Postulates (T1–3) guarantee that, for any combination of price vector $p = (p_j)$ and carbon tax rate θ^ν, the optimum combination (x^ν, a^ν) of production vector x^ν and CO_2 emissions a^ν always exists and is uniquely determined.

For any combination of price vector $p = (p_j)$ and carbon tax rate θ^ν, the vector of the optimum activity levels $\xi^\nu = (\xi_s^\nu)$ may be characterized by the following marginality conditions, where $r^\nu = (r_\ell^\nu)$ denotes the vector of the imputed rental prices of factors of production:

(i)′ For each activity s, marginal net profits $px^\nu_{\xi_s^\nu}(\xi^\nu) - \theta^\nu a^\nu_{\xi_s^\nu}(\xi^\nu)$ are less than or equal to marginal factor costs $r^\nu K^\nu_{\xi_s^\nu}(\xi^\nu)$:

$$px^\nu_{\xi_s^\nu}(\xi^\nu) - \theta^\nu a^\nu_{\xi_s^\nu}(\xi^\nu) \leqq r^\nu K^\nu_{\xi_s^\nu}(\xi^\nu) \quad (\text{mod.}\, \xi^\nu) \tag{6}$$

with equality when activity s is operated at a positive level $\xi_s^\nu > 0$.

(ii)′ For each factor of production ℓ, the required employment $K_\ell^\nu(\xi^\nu)$ does not exceed the endowments K_ℓ^ν:

$$K_\ell^\nu(\xi^\nu) \leqq K_\ell^\nu \quad (\text{mod.}\, r^\nu) \tag{7}$$

with equality when the rental price of factor r^ν of production ℓ is positive: $r_\ell^\nu > 0$.

We multiply both sides of (6) by ξ_s^ν and sum over s to obtain

$$px^\nu_{\xi^\nu}(\xi^\nu)\xi^\nu - \theta^\nu a^\nu_{\xi^\nu}(\xi^\nu)\xi^\nu = r^\nu K^\nu_{\xi^\nu}(\xi^\nu)\xi^\nu,$$

which, in view of the constant-returns-to-scale conditions, yields

$$px^\nu(\xi^\nu) - \theta^\nu a^\nu(\xi^\nu) = r^\nu K^\nu(\xi^\nu).$$

Hence, in view of condition (7), we have

$$px^\nu - \theta^\nu a^\nu = r^\nu K^\nu.$$

That is, the net evaluation of output is equal to the sum of the rental payments to the factors of production.

The Case of Simple Linear Technologies

In the simplest case, the vector of activity levels $\xi^\nu = (\xi_s^\nu)$ may be identified with the vector of produced quantities of goods $x^\nu = (x_j^\nu)$, and all technological coefficients are assumed to be constant. Then the CO_2 emissions $a^\nu(x^\nu)$ and the quantities of factors of production $K^\nu(x^\nu)$ required to produce $x^\nu = (x_j^\nu)$ are, respectively, represented by

$$a^\nu(x^\nu) = \alpha^\nu x^\nu, \quad K^\nu(x^\nu) = A^\nu x^\nu,$$

where $\alpha^\nu = (\alpha_j^\nu)$ is the vector of technological coefficients specifying the amount of CO_2 emissions associated with the production of goods, and $A^\nu = (A_{\ell j}^\nu)$ is the matrix of technological coefficients specifying the quantities of factors of production required in the production of goods. Then the production possibility set T^ν of country ν may be given by

$$T^\nu = \{(x^\nu, a^\nu): x^\nu \geqq 0,\ A^\nu x^\nu \leqq K^\nu,\ a^\nu \geqq \alpha^\nu x^\nu\}.$$

In this simple linear case, the marginality conditions for the producer optimum are given by

$$p_j - \theta^\nu \alpha_j^\nu \leqq \sum_\ell r_\ell^\nu A_{\ell j}^\nu$$

with equality when $x_j^\nu > 0$, and

$$\sum_j A_{\ell j}^\nu x_j^\nu \leqq K_\ell^\nu$$

with equality when $r_\ell^\nu > 0$.

NOTE. For any given combination (x^ν, a^ν) of production vector x^ν and CO_2 emissions a^ν, let us define the set of quantities of factors of production $T^\nu(x^\nu, a^\nu)$ by

$$T^\nu(x^\nu, a^\nu) = \{R^\nu: R^\nu \geqq K^\nu(\xi^\nu), x^\nu(\xi^\nu) \geqq x^\nu, a^\nu(\xi^\nu) \leqq a^\nu, \text{ for some } \xi^\nu \geqq 0\}.$$

The set $T^\nu(x^\nu, a^\nu)$ thus defined is a closed convex set in the L-dimensional vector space of the vectors of quantities of factors of production. When the number of factors of production is more than one ($L > 1$), the functions specifying the minimum quantities of factors of production required to produce (x^ν, a^ν) as introduced earlier in this section,

$$f^\nu(x^\nu, a^\nu) = \left(f_1^\nu(x^\nu, a^\nu), \ldots, f_L^\nu(x^\nu, a^\nu)\right),$$

are generally not well defined.

However, all the analyses developed in this book remain valid for the general case formulated in terms of activity analysis. For the sake of expository simplicity and intuitive reasoning, our discussion will be carried out in terms of the functional approach.

3. GLOBAL WARMING AND DEFERENTIAL EQUILIBRIUM

The phenomenon of global warming exhibits the basic features of public goods in the sense introduced by Paul Samuelson in his classic paper (Samuelson 1954). Thus, it is necessary to introduce some sort of institutional arrangements to realize socially acceptable patterns of resource allocation and income distribution. This is particularly relevant in our discussion of global warming because the participants in the global warming problem are not individual members of society, but rather the principal agents are the nations in the world. No definite rules or established customs concerning global warming exist that are binding on the nations involved.

To begin with, we explore the implications of market solutions for global warming. We assume that produced goods are freely traded between the countries in the world, whereas factors of production are not traded between the countries. We confine ourselves to the static circumstances under which the endowments of factors of production in individual countries and the stock of CO_2 accumulated in the atmosphere all remain constant. All the notations and postulates introduced in the previous sections are retained.

Global Warming and Competitive Equilibrium

Prices of goods on the world market are denoted by price vector $p = (p_j)$. The producers in country ν choose those combinations (x^ν, a^ν) of production vectors and CO_2 emissions that maximize net profits

$$px^\nu = px^\nu - 0a^\nu$$

over $(x^\nu, a^\nu) \in T^\nu$. Note that, in the case of perfectly competitive markets, no carbon taxes would be levied for CO_2 emissions; that is, $\theta^\nu = 0$.

In each country ν, the optimum levels of production x^ν and CO_2 emissions a^ν are determined at the levels at which, marginal factor costs for the production of goods are equated to the prices on the world market with the highest CO_2 emissions technologically possible; that is, in the case of perfectly competitive markets, the producer optimum is characterized by conditions (3), (4), and (5) with $\theta^\nu = 0$.

The consumer optimum, on the other hand, is obtained by maximizing utility function

$$u^\nu(c^\nu, a) = \varphi(a)u^\nu(c^\nu)$$

subject to the budget constraints

$$pc^\nu = y^\nu, c^\nu \geqq 0,$$

where y^ν is national income of country ν to be given by

$$y^\nu = r^\nu K^\nu = px^\nu.$$

The optimum vector of consumption c^ν is obtained by solving the following marginality conditions:

$$\varphi(a)u^\nu_{c^\nu}(c^\nu) = \lambda^\nu p,$$

where λ^ν is the Lagrange unknown associated with the budgetary constraint.

Total CO_2 emissions a are given by

$$a = \sum_\nu a^\nu.$$

Competitive market equilibrium for the world economy is obtained if we find a vector of prices p at which total demand for goods and services is equal to total supply

$$\sum_\nu c^\nu = \sum_\nu x^\nu.$$

The emission of CO_2 plays the role of a public "bad" provided to the producers in each country "free of charge"; thus, an excess amount of CO_2 is emitted into the atmosphere with a negative impact on world welfare. However, it is not immediately apparent that this is indeed the case. Instead we consider market equilibrium under a different behavioral postulate. We term such a market equilibrium *deferential equilibrium* because we believe that a certain sense of decency and awe to nature are embodied in the behavioral postulates of the model.

Deferential Equilibrium and Proportional Carbon Taxes

Deferential equilibrium is obtained if, when each country decides the levels of production activities, it takes into account the negative impact on its own utility level brought about by its CO_2 emissions. Formally, *deferential equilibrium* is defined as follows:

Consider the situation in which a combination (x^ν, a^ν) of production vector x^ν and CO_2 emissions a^ν is chosen in country ν. Suppose CO_2 emissions in country ν are increased by the marginal quantity. This would imply a marginal decrease in country ν's utility. Deferential equilibrium is obtained if this marginal decrease in country ν's utility is balanced with its marginal increase in utility caused by the accompanying marginal increase in the levels of production due to the marginal increase in CO_2 emissions in country ν. One can easily see that deferential equilibrium precisely corresponds to the Nash solution in game theory.

Hence, the choice of the levels of consumption, production, and CO_2 emissions under the deferential behavioristic postulate may be regarded as the optimum solution to the following maximum problem for country ν:

Maximum Problem for Deferential Equilibrium. Find the combination (c^ν, x^ν, a^ν, a) of consumption vector c^ν, production vector x^ν, CO_2 emissions a^ν, and virtual level of total CO_2 emissions a that maximizes country ν's utility

$$u^\nu(c^\nu, a) = \varphi(a)u^\nu(c^\nu)$$

subject to the constraints that

(i) Consumption expenditures are equal to national income $y^\nu = px^\nu$:

$$pc^\nu = y^\nu, \; c^\nu \geqq 0. \tag{8}$$

(ii) For each country ν, employment of factors of production is within the availability K_ℓ^ν:

$$f^\nu(x^\nu, a^\nu) \leqq K^\nu. \tag{9}$$

(iii) The virtual level of total CO_2 emissions a is thought to be increased by whatever amount a^ν of CO_2 is emitted by country ν; that is,

$$a = a^{-\nu} + a^\nu, \tag{10}$$

where $a^{-\nu}$ is the sum of CO_2 emissions by the rest of the world regarded as given.

The maximum problem is solved by introducing the Lagrangian unknowns associated with the constraints (8), (9), and (10) to be denoted, respectively, by $\lambda^\nu, \lambda^\nu r^\nu, \lambda^\nu \theta^\nu$. The reason the Lagrangian unknowns associated with constraints (9) and (10) are denoted by $\lambda^\nu r^\nu, \lambda^\nu \theta^\nu$ will become clear shortly.

The Lagrangian form is defined by

$$L^\nu(c^\nu, x^\nu, a^\nu, a; \lambda^\nu, \lambda^\nu r^\nu, \lambda^\nu \theta^\nu) = \varphi(a)u^\nu(c^\nu) + \lambda^\nu(px^\nu - pc^\nu) + \lambda^\nu r^\nu[K^\nu - f^\nu(x^\nu, a^\nu)] + \lambda^\nu \theta^\nu(a - a^{-\nu} - a^\nu),$$

where $a^{-\nu}$ is given.

The optimum combination (c^ν, x^ν, a^ν, a) of consumption vector c^ν, production vector x^ν, CO_2 emissions a^ν, and virtual level of total CO_2 emissions a is obtained as follows:

Partially differentiate Lagrangian form L^ν with respect to c^ν, x^ν, a^ν, a and equate them to zero to obtain

$$\varphi(a)u^\nu_{c^\nu}(c^\nu) = \lambda^\nu p \tag{11}$$

$$\lambda^\nu p = \lambda^\nu r^\nu f^\nu_{x^\nu}(x^\nu, a^\nu) \tag{12}$$

$$\lambda^\nu \theta^\nu = \lambda^\nu r^\nu[-f^\nu_{a^\nu}(x^\nu, a^\nu)] \tag{13}$$

$$\lambda^\nu \theta^\nu = [-\varphi'(a)]u^\nu(c^\nu) \tag{14}$$

together with feasibility conditions (8), (9), and (10).

NOTE. To be precise, for maximum problems in general, Lagrange conditions (11–14) are necessary conditions for the optimum but are not necessarily sufficient conditions. However, the neoclassical conditions postulated above ensure that conditions (11–14) are indeed sufficient (see, e.g., Arrow, Hurwicz, and Uzawa 1958).

Relation (11) expresses the standard proposition that, at the optimum, marginal utilities of goods are proportional to market prices.

Relation (12) means that, at the optimum, production of goods is so arranged that marginal factor costs are equal to market prices when $\lambda^\nu r^\nu$ are interpreted as the imputed rental prices of factors of production measured in units of country ν's utility.

Relation (13) similarly means that CO_2 emissions of country ν are so controlled that the marginal loss due to the marginal increase in CO_2 emissions a^ν of country ν is equal to the imputed price $\lambda^\nu \theta^\nu$, for country ν, of the virtual level of total CO_2 emissions, all measured in units of country ν's utility.

Relation (14) means that the virtual level of total CO_2 emissions is so controlled that the marginal loss (evaluated in units of country ν's utility) associated with the marginal increase in the virtual level of total CO_2 emissions due to the marginal increase in CO_2 emissions a^ν of country ν is equal to the imputed price $\lambda^\nu \theta^\nu$ of CO_2 emissions measured in units of country ν's utility.

To express marginality relations (11)–(14) in units of market prices, we divide both sides of these relations by λ^ν to obtain the following relations:

$$\alpha^\nu \varphi(a) u^\nu_{c^\nu}(c^\nu) = p \tag{15}$$

$$p = r^\nu f^\nu_{x^\nu}(x^\nu, a^\nu) \tag{16}$$

$$\theta^\nu = r^\nu[-f^\nu_{a^\nu}(x^\nu, a^\nu)] \tag{17}$$

$$\theta^\nu = \alpha^\nu[-\varphi'(a)] u^\nu(c^\nu), \tag{18}$$

where $\alpha^\nu = \dfrac{1}{\lambda^\nu} > 0$.

We now derive two relations that will play a central role in our analysis of global warming. By multiplying both sides of relation (15) by c^ν, we obtain

$$\alpha^\nu \varphi(a) u^\nu_{c^\nu}(c^\nu) c^\nu = pc^\nu = px^\nu = y^\nu. \tag{19}$$

On the other hand, in view of the homogeneity hypothesis with respect to utility function $u^\nu(c^\nu)$, we have

$$u^\nu(c^\nu) = u^\nu_{c^\nu}(c^\nu) c^\nu.$$

Hence, the following basic relation holds:

$$\alpha^{\nu}\varphi(a)u^{\nu}(c^{\nu}) = y^{\nu},$$

which may be substituted into the right-hand side of (18) to obtain

$$\theta^{\nu} = \tau(a)y^{\nu}, \tag{20}$$

where $\tau(a)$ is the impact coefficient of global warming

$$\tau(a) = -\frac{\varphi'(a)}{\varphi(a)}$$

and $y^{\nu} = px^{\nu}$ is national income of country ν.

On the other hand, relations (16) and (17) put together mean that the optimum combination (x^{ν}, a^{ν}) of production vector x^{ν} and CO_2 emissions a^{ν} is obtained by maximizing

$$px^{\nu} - \theta^{\nu}a^{\nu}$$

over the technological possibility set $(x^{\nu}, a^{\nu}) \in T^{\nu}$, where θ^{ν}, given by (20), is interpreted as the tax rate that producers in country ν have to pay for the emission of CO_2.

The discussion carried out so far shows that deferential equilibrium may be obtained as the standard market equilibrium when, in each country ν, carbon taxes are levied where the rate θ^{ν} is proportional to national income y^{ν} of country ν with the impact coefficient of global warming $\tau(a)$ as the coefficient of proportion. On the other hand, it is straightforward to see that the converse is true. That is, standard market equilibrium with carbon tax rate $\tau(a)y^{\nu}$ is a deferential equilibrium. Thus, we have established the following proposition.

Proposition 1. *Deferential equilibrium corresponds precisely to the standard market equilibrium under proportional carbon taxes when, in each country ν, carbon taxes are levied where the tax rate θ^{ν} is proportional to national income y^{ν} with the impact coefficient of global warming $\tau(a)$ as the coefficient of proportion*

$$\theta^{\nu} = \tau(a)y^{\nu}, \quad \tau(a) = -\frac{\varphi'(a)}{\varphi(a)}.$$

4. UNIFORM CARBON TAXES AND SOCIAL OPTIMUM

In the previous section, we have seen that deferential equilibrium may be obtained as the standard market equilibrium provided the carbon tax rate θ^ν in each country ν is equal to $\tau(a)y^\nu$, where $\tau(a)$ is the impact coefficient of global warming and y^ν is national income of country ν. We would like to move a step forward and to explore the implications of market equilibrium under the *uniform carbon tax* scheme, where the tax rate θ is proportional to the aggregate national income y of the whole world with the impact coefficient of global warming $\tau(a)$ as the coefficient of proportion:

$$\theta = \tau(a)y, \tag{21}$$

where

$$\tau(a) = -\frac{\varphi'(a)}{\varphi(a)}, \quad y = \sum_\nu y^\nu.$$

The conditions for market equilibrium under such a uniform carbon tax scheme are obtained in exactly the same manner as in the case of the proportional carbon tax scheme discussed in the previous section.

(i) For each country ν, the vector of consumption c^ν maximizes country ν's utility function

$$u^\nu(c^\nu, a) = \varphi(a)u^\nu(c^\nu)$$

subject to the budgetary constraints

$$pc^\nu = px^\nu, \ c^\nu \geqq 0,$$

where the world total of CO_2 emissions a is assumed to be given.

(ii) For each country ν, the combination (x^ν, a^ν) of production vector and CO_2 emissions maximizes net profits

$$px^\nu - \theta a^\nu$$

over the technological possibility set $(x^\nu, a^\nu) \in T^\nu$.

(iii) At the vector of prices p, total demand for goods is equal to total supply:

$$\sum_\nu c^\nu = \sum_\nu x^\nu.$$

(iv) Total CO_2 emissions a are given by

$$a = \sum_\nu a^\nu.$$

Market equilibrium under such a uniform carbon tax scheme is characterized by the following conditions:

(i) Marginal utilities are proportional to market prices:

$$\varphi(a)u^\nu_{c^\nu}(c^\nu) = \lambda^\nu p \quad [\lambda^\nu > 0]. \tag{22}$$

(ii) Net profits

$$px^\nu - \theta a^\nu$$

are maximized over $(x^\nu, a^\nu) \in T^\nu$.

We may write the marginality conditions (22) in units of market prices:

$$\alpha^\nu \varphi(a)u^\nu_{c^\nu}(c^\nu) = p, \tag{23}$$

where $\alpha^\nu = \dfrac{1}{\lambda^\nu} > 0$.

Equation (23) expresses the familiar relations that the price of each good is exactly equal to its marginal utility when the utility of each country ν is measured in units of world prices.

Exactly as in the previous case, marginality condition (23) and the linear homogeneity hypothesis on utility functions yield the following basic relation:

$$\alpha^\nu \varphi(a)u^\nu(c^\nu) = pc^\nu. \tag{24}$$

Let us now calculate the disutility of global warming due to CO_2 emissions measured in terms of the same utility units:

$$\sum_\nu \alpha^\nu[-\varphi'(a)]u^\nu(c^\nu),$$

which, through substitution of (24), may be expressed as follows:

$$\sum_\nu \alpha^\nu[-\varphi'(a)]u^\nu(c^\nu) = \tau(a)\sum_\nu \alpha^\nu \varphi(a)u^\nu(c^\nu)$$

$$= \tau(a)\sum_\nu pc^\nu = \tau(a)\sum_\nu px^\nu = \tau(a)y.$$

By noting the definition of θ, (21), we obtain

$$\sum_{\nu} \alpha^{\nu}[-\varphi'(a)]u^{\nu}(c^{\nu}) = \theta. \tag{25}$$

Relations (24) and (25) together with condition (ii) above may be interpreted as follows:

Define the world utility W as the sum of utilities of individual countries measured in units of world prices; that is,

$$W = \sum_{\nu} \alpha^{\nu}\varphi(a)u^{\nu}(c^{\nu}). \tag{26}$$

Then (24) and (25) are expressed as

$$\frac{\partial W}{\partial c^{\nu}} = p \tag{27}$$

$$\frac{\partial W}{\partial a} = -\theta. \tag{28}$$

Two relations, (27) and (28), together with condition (ii), are nothing but the Euler–Lagrange conditions for the following Lagrangian form:

$$L(c^1, \ldots, c^n, x^1, \ldots, x^n, a^1, \ldots, a^n, a; p, \theta) = \sum_{\nu} \alpha^{\nu}\varphi(a)u^{\nu}(c^{\nu})$$

$$+ p\left[\sum_{\nu} x^{\nu} - \sum_{\nu} c^{\nu}\right] + \theta\left[a - \sum_{\nu} a^{\nu}\right], \quad (x^{\nu}, a^{\nu}) \in T^{\nu}. \tag{29}$$

Applying the classic Kuhn–Tucker theorem on concave programming, one can readily see that Lagrangian form (29) is associated with the following maximum problem. The Lagrangian unknowns p, θ exactly correspond to those introduced above. (In the mathematical notes at the end of this chapter, a brief description of the Kuhn–Tucker theorem on concave programming will be presented.)

Social Optimum Problem

Find the pattern of consumption and production of goods for individual countries, the pattern of CO_2 emissions by individual countries, and total CO_2 emissions of the world $(c_*^1, \ldots, c_*^n, x_*^1, \ldots, x_*^n, a_*^1, \ldots, a_*^n, a_*)$ that maximize the world utility W defined by (26) among all feasible patterns of allocation $(c^1, \ldots, c^n, x^1, \ldots, x^n, a^1, \ldots, a^n, a)$:

$$\sum_{\nu} c^{\nu} = \sum_{\nu} x^{\nu}, \quad a = \sum_{\nu} a^{\nu}, \quad (x^{\nu}, a^{\nu}) \in T^{\nu}.$$

The analysis we have carried out so far may be summarized as the following proposition.

Proposition 2. *Consider the uniform carbon tax scheme with the same rate θ for all countries in the world where the rate θ is proportional to the aggregate national income y of the whole world with the impact coefficient of global warming $\tau(a)$ as the coefficient of proportion:*

$$\theta = \tau(a)y,$$

where

$$\tau(a) = -\frac{\varphi'(a)}{\varphi(a)}, \quad y = \sum_{\nu} y^{\nu}.$$

Then market equilibrium obtained under such a uniform carbon tax scheme is a social optimum in the sense that a set of positive weights exists for the utilities of individual countries $(\alpha^1, \ldots, \alpha^n)$, $[\alpha^{\nu} > 0]$ such that the world utility

$$W = \sum_{\nu} \alpha^{\nu} \varphi(a) u^{\nu}(c^{\nu})$$

is maximized among all feasible patterns of allocation $(c^1, \ldots, c^n, x^1, \ldots, x^n, a^1, \ldots, a^n, a)$:

$$\sum_{\nu} c^{\nu} = \sum_{\nu} x^{\nu}, \quad a = \sum_{\nu} a^{\nu}, \quad (x^{\nu}, a^{\nu}) \in T^{\nu}.$$

The social optimum may be defined for any arbitrarily given set of positive weights for the utilities of individual countries $(\alpha^1, \ldots, \alpha^n)$, $[\alpha^{\nu} > 0]$. A pattern of allocation $(c^1_*, \ldots, c^n_*, x^1_*, \ldots, x^n_*, a^1_*, \ldots, a^n_*, a_*)$ is a *social optimum* if the world utility W defined by (26) with positive weights $(\alpha^1, \ldots, \alpha^n)$, $[\alpha^{\nu} > 0]$ is maximized among all feasible patterns of allocation $(c^1, \ldots, c^n, x^1, \ldots, x^n, a^1, \ldots, a^n, a)$.

The social optimum necessarily implies the existence of the uniform carbon tax scheme with the universal rate $\theta = \tau(a)y$. However, the balance-of-payments conditions

$$pc^{\nu} = px^{\nu}$$

are generally not satisfied. It is often the case that the set of positive weights for the utilities of individual countries, $(\alpha^1, \ldots, \alpha^n)$, $[\alpha^{\nu} > 0]$, for which the balance-of-payments conditions are satisfied, is uniquely (except for proportionality) determined.

It is apparent that, if a social optimum satisfies the balance-of-payments conditions, it corresponds to the market equilibrium under the uniform carbon tax scheme. The existence of such a social optimum is guaranteed by the following proposition. The proof of Proposition 3 will be given in the mathematical notes at the end of this chapter.

Proposition 3. *There always exists a set of positive weights for the utilities of individual countries* $(\alpha^1, \dots, \alpha^n)$, $[\alpha^\nu > 0]$ *such that the social optimum with respect to the world utility*

$$W = \sum_\nu \alpha^\nu \varphi(a) u^\nu(c^\nu)$$

satisfies the balance-of-payments conditions:

$$pc^\nu = px^\nu$$

and, accordingly, the corresponding pattern of allocation $(c^1, \dots, c^n, x^1, \dots, x^n, a^1, \dots, a^n, a)$, *in conjunction with prices of goods p and the uniform carbon tax scheme with the rate* $\theta = \tau(a)y$, *constitutes a market equilibrium.*

5. GLOBAL WARMING AND LINDAHL EQUILIBRIUM

The concept of Lindahl equilibrium was originally introduced by Lindahl in his classic paper (Lindahl 1919). Many contributions were made to clarify the welfare implications of the concept of Lindahl equilibrium in the theory of public goods such as those, in particular, by Johansen (1963), Fabre-Sender (1969), Foley (1967, 1970), Malinvaud (1971), Milleron (1972), Roberts (1974), Kaneko (1977), and Mas-Colell (1980). With respect to global warming, the existence of Lindahl equilibrium and the implications for the welfare effect of global warming were examined in detail by Mäler and Uzawa (1994).

Within the context of global warming, the concept of Lindahl equilibrium corresponds to the situation in which the present level a of total CO_2 emissions is exactly equal to the level that would be chosen by each country ν when it would be free to choose the most desirable level on the assumption that the price to be paid would be equal to that country's marginal disutility. Formally, we define the concept of Lindahl equilibrium as follows.

A pattern of consumption, production, and CO_2 emissions (c_*^ν, x_*^ν, a_*^ν) for each country ν, and total CO_2 emissions a_* is a *Lindahl equilibrium* if a price vector $p = (p_j)$ exists such that

(i) In each country ν, the combination of production plan and CO_2 emissions (x_*^ν, a_*^ν) is so chosen as to maximize net profits under the uniform carbon tax scheme

$$px^\nu - \theta a^\nu$$

over the technological possibility set $(x^\nu, a^\nu) \in T^\nu$, where

$$\theta = \tau(a_*)y_*$$

$$\tau(a_*) = -\frac{\varphi'(a_*)}{\varphi(a_*)}, \quad y_* = \sum_\nu y_*^\nu, \quad y_*^\nu = px_*^\nu.$$

(ii) In each country ν, the combination of consumption vector and the level of total CO_2 emissions (c_*^ν, a_*) maximizes country ν's utility

$$\varphi(a^{(\nu)})u^\nu(c^\nu)$$

subject to the budgetary constraints

$$pc^\nu - \theta^\nu a^{(\nu)} = px_*^\nu - \theta a_*^\nu,$$

where θ^ν is the marginal rate of substitution between CO_2 emissions and produced goods for country ν; that is,

$$\theta^\nu = \tau(a_*)y_*^\nu.$$

(iii) Total CO_2 emissions a_* are equal to the sum of CO_2 emissions of individual countries:

$$a_* = \sum_\nu a_*^\nu.$$

(iv) World markets for produced goods are in equilibrium:

$$\sum_\nu c_*^\nu = \sum_\nu x_*^\nu.$$

Thus, Lindahl equilibrium coincides with the market equilibrium under the uniform carbon tax scheme with the system of transfer payments

$$t^\nu = \theta^\nu a_* - \theta a_*^\nu.$$

If no transfer payments are required at a Lindahl equilibrium, then the following relations are satisfied:

$$\theta^\nu a_* = \theta a_*^\nu.$$

Hence,

$$\frac{a_*^\nu}{a_*} = \frac{\theta^\nu}{\theta} = \frac{y^\nu}{y}.$$

That is, CO_2 emissions in individual countries ν are proportional to their national incomes.

The existence of Lindahl equilibrium is ensured by the following proposition, the proof of which will be given in the mathematical notes at the end of this chapter.

Proposition 4. *There always exists a Lindahl equilibrium.*

6. UTILITY MEASURED IN CO_2 STANDARDS

The analysis of global warming we have pursued so far is based on the ordinalist approach in the sense that preference relations are essentially orderings, and any conclusion of the analysis should not depend on a particular choice of utility index. In this section, we propose a particular way of measuring utilities that is pertinent to the analysis of global warming. It may appropriately be termed the *utility measured in* CO_2 *standards*.

As in the previous sections, we assume that the preference ordering of country ν is strongly separable with respect to vector of consumption c^ν and total CO_2 emissions a and that, as a utility index, the utility function of the form

$$u^\nu(c^\nu, a) = \varphi(a)u^\nu(c^\nu)$$

may be chosen, where all the properties postulated above are retained.

We begin with the situation in which the utility level associated with the combination (c^ν, a) of vector of consumption c^ν and total CO_2 emissions a is at a certain level u^ν, $[u^\nu > 0]$:

$$\varphi(a)u^\nu(c^\nu) = u^\nu. \tag{30}$$

We calculate the real cost-of-living index for the given utility level u^ν. Suppose that the prices of commodities at the base year measured in CO_2 standards are given by the price vector, $p^0 = (p_1^0, \ldots, p_j^0)$; that is, for each commodity j, p_j^0 is equal to the normal amount of CO_2 emitted into the atmosphere in the processes of production and consumption of one unit of commodity j. To simplify the exposition, we assume that the units of measurement for commodities are so chosen that the price vector at the base year is given by $p^0 = \mathbf{1} = (1, \ldots, 1)$.

We also assume that a vector of consumption c_0^ν exists such that partial derivatives $u_{c^\nu}^\nu(c_0^\nu)$ are proportional to the price vector $\mathbf{1}$:

$$u_{c^\nu}^\nu(c_0^\nu) = \beta^\nu \mathbf{1}, \quad \beta^\nu > 0.$$

Because partial derivatives $u_{c^\nu}^\nu(c^\nu)$ are homogeneous of order 0, we may without loss of generality assume that

$$\mathbf{1}c_0^\nu = 1.$$

Because utility function $u^\nu(c^\nu)$ is homogeneous of order 1, we have

$$u^\nu(c_0^\nu) = u_{c^\nu}^\nu(c_0^\nu)c_0^\nu = \beta^\nu \mathbf{1}c_0^\nu = \beta^\nu.$$

Let us define a new utility index by

$$\overline{u}^\nu(c^\nu) = \frac{1}{\beta^\nu} u^\nu(c^\nu).$$

Then, the following relations hold:

$$\overline{u}^\nu(c_0^\nu) = 1, \quad \overline{u}_{c^\nu}^\nu(c_0^\nu) = \mathbf{1}, \quad \mathbf{1}c_0^\nu = 1.$$

If we choose such a utility index from the beginning, we may assume that, for the utility function $u^\nu(c^\nu)$ of each country ν, a vector of consumption c_0^ν exists such that

$$u^\nu(c_0^\nu) = 1, \quad u_{c^\nu}^\nu(c_0^\nu) = \mathbf{1}, \quad \mathbf{1}c_0^\nu = 1.$$

Then, the real-cost-of living index in CO_2 standards w^ν for the combination (c^ν, a) of vector of consumption c^ν and total CO_2 emissions a is given by

$$w^\nu = \mathbf{1}c^\nu - a = \sum_\nu c^\nu - a, \quad [\mathbf{1} = (1, \ldots, 1)].$$

The utility measured in CO_2 standards w^ν for utility level u^ν may be defined as the minimum expenditures measured in CO_2 standards to attain the utility at the level u^ν. That is, the utility measured in CO_2 standards w^ν for utility level u^ν is obtained as the solution to the following minimum problem:

Find $(c^\nu_*, a^{(\nu)}_*)$ that minimizes the real cost-of-living index

$$w^\nu = \mathbf{1}c^\nu_* - a^{(\nu)}_*$$

subject to the constraint

$$\varphi(a^{(\nu)}_*)u^\nu(c^\nu_*) = u^\nu. \tag{31}$$

An excuse may be necessary to justify the use of such a tedious notation system. The variables c^ν_*, $a^{(\nu)}_*$ in the minimum problem denote, respectively, the vector of consumption and total CO_2 emissions to be chosen by country ν. They are distinct from the vector of consumption c^ν and total CO_2 emissions a that are the determining variables for the utility level u^ν, as in (30).

The minimum problem may be solved by the Lagrangian method. We first take the logarithm of both sides of constraint (31):

$$\log \varphi(a^{(\nu)}_*) + \log u^\nu(c^\nu_*) = \log u^\nu. \tag{32}$$

Let us denote by λ^ν the Lagrangian unknown for the constraint (32); then, the Lagrangian form is given by

$$L^\nu(c^\nu_*, a^{(\nu)}_*; \lambda^\nu) = (\mathbf{1}c^\nu_* - a^{(\nu)}_*) - \lambda^\nu[\log \varphi(a^{(\nu)}_*) + \log u^\nu(c^\nu_*) - \log u^\nu].$$

The Euler–Lagrange conditions for this Lagrangian form are

$$\mathbf{1} = \lambda^\nu \frac{u^\nu_{c^\nu}(c^\nu_*)}{u^\nu(c^\nu_*)} \tag{33}$$

$$1 = \lambda^\nu \tau(a^{(\nu)}_*), \tag{34}$$

where

$$\tau(a^{(\nu)}_*) = -\frac{\varphi'(a^{(\nu)}_*)}{\varphi(a^{(\nu)}_*)}$$

is the impact coefficient of global warming at $a^{(\nu)}_*$.

Multiplying both sides of (33) by c_*^ν and noting the Euler identity for utility function $u^\nu(c^\nu)$, we obtain

$$\mathbf{1}c_*^{(\nu)} = \lambda^\nu.$$

Let us denote by c_0^ν the standard vector of consumption introduced above:

$$u^\nu(c_0^\nu) = 1, \quad u_{c^\nu}^\nu(c_0^\nu) = \mathbf{1}, \quad \mathbf{1}c_0^\nu = 1.$$

The optimum vector of consumption c_*^ν may be expressed as

$$c_*^\nu = \lambda^\nu c_0^\nu.$$

Then constraint (31) may be written as

$$\lambda^\nu \varphi(a_*^{(\nu)}) = u^\nu, \quad \text{or} \quad \lambda^\nu = \frac{u^\nu}{\varphi(a_*^{(\nu)})}.$$

The optimum value of λ^ν is simply obtained by finding the value of $a_*^{(\nu)}$ that maximizes

$$w^\nu = \lambda^\nu - a_*^{(\nu)} = \frac{u^\nu}{\varphi(a_*^{(\nu)})} - a_*^{(\nu)}. \tag{35}$$

Differentiate the right-hand side of (35) with respect to $a_*^{(\nu)}$ and equate it with 0 to obtain

$$-\frac{\varphi'(a_*^{(\nu)})}{[\varphi(a_*^{(\nu)})]^2} u^\nu - 1 = 0.$$

Hence, we have

$$\frac{\varphi(a_*^{(\nu)})}{\tau(a_*^{(\nu)})} = u^\nu. \tag{36}$$

The left-hand side of Equation (36) is a strictly decreasing function of $a_*^{(\nu)}$, and the value of $a_*^{(\nu)}$ that satisfies Equation (36) generally always exists and is uniquely determined. Logarithmically differentiate both sides of Equation (36) to obtain

$$\left[\frac{\varphi'(a_*^{(\nu)})}{\varphi(a_*^{(\nu)})} - \frac{\tau'(a_*^{(\nu)})}{\tau(a_*^{(\nu)})}\right] da_*^{(\nu)} = \frac{du^\nu}{u^\nu},$$

which, by substitution of (36) and rearrangement, yields

$$\frac{da_*^{(\nu)}}{du^\nu} = -\frac{[\tau(a_*^{(\nu)})]^2}{[\tau(a_*^{(\nu)})]^2 + \tau'(a_*^{(\nu)})} \frac{1}{\varphi(a_*^{(\nu)})} < 0. \tag{37}$$

The utility measured in CO_2 standards w^ν now is expressed as

$$w^\nu = \ell(u^\nu),$$

where the function $\ell(\cdot)$ is identical for all countries. The derivative of function $w^\nu = \ell(u^\nu)$ at u^ν may be calculated by differentiating both sides of (35) with respect to u^ν and taking note of relation (36):

$$\ell'(u^\nu) = \frac{dw^\nu}{du^\nu} = \frac{1}{\varphi(a_*^{(\nu)})} > 0. \tag{38}$$

Differentiate both sides of (38) further with respect to $a_*^{(\nu)}$ and take note of relation (37) to obtain

$$\ell''(u^\nu) = \frac{d}{du^\nu}\left(\frac{dw^\nu}{du^\nu}\right) = -\frac{[\tau(a_*^{(\nu)})]^3}{[\tau(a_*^{(\nu)})]^2 + \tau'(a_*^{(\nu)})} \frac{1}{[\varphi(a_*^{(\nu)})]^2} < 0. \tag{39}$$

Relations (38) and (39) indicate that the real cost-of-living index function $w^\nu = \ell(u^\nu)$ is a strictly increasing and strictly concave function of utility level u^ν. The immediately discussion preceding may be summarized in the following proposition:

Proposition 5. *The utility measured in CO_2 standards w^ν corresponding to utility level u^ν is defined as the minimum expenditure evaluated at the base year price vector $p^0 = \mathbf{1}$ necessary to attain a utility level at least as high as u^ν, and it is expressed by the following functional form:*

$$w^\nu = \ell(u^\nu), \quad u^\nu = \varphi(a)u^\nu(c^\nu),$$

where the function $\ell(\cdot)$ is identical for all countries provided that the unit of the utility for each country ν is chosen so that the vector of optimum consumption c_0^ν at the base year price vector $p^0 = \mathbf{1}$ satisfies the following conditions:

$$u^\nu(c_0^\nu) = 1, \quad \mathbf{1}c_0^\nu = 1, \quad u_{c^\nu}^\nu(c_0^\nu) = \mathbf{1}.$$

The cost-of-living index function $w^\nu = \ell(u^\nu)$ is a strictly increasing and strictly concave function of utility level u^ν.

The world utility measured in CO_2 standards is now defined by

$$W = \sum_\nu w^\nu, \quad w^\nu = \ell(u^\nu), \quad u^\nu = \varphi(a)u^\nu(c^\nu).$$

The social optimum with respect to the world utility measured in CO_2 standards W is the pattern of consumption and production of goods and services for individual countries, the pattern of CO_2 emissions by individual countries, and total CO_2 emissions of the world $(c_*^1, \ldots, c_*^n, x_*^1, \ldots, x_*^n, a_*^1, \ldots, a_*^n, a_*)$ that maximize the world utility W among all feasible patterns of allocation $(c^1, \ldots, c^n, x^1, \ldots, x^n, a^1, \ldots, a^n, a)$:

$$\sum_\nu c^\nu = \sum_\nu x^\nu, \quad a = \sum_\nu a^\nu, \quad f^\nu(x^\nu, a^\nu) \leqq K^\nu.$$

The following proposition follows easily from Proposition 3.

Proposition 6. *There exists a system of transfer payments in CO_2 standards $\{t^\nu\}$*

$$\sum_\nu t^\nu = 0$$

such that the social optimum with respect to the world utility measured in CO_2 standards W is obtained as the market equilibrium $(c_*^1, \ldots, c_*^n, x_*^1, \ldots, x_*^n, a_*^1, \ldots, a_*^n, a_*)$ when the uniform carbon taxes are levied, where the rate θ is proportional to the world income y_* with the impact coefficient of global warming $\tau(a_*)$ as the coefficient of proportion as follows:

$$\theta = \tau(a_*)y_* \quad \tau(a_*) = -\frac{\varphi'(a_*)}{\varphi(a_*)}, \quad y_* = \sum_\nu y_*^\nu.$$

That is, a vector of prices p exists such that

(i) *For each country ν, the vector of consumption c_*^ν maximizes country ν's utility measured in CO_2 standards*

$$w^\nu = \ell(u^\nu), \quad u^\nu = \varphi(a)u^\nu(c^\nu)$$

subject to the budgetary constraints that

$$pc^\nu = px_*^\nu + t^\nu,$$

where the world total of CO_2 emissions is assumed to be given at a_* as

$$a_* = \sum_\nu a_*^\nu.$$

(ii) *For each country ν, the combination (x_*^ν, a_*^ν) of production vector and CO_2 emissions maximizes net profits*

$$px^\nu - \theta a^\nu$$

over the technological possibility set $(x^\nu, a^\nu) \in T^\nu$.

MATHEMATICAL NOTES

7. KUHN–TUCKER THEOREM ON CONCAVE PROGRAMMING

The Lagrangian Method

To solve problems of constrained extrema, it is customary in calculus to use the method of the Lagrangian multiplier. Let us, for example, consider the following maximization problem:

Maximize $f(x_1, \ldots, x_n)$ subject to the restrictions

$$g_\ell(x_1, \ldots, x_n) = 0 \quad (\ell = 1, \ldots, L).$$

First, formulate the so-called Lagrangian form

$$L(x, p) = f(x_1, \ldots, x_n) + \sum_\ell p_\ell g_\ell(x_1, \ldots, x_n),$$

where unknowns $p_1, \ldots, p_L$ are called the Lagrangian multipliers. Then solutions $x_1, \ldots, x_n$ are found among extreme points of $L(x, p)$, with unrestricted x and p, which in turn are characterized as the solutions of

$$\frac{\partial L}{\partial x_j} = \frac{\partial f}{\partial x_j} + \sum_\ell y_\ell \frac{\partial g_\ell}{\partial x_j} = 0 \quad (j = 1, \ldots, n)$$

$$\frac{\partial L}{\partial p_\ell} = g_\ell(x_1, \ldots, x_n) = 0 \quad (\ell = 1, \ldots, L).$$

This method, although not necessarily true without certain qualifications, has been found to be useful in many particular problems of constrained extrema.

The method is also applied with a suitable modification to solve the programming problems in which we are concerned with maximizing a function

$$f(x_1, \ldots, x_n)$$

subject to the restrictions

$$x_j \geqq 0 \qquad (j = 1, \ldots, n)$$
$$g_\ell(x_1, \ldots, x_n) \geqq 0 \quad (\ell = 1, \ldots, L).$$

Kuhn and Tucker (1951) first proved that under certain constraint qualifications, concave programming is reduced to finding a saddlepoint of the Lagrangian form $L(x, p)$. The Kuhn–Tucker theorem was further elaborated by Arrow and Hurwicz (1956) to handle nonconcave programming. In this book, we make frequent use of the Kuhn–Tucker theorem for concave programming under different qualifications, which is an approach originally proved in Arrow, Hurwicz, and Uzawa (1958).

Maximum Problem and Saddlepoint Problem

Let $f(x)$ be a real-valued function and $g(x) = (g_\ell(x), \ldots, g_L(x))$ be an L-dimensional vector-valued function both defined for nonnegative vectors $x = (x_1, \ldots, x_n)$.

Maximum Problem
Find a vector $\bar{x}$ that maximizes

$$f(x)$$

subject to the restrictions

$$x \geqq 0, \quad g(x) \geqq 0. \tag{1}$$

A vector x is *feasible* if it satisfies (1), and a feasible vector $\bar{x}$ maximizing $f(x)$ subject to (1) is called an *optimum solution* to the maximum problem.

Associated with the maximum problem, the *Lagrangian form* is defined by

$$L(x, p) = f(x) + pg(x).$$

A pair of vectors $(\overline{x}, \overline{p})$ is termed a nonnegative saddlepoint of $L(x, p)$ if

$$\overline{x} \geqq 0, \quad \overline{p} \geqq 0$$
$$L(x, \overline{p}) \leqq L(\overline{x}, \overline{p}) \leqq L(\overline{x}, p).$$

In other words,

$$L(\overline{x}, \overline{p}) = \min_{p \geqq 0} \max_{x \geqq 0} L(x, p) = \max_{x \geqq 0} \min_{p \geqq 0} L(x, p).$$

Saddlepoint Implies the Optimality

Theorem 1. *If $(\overline{x}, \overline{p})$ is a nonnegative saddlepoint of $L(x, p)$, then $\overline{x}$ is an optimum solution to the maximum problem.*

Proof. If $(\overline{x}, \overline{p})$ is a nonnegative saddlepoint of $L(x, p)$, then we have

$$f(x) + \overline{p}g(x) \leqq f(\overline{x}) + \overline{p}g(\overline{x}) \leqq f(\overline{x}) + pg(\overline{x}), \quad \text{for all } x \geqq 0,\ p \geqq 0.$$

Because the second inequality of the saddlepoint inequalities holds for any $p \geqq 0$, it follows that $g(\overline{x})$ cannot have a negative component and that $\overline{p}g(\overline{x})$ must be zero:

$$g(\overline{x}) \geqq 0, \quad \overline{p}g(\overline{x}) = 0.$$

Thus, the first inequality of the saddlepoint inequalities may be written as

$$f(x) + \overline{p}g(x) \leqq f(\overline{x}), \quad \text{for all } x \geqq 0.$$

Because we have $\overline{p}g(x) \geqq 0$, for any feasible vector x it follows that

$$f(x) \leqq f(x) + \overline{p}g(x) \leqq f(\overline{x}),$$

thus showing that $\overline{x}$ is an optimum solution to the maximum problem.

Q. E. D.

The Kuhn–Tucker Theorem on Concave Programming

Theorem 2. *Suppose that $f(x)$ and $g(x)$ are concave functions on $x \geqq 0$ and that $g(x)$ satisfies the following condition due to Slater (1950):*

(S) There exists an $x^0 \geqq 0$ such that $g(x^0) > 0$.

Then a vector $\overline{x}$ is optimum if, and only if, there is a vector $\overline{p} \geqq 0$ such that $(\overline{x}, \overline{p})$ is a saddlepoint of the Lagrangian form $L(x, p)$.

Proof. Let $\overline{x}$ be optimum. We define the two sets A and B in the $(L+1)$-dimensional vector space:

$$A = \left\{ \begin{pmatrix} z_0 \\ z \end{pmatrix} : \ \begin{pmatrix} z_0 \\ z \end{pmatrix} \leqq \begin{pmatrix} f(x) \\ g(x) \end{pmatrix} \quad \text{for some } x \geqq 0 \right\}$$

$$B = \left\{ \begin{pmatrix} z_0 \\ z \end{pmatrix} : \ \begin{pmatrix} z_0 \\ z \end{pmatrix} > \begin{pmatrix} f(\overline{x}) \\ 0 \end{pmatrix} \right\}.$$

Because $f(x)$ and $g(x)$ are concave functions of x, the set A is a convex set. Because $\overline{x}$ is optimum, A and B have no vector in common. Therefore, by the separation theorem for convex sets, there is a nonzero vector $\langle \nu_0, \nu \rangle \neq 0$ such that

$$\nu_0 z_0 + \nu \cdot z \leqq \nu_0 u_0 + \nu \cdot u \quad \text{for all} \begin{pmatrix} z_0 \\ z \end{pmatrix} \in A, \ \begin{pmatrix} u_0 \\ u \end{pmatrix} \in B.$$

By the definition of B, we have $\langle \nu_0, \nu \rangle \geqq 0$. Because $(f(\overline{x}), 0)$ is on the boundary of B, we also have, by the definition of A,

$$\nu_0 f(x) + \nu g(x) \leqq \nu_0 f(\overline{x}) \quad \text{for all } x \geqq 0.$$

Now we show that $\nu_0 > 0$. Otherwise, we would have $\nu \geq 0$ and $\nu \cdot g(x) \leqq 0$ for all $x \geqq 0$, contradicting the condition (S).

Let $\overline{p} = \dfrac{\nu}{\nu_0}$. Then, we have

$$\overline{p} \geqq 0$$
$$f(x) + \overline{p} g(x) \leqq f(\overline{x}) \quad \text{for all } x \geqq 0.$$

Hence,

$$\overline{p} g(\overline{x}) \leqq 0, \quad g(\overline{x}) \geqq 0,$$

thus implying that

$$\overline{p} g(\overline{x}) = 0. \qquad \text{Q.E.D.}$$

8. PROOF OF PROPOSITION 3

Proposition 3 may be proved along the lines originally devised by Arrow and Debreu (1954). We consider the $n-1$-dimensional simplex

S defined by

$$S = \left\{\alpha = (\alpha^\nu) \colon \alpha^\nu \geqq 0,\ \sum_\nu \alpha^\nu = 1\right\}.$$

We denote the optimum vectors and the vector of imputed prices associated with the social optimum with utility weight vector α, respectively, by $c^\nu(\alpha)$, $x^\nu(\alpha)$, $a^\nu(\alpha)$, $a(\alpha)$, and $p(\alpha)$, $\theta(\alpha)$. Then the following conditions are satisfied:

$$\sum_\nu c^\nu(\alpha) = \sum_\nu x^\nu(\alpha)$$

$$a(\alpha) = \sum_\nu a^\nu(\alpha)$$

$$\alpha^\nu \varphi(a(\alpha)) u^\nu_{c^\nu}(c^\nu(\alpha)) = p(\alpha) \tag{2}$$

$$(x^\nu(\alpha), a^\nu(\alpha)) \in T^\nu$$

$$p(\alpha)x^\nu(\alpha) - \theta(\alpha)a^\nu(\alpha) \geqq p(\alpha)x^\nu - \theta(\alpha)a^\nu \quad \text{for all } (x^\nu, a^\nu) \in T^\nu$$

$$\theta(\alpha) = \sum_\nu \alpha^\nu[-\varphi'(a(\alpha))]u^\nu(c^\nu(\alpha)) = \tau(a) \sum_\nu \alpha^\nu \varphi(a(\alpha))u^\nu(c^\nu(\alpha)). \tag{3}$$

We have from (2) and the homogeneity assumption of utility functions $u^\nu(c^\nu)$ that

$$\alpha^\nu \varphi(a(\alpha))u^\nu(c^\nu(\alpha)) = p(\alpha)c^\nu(\alpha).$$

Hence, we have, in view of relation (3), that

$$\theta(\alpha) = \tau(a) \sum_\nu p(\alpha)c^\nu(\alpha) = \tau(a) \sum_\nu p(\alpha)x^\nu(\alpha) = \tau(a)y(\alpha)$$

$$y(\alpha) = \sum_\nu y^\nu(\alpha), \quad y^\nu(\alpha) = p(\alpha)x^\nu(\alpha).$$

Let us define $z^\nu(\alpha)$ by

$$z^\nu(\alpha) = p(\alpha)c^\nu(\alpha) - p(\alpha)x^\nu(\alpha).$$

Then we have

$$\sum_\nu z^\nu(\alpha) = 0 \quad \text{for all } \alpha \in S. \tag{4}$$

For each $\alpha \in S$ and each ν, we define $\overline{\alpha}^\nu$ and $\overline{c}^\nu$ by the following conditions:

$$\overline{\alpha}^\nu \varphi(a(\alpha)) u^\nu_{c^\nu}(c^\nu(\alpha)) = p(\alpha) \tag{5}$$

$$p(\alpha)\overline{c}^\nu = p(\alpha)x^\nu(\alpha). \tag{6}$$

It is apparent that, for each ν, such a $\overline{c}^\nu$ is obtained as the optimum solution to the maximum problem as follows:

Maximize $u^\nu(c^\nu)$ subject to the constraints

$$p(\alpha)c^\nu \leqq p(\alpha)x^\nu(\alpha), \quad c^\nu \geqq 0.$$

The value of $\overline{\alpha}^\nu$ is obtained as the inverse of the Lagrangian multiplier associated with this maximum problem, and it is uniquely determined.

Note that $\overline{\alpha} = (\overline{\alpha}^\nu)$ is defined and continuous for all $\alpha \in S$ and $\overline{\alpha} = (\overline{\alpha}^\nu) > 0$. We define $\beta(\alpha) = (\beta^\nu(\alpha))$ by

$$\beta^\nu(\alpha) = \frac{1}{\lambda(\alpha)}\overline{\alpha}^\nu, \quad \text{for all } \nu$$

$$\lambda(\alpha) = \sum_\nu \overline{\alpha}^\nu > 0, \quad \text{for all } \alpha \in S.$$

Then $\beta(\alpha) \in S$ for all $\alpha \in S$, and $\alpha \to \beta(\alpha)$ is a continuous mapping from S onto itself. Hence, an application of Brouwer's fixed-point theorem guarantees that an $\alpha \in S$ exists such that

$$\beta(\alpha) = \alpha; \text{ that is, } \overline{\alpha}^\nu = \lambda(\alpha)\alpha^\nu \text{ for all } \nu.$$

We can now show that

$$\lambda(\alpha) = 1. \tag{7}$$

Suppose to the contrary that $\lambda(\alpha) < 1$. Then, relations (5) and (6) imply that

$$p(\alpha)c^\nu(\alpha) < p(\alpha)\overline{c}^\nu = p(\alpha)x^\nu(\alpha), \quad \text{for all } \nu.$$

Hence, $z^\nu(\alpha) > 0$, for all ν, and $\sum_\nu z^\nu(\alpha) > 0$, thus contradicting (4). Similarly, $\lambda(\alpha) > 1$ leads to a contradiction. Thus, (7) must be satisfied, implying that $\overline{\alpha}^\nu = \alpha^\nu$ and $z^\nu(\alpha) = 0$ for all ν. Q. E. D.

9. PROOF OF PROPOSITION 4

The proof of Proposition 4 may be carried out in exactly the same manner as the one for Proposition 3 with the following modifications:

$$z^\nu(\alpha) = [p(\alpha)x(\alpha) - \theta(\alpha)a^\nu(\alpha)] - [p(\alpha)c^\nu(\alpha) - \theta^\nu(\alpha)a(\alpha)]$$
$$\theta^\nu(\alpha) = -\alpha^\nu\varphi'(a(\alpha))u^\nu(c^\nu(\alpha)).$$

Then we have

$$\sum_\nu z^\nu(\alpha) = 0 \quad \text{for all } \alpha \in S,$$

and $(c^1(\alpha), \ldots, c^N(\alpha); a(\alpha))$ is a Lindahl equilibrium if, and only if,

$$z^\nu(\alpha) = 0, \quad \text{for all } \nu.$$

For each $\alpha = (\alpha^\nu) \in S$, we define by $(\bar{c}^\nu, \bar{a}^{(\nu)})$ the following conditions:

$$\bar{\alpha}^\nu\varphi(\bar{a}^{(\nu)})u^\nu_{c^\nu}(\bar{c}^\nu) = p(\alpha)$$
$$-\bar{\alpha}^\nu\varphi'(\bar{a}^{(\nu)})u^\nu(\bar{c}^\nu) = \theta^\nu(\alpha)$$
$$p(\alpha)\bar{c}^\nu - \theta^\nu(\alpha)\bar{a}^\nu = p(\alpha)x(\alpha) - \theta(\alpha)a^\nu(\alpha).$$

For each ν, $(\bar{c}^\nu, \bar{a}^{(\nu)})$ is obtained as the optimum solution to the maximum problem:

Find $(\bar{c}^\nu, \bar{a}^{(\nu)})$ that maximizes $\varphi(a^{(\nu)})u^\nu(c^\nu)$ subject to the constraints that

$$p(\alpha)c^\nu - \theta^\nu(\alpha)a^{(\nu)} = p(\alpha)x(\alpha) - \theta(\alpha)a^\nu(\alpha), \quad c^\nu, a^{(\nu)} \geqq 0.$$

Such a $(\bar{c}^\nu, \bar{a}^{(\nu)})$ is uniquely determined, and

$$\bar{a}^{(\nu)} \geqq a(\alpha), \quad \text{or} \quad \bar{a}^{(\nu)} \leqq a(\alpha)$$

on the basis of whether

$$z^{(\nu)} \geqq 0 \quad \text{or} \quad z^{(\nu)} \leqq 0. \qquad \text{Q.E.D.}$$

2

Pareto Optimality and Social Optimum

1. INTRODUCTION

In the previous chapter, we showed, as Proposition 2, that the market equilibrium obtained under the uniform carbon tax scheme is a social optimum in the sense that a set of positive weights exists for the utilities of individual countries $(\alpha^1, \ldots, \alpha^n)$, $[\alpha^\nu > 0]$ such that the world utility

$$W = \sum_\nu \alpha^\nu \varphi(a) u^\nu(c^\nu)$$

is maximized among all feasible patterns of allocation $(c^1, \ldots, c^n, x^1, \ldots, x^n, a^1, \ldots, a^n, a)$.

The converse of this proposition does not hold. The pattern of allocation at a social optimum exhibits all the conditions necessary for market equilibrium under the universal carbon tax scheme except for the balance-of-payments conditions. One of the primary functions of the institutions of markets for tradable emission permits is the arrangement of the initial allotment of tradable emission permits among individual countries so that the balance-of-payments conditions are satisfied at the social optimum corresponding to the uniform carbon tax regime.

The new era of economic thinking was ushered in by Arrow and Debreu (1954), and many contributions since have been made concerning the existence and stability of general equilibrium systems involving both private and public goods. They are all noted for the precision and generality of their theoretical premises and for the rigor and elegance of the deductive and analytical approaches used to derive propositions of both theoretical and practical relevance. They are primarily concerned with pursuing theoretical premises that minimize the qualifying constraints required to derive relevant propositions. This tendency is particularly manifest in the analysis of consumer behavior, where preference ordering has replaced the more restrictive assumption of cardinal utility.

In this chapter, however, we confine ourselves to the realm of cardinal utility and the analysis of the existence and stability of competitive equilibrium. Our approach is more restrictive, albeit only slightly, than the standard one formulated in terms of preference ordering and the dynamic process in terms of the adjustment of the weights assigned to individual utility levels contrary to the classic, more realistic process of price adjustment in terms of the divergence between demand and supply. It is possible, however, to obtain far-reaching conclusions concerning the stability of competitive equilibrium. Indeed, we prove that the adjustment process for utility weights, as precisely defined in Section 4, is always globally stable, without imposing further qualifying constraints on the nature of the utility functions of individual consumers or on the number of individual consumers. We also prove that the set of all competitive equilibria is locally convex and piecewise connected – the latter in the sense that the whole domain of equilibrium vectors of utility weights is partitioned into a finite number of disjoint subsets such that any pair of two competitive equilibria in the same subset may be connected by a smooth (continuously differentiable) curve.

The analysis is then extended to the general case involving public goods in the Samuelsonian sense. We show that Lindahl equilibrium always exists and that the set of all Lindahl equilibria is locally convex and piecewise connected. The dynamic processes of the adjustment with respect to utility weights are shown to be always globally stable. It is possible to derive similar results for the model of global warming, where the emission of greenhouse gases produces public goods – all with negative marginal utilities. The classic concept of Lindahl equilibrium is introduced specifically with global warming in mind, the existence of Lindahl equilibrium involving emissions of greenhouse gases is proved, and the adjustment processes in terms of utility weights are shown to be always globally stable. The set of all Lindahl equilibria is locally convex and piecewise connected.

Some of the propositions discussed in this chapter are so esoteric that they may seem to have no relevance for practical and policy purposes. However, they help us to understand the complicated interrelationships that exist between the basic concepts and relevant variables that are routinely utilized in economic arguments, on the one hand, and to examine the welfare implications of various institutional arrangements and policy measures that have been devised to control the emission of carbon dioxide and other greenhouse gases and to effectively abate processes of global warming, as will be discussed in Chapter 3 in relation to the choice of the initial allotment of tradable emission permits.

Regarding the principle of judging the distribution of welfare among individual members of the society with public goods in the Samuelsonian sense or social overhead capital in general, the most important role is played by the concept of the Lindahl solution, as briefly discussed in Chapter 1. The Lindahl solution is obtained when the amount of public goods or social overhead capital actually provided by the society is precisely equal to the amount each member of the society wishes to have under the budgetary constraints he or she is subject to.

As mentioned in Chapter 1, many contributions have been made to reinforce the proposition that the Lindahl solution concretely formulates the sense of equity and social justice prevailing in the society. It has turned out, however, in the case of the market for tradable emission permits that the Lindahl solution has a tendency to reinforce, rather than mitigate, the inequality that exists for the initial distribution of welfare among individual members of the society. The concept of the Lindahl solution has been defined so esoterically that this basic property has been extremely difficult to see; a few economists have noticed it but have confined their remarks to oral comments made at various seminars on the Lindahl solution. Indeed, this observation will be one of the major conclusions in Chapter 3, where the function of markets for tradable emission permits will be examined in detail.

2. PARETO OPTIMALITY AND SOCIAL OPTIMUM

The concept of Pareto optimality plays a central role in the analysis of the welfare implications of institutional arrangements for the allocation of scarce resources – both private and public. It has been extensively examined in the literature, particularly in terms of abstract preference relations, as described in detail in virtually every textbook on price theory. The existing body of propositions concerning the concept of Pareto optimality, however, is not particularly well suited to the analysis of the various institutional arrangements and policy measures – particularly carbon taxes and tradable emission permits – that have been proposed to effectively abate processes of global warming.

Pareto Optimality in a Purely Private Economy

Before we begin our discussion, we would like to consider an alternative formulation of Pareto optimality in which the welfare implications are more explicitly brought out.

We consider an economy consisting of a finite number of individual economic agents, generically denoted by $\nu = 1, \ldots, n$. Each economic agent is assumed to play the role of both a consumer and a producer. For each economic agent ν, the preference relation is represented by a utility function $u^\nu(c^\nu)$, which satisfies the following conditions:

(U1) $u^\nu(c^\nu)$ is defined for all nonnegative J-dimensional vectors $c^\nu = (c_j^\nu) > 0$ and is continuous and continuously twice-differentiable everywhere.

(U2) Marginal utilities are always positive; that is,

$$u_{c^\nu}^\nu > 0 \quad \text{for all} \quad c^\nu > 0.$$

(U3) Marginal rates of substitution between various goods are diminishing; that is, $u^\nu(c^\nu)$ is strictly concave with respect to c^ν:

$$u^\nu((1-\theta)c_0^\nu + \theta c_1^\nu) > (1-\theta)u^\nu(c_0^\nu) + \theta u^\nu(c_1^\nu)$$
$$\text{for all } c_0^\nu \neq c_1^\nu, \text{ and } 0 < \theta < 1.$$

Condition (U3) may be formulated alternatively as

(U3)′ $u^\nu(c_1^\nu) - u^\nu(c_0^\nu) < u_{c^\nu}^\nu(c_0^\nu)(c_1^\nu - c_0^\nu)$ for all $c_0^\nu \neq c_1^\nu$

or, in a stronger form, as follows:

(U3)″ The matrix of second-order partial derivatives $(u_{c^\nu c^\nu}^\nu)$ is negative-definite for all $c^\nu > 0$.

NOTE. If a preference ordering on the conceivable set of vectors of consumption is strictly concave and smooth in the sense that each indifference surface is continuously twice-differentiable, then, in any compact set of vectors of consumption, the preference ordering may be represented by a utility function that is strictly concave and continuously twice-differentiable. This classic theorem is due to Fenchel (Fenchel 1953, pp. 133–4).

For each economic agent ν, the endowments of factors of production and available technologies are represented by the production possibility set T^ν consisting of all commodity vectors $x^\nu = (x_j^\nu)$ that are feasibly produced by economic agent ν. We assume that

(T1) For each economic agent ν, production possibility set T^ν is nonempty and compact (closed and bounded). All vectors in T^ν are nonnegative.

(T2) For any vector of nonzero, nonnegative prices $p = (p_j) \geq 0$, the output vector $x^\nu(p)$ that maximizes px^ν among all feasible vectors $x^\nu \in T^\nu$ is uniquely determined and continuously twice-differentiable for all $p \geq 0$. It is also assumed that $px^\nu(p) > 0$ for all $p > 0$.

The assumption that the production possibility set T^ν is defined for each economic agent ν is introduced, primarily on the basis of our concern with markets for tradable permits for the emission of carbon dioxide and other greenhouse gases, where each economic agent is a country rather than an individual person or enterprise. The standard formulation, traditionally adopted in the literature on the theory of general equilibrium, as in Arrow and Debreu (1954), may readily be reduced to our model. Suppose there are a finite number of producers, generically denoted by η, distinct from the consumers, denoted by ν, who are solely engaged in consumption. The production possibility set T^η for each producer η is assumed to satisfy hypotheses (T1) and (T2), and the optimum vector corresponding to price vector p is denoted by $x^\eta(p)$. We assume that the fraction of the profits of producer η distributed to consumer ν is a constant to be denoted by $s^{\nu\eta}$. We define the production possibility set T^ν for consumer ν as follows:

$$T^\nu = \sum_\eta s^{\nu\eta} T^\eta + \omega^\nu = \left\{ x = \sum_\eta s^{\nu\eta} x^\eta + \omega^\nu : x^\eta \in T^\eta \right\},$$

where ω^ν is the vector of endowments for agent ν. The production possibility sets T^ν thus defined satisfy (T1) and (T2).

A pattern of vectors of consumption and production $(c^1, \ldots, c^n; x^1, \ldots, x^n)$ is a *feasible allocation* if a system of vectors of production exists such that the following conditions are satisfied:

$$\sum_\nu c^\nu \leqq \sum_\nu x^\nu, \quad c^\nu \geqq 0, \quad x^\nu \in T^\nu \quad \text{for all } \nu.$$

A feasible allocation $(c_*^1, \ldots, c_*^n; x_*^1, \ldots, x_*^n)$ is a *Pareto optimum* if no other feasible allocation $(c^1, \ldots, c^n; x^1, \ldots, x^n)$ exists such that

$$u^\nu(c^\nu) \geqq u^\nu(c_*^\nu) \quad \text{for all } \nu$$
$$u^\nu(c^\nu) > u^\nu(c_*^\nu) \quad \text{for some } \nu.$$

Similar concepts may be defined in reference to the pattern of vectors of consumption $(c^1, \ldots, c^n)$.

The following proposition is basic to our discussion. The proof of Proposition 1 and other propositions will be given in the mathematical notes at the end of this chapter.

Proposition 1. *Let assumptions* (U1),(U2),(U3) *and* (T1),(T2) *be satisfied. Then a feasible allocation* $(c_*^1, \ldots, c_*^n; x_*^1, \ldots, x_*^n)$ *is a Pareto optimum if, and only if, there exists a positive vector* $\alpha = (\alpha^\nu)$, $[\alpha^\nu > 0$ *for all* $\nu]$ *uniquely determined, except for proportionality, such that* $(c_*^1, \ldots, c_*^n; x_*^1, \ldots, x_*^n)$ *is the optimum solution to the following maximum problem:*

Find an allocation $(c_*^1, \ldots, c_*^n; x_*^1, \ldots, x_*^n)$ *that maximizes social utility*

$$W = \sum_\nu \alpha^\nu u^\nu(c^\nu)$$

among all feasible allocations.

Proposition 1 establishes a one-to-one correspondence between Pareto-optimal allocations and weight vectors for individual utilities (except for proportionality), confirming the familiar observation that the concept of Pareto optimality exclusively concerns efficiency properties of allocative processes and entirely disregards equity considerations for individual consumers in the economy.

3. SOCIAL OPTIMUM AND IMPUTED PRICES

Let $\alpha = (\alpha^\nu)$ be a nonnegative, nonzero vector of weights for individual utilities and consider the following optimum problem:

Find an allocation $(c^1_*, \ldots, c^n_*; x^1_*, \ldots, x^n_*)$ that maximizes the weighted total utility

$$W = \sum_\nu \alpha^\nu u^\nu(c^\nu)$$

among all feasible allocations $(c^1, \ldots, c^n; x^1, \ldots, x^n)$.

Assumptions (U1), (U2), (U3) and (T1), (T2) introduced in the previous section ensure that the optimum allocation $(c^1_*, \ldots, c^n_*; x^1_*, \ldots, x^n_*)$ always exists and is uniquely determined. The optimum problem is a concave programming problem, and the Kuhn–Tucker theorem on concave programming may be applied to show the existence of the nonnegative vector of imputed prices $p = (p_j)$ satisfying the following marginality conditions (see the mathematical notes at the end of Chapter 1 and also Arrow, Hurwicz, and Uzawa 1958):

(i) $$\sum_\nu c^\nu_* \leqq \sum_\nu x^\nu_*, \quad x^\nu_* = x^\nu(p).$$

(ii) $$\sum_\nu \alpha^\nu u^\nu_{c^\nu}(c^\nu_*) \leqq p \quad (\text{mod. } c^\nu_*),$$

meaning that $\sum_\nu \alpha^\nu_j u^\nu_{c^\nu}(c^\nu_*) \leqq p^\nu_j$ with equality for those components j for which $c^\nu_{j*} > 0$.

Such a vector of imputed prices $p = (p_j)$ is uniquely determined. All relevant variables are also uniquely determined for the given weight vector $\alpha = (\alpha^\nu)$. Hence, they may be denoted as $c^\nu(\alpha)$, $x^\nu(\alpha)$, and $p(\alpha)$.

Conversely, if conditions (i) and (ii) are satisfied, then the given allocation $(c^1_*, \ldots, c^n_*; x^1_*, \ldots, x^n_*)$ is the optimum allocation with respect to the vector of utility weights $\alpha = (\alpha^\nu)$.

Because α is nonnegative, nonzero, the vector of imputed prices $p(\alpha)$ is positive:

$$p(\alpha) > 0; \text{ that is, } \quad p_j(\alpha) > 0, \quad \text{for all } j.$$

4. COMPETITIVE EQUILIBRIUM AND SOCIAL OPTIMUM

A feasible allocation $(c^1_*, \ldots, c^n_*; x^1_*, \ldots, x^n_*)$ is a *competitive equilibrium* if there exists a nonnegative, nonzero vector of prices $p = (p_j)$

that satisfy the following conditions:

(i) $x_*^\nu = x^\nu(p)$ for all ν.
(ii) For each ν, c_*^ν maximizes $u^\nu(c^\nu)$ subject to $pc^\nu \leqq px_*^\nu$.

Proposition 2. *Let assumptions* (U1), (U2), (U3), *and* (T1), (T2) *be satisfied. Then there always exists a competitive equilibrium* $(c_*^1, \ldots, c_*^n; x_*^1, \ldots, x_*^n)$.

In view of Proposition 1, Proposition 2 implies that, if $(c_*^1, \ldots, c_*^n; x_*^1, \ldots, x_*^n)$ is an allocation associated with a competitive equilibrium, it is a Pareto optimum. On the other hand, any Pareto-optimal allocation $(c_*^1, \ldots, c_*^n; x_*^1, \ldots, x_*^n)$ may be represented as a competitive equilibrium with suitable vectors of endowments (ω^ν). Indeed, let $\alpha = (\alpha^\nu)$ be a vector of positive weights for utilities associated with the given Pareto-optimal allocation $(c_*^1, \ldots, c_*^n; x_*^1, \ldots, x_*^n)$, and let $p_* = p(\alpha)$ be the vector of imputed prices corresponding to the vector of utility weights α. Then, there exist transfer vectors $\Delta\omega^\nu$ such that

$$\sum_\nu p_* \Delta\omega^\nu = 0,$$

and $(p_*, c_*^1, \ldots, c_*^n; x_*^1, \ldots, x_*^n)$ is a competitive equilibrium with vectors of endowments $\overline{\omega}^\nu = \omega^\nu + \Delta\omega^\nu$, where ω^ν are the vectors of initial endowments .

A vector of utility weights $\alpha = (\alpha^\nu)$ is an *equilibrium vector of utility weights* if the optimum allocation $(c^\nu(\alpha), x^\nu(\alpha))$ and the associated price vector $p(\alpha)$ are a competitive equilibrium.

We introduce an adjustment process with respect to the vector of utility weights $\alpha(t) = (\alpha^\nu(t))$ defined by the following system of differential equations:

$$\text{(A)} \qquad \dot{\alpha}^\nu(t) = \alpha^\nu(t)\left\{u^\nu(\bar{c}^\nu(t)) - u^\nu(c^\nu(t))\right\},$$

with initial condition $\alpha(0) = \alpha_0$, where $c^\nu(t) = c^\nu(\alpha(t))$, $p(t) = p(\alpha(t))$, and $\bar{c}^\nu(t)$ is obtained as the optimum solution to the following maximum problem:

Find $\bar{c}^\nu(t)$ that maximizes $u^\nu(c^\nu)$ subject to the budget constraint

$$c^\nu \geqq 0,\ p(t)c^\nu = p(t)x^\nu(p(t)).$$

Assumptions (U1), (U2), (U3), and (T1), (T2) ensure that the solution path $\alpha(t)$ to the system of differential equations (A) uniquely exists for any given initial condition $\alpha_0 > 0$. It may be denoted by $\alpha(t;\alpha_0)$ to indicate explicitly the dependency on initial condition α_0. At each time t, $\alpha(t;\alpha_0)$ is continuous and continuously differentiable with respect to initial condition α_0.

Our adjustment process is formulated in terms of the vector of weights for individual utilities in contrast to the process of the market mechanism, which concerns price adjustment with regard to demand and supply. The stability of such an adjustment process may be of some interest – particularly in relation to the analysis of markets for tradable emission permits – as will be discussed in detail in Chapter 3. The proof of Proposition 3 is described in the mathematical notes at the end of this chapter.

Proposition 3. *Let assumptions* (U1),(U2),(U3), *and* (T1),(T2) *be satisfied. For any initial condition* $\alpha_0 > 0$, *the solution path* $\alpha(t;\alpha_0)$ *to the system of differential equations* (A) *uniquely exists and converges to an equilibrium vector of utility weights* α_*.

In what follows, we examine the structure of the set of all equilibrium vectors denoted by Γ_*.

The set of all equilibrium vectors Γ_* is a cone; that is, if $\alpha = (\alpha^\nu)$ is an equilibrium vector of utility weights, then, for any positive number $t > 0$, $t\alpha$ is also an equilibrium vector:

$$\alpha \in \Gamma_* \Rightarrow t\alpha \in \Gamma_*, \quad \text{for all } t > 0.$$

A set Γ of weight vectors is *locally convex* if, for any vector $\alpha_0 \in \Gamma$, there exists a positive number $\varepsilon(\varepsilon > 0)$ such that the ε- neighborhood of α_0

$$V = \{\alpha : \alpha \in \Gamma, \|\alpha - \alpha_0\| < \varepsilon\}$$

is a convex set.

A set Γ of weight vectors is *piecewise connected* if the set Γ is divided into several disjoint subsets $\{\Gamma_1, \ldots, \Gamma_M\}$ such that, for any pair of two weight vectors α_0 and α_1 in the same subset Γ_m, there exists a smooth curve connecting them; that is, there exists a continuous curve $\alpha(t), 0 \leqq t \leqq 1$ such that $\alpha(0) = \alpha_0, \alpha(1) = \alpha_1, \alpha(t) \in \Gamma_m$, and $\alpha(t)$ is continuously differentiable with respect to t for all $0 \leqq t \leqq 1$.

Proposition 4. *Let assumptions* (U1), (U2), (U3), *and* (T1), (T2) *be satisfied. Then the set* Γ_* *of all equilibrium vectors of utility weights is a nonempty cone that is locally convex and piecewise connected.*

The proof of Proposition 4, which will be described in the mathematical notes at the end of this chapter, is rather complicated and relies heavily on the stability of the adjustment process with respect to vectors of utility weights, as introduced by (A).

5. PUBLIC GOODS AND LINDAHL EQUILIBRIUM

The analysis we have developed in the previous sections may easily be extended to an economy involving private goods as well as public goods in the sense defined by Samuelson (1954). The analysis of economies involving public goods in the Samuelsonian sense is focused on the elaboration and extension of the concept of Lindahl equilibrium (Lindahl 1919). It has been studied extensively by Johansen (1963), Foley (1967, 1970), Fabre-Sender (1969), Malinvaud (1971), Milleron (1972), Roberts (1974), Kaneko (1977), and Mas-Colell (1980, 1985), among others. In the following analysis, we adopt the approaches developed by Foley (1970) and Roberts (1974).

An Economy with Public Goods

The economy we consider in the following discussion involves finite numbers of private goods and public goods respectively denoted by $j = 1, \ldots, J$, and $k = 1, \ldots, K$. There exist n consumers, to be denoted by $\nu = 1, \ldots, n$, but only one producer.

For each consumer ν, the preference relation is defined with respect to quantities of consumption of private goods as well as those of public goods provided for all members of the economy to be represented by (c^ν, a), where $c^\nu = (c_j^\nu)$ is the vector of private goods consumed by ν, whereas $a = (a_k)$ is the vector of public goods available in the economy. The preference relation of consumer ν is assumed to be represented by a utility function $u^\nu(c^\nu, a)$ for which the following conditions are satisfied:

(U1′) $u^\nu(c^\nu, a)$ is defined, continuous, and continuously twice-differentiable for all nonnegative $(c^\nu, a) > (0, 0)$.

(U2′) Marginal utilities are always positive; that is,

$$u^{\nu}_{c^{\nu}} > 0, u^{\nu}_{a} > 0 \quad \text{for all } (c^{\nu}, a) > (0, 0).$$

(U3′) $u^{\nu}(c^{\nu}, a)$ is strictly concave with respect to (c^{ν}, a); that is,

$$u^{\nu}(c^{\nu}(\theta), a(\theta)) > (1-\theta)u^{\nu}(c^{\nu}_0, a_0) + \theta u^{\nu}(c^{\nu}_1, a_1)$$
$$\text{for all } (c^{\nu}_0, a_0) \neq (c^{\nu}_1, a_1), 0 < \theta < 1,$$

where $c^{\nu}(\theta) = (1-\theta)c^{\nu}_0 + \theta c^{\nu}_1$, $a(\theta) = (1-\theta)a_0 + \theta a_1$.
or in a stronger form, as follows:

(U3′)′ The matrix of second-order partial derivatives

$$\begin{pmatrix} u_{c^{\nu}c^{\nu}} & u_{c^{\nu}} \\ u_{ac^{\nu}} & u_{aa} \end{pmatrix}_{(c^{\nu}, a)}$$

is negative definite for all $(c^{\nu}, a) > (0, 0)$.

The set of all production plans (x, a), each consisting of vectors of aggregate private goods $x = (x_j)$ and public goods $a = (a_k)$, that are technologically possible with given endowments of factors of production, is denoted by the production possibility set T.

(T1′) Production possibility set T is nonempty and compact. All vectors (x, a) in T are nonnegative; that is, $(x, a) \geqq (0, 0)$ for all $(x, a) \in T$, and $(0, 0) \in T$.

(T2′) For any vector of nonzero, nonnegative prices $(p, q) \geq (0, 0)$, the production plan $(x(p, q), a(p, q))$ that maximizes $px + qa$ among all feasible production plans $(x, a) \in T$ is uniquely determined and continuously twice-differentiable, and

$$px(p, q) + qa(p, q) > 0, \quad \text{for all } (p, q) > (0, 0).$$

Conditions (T2′) imply that, for price vector $(p, q) > (0, 0)$, the matrix of second-order partial derivatives

$$\begin{pmatrix} x_p & a_p \\ x_a & a_q \end{pmatrix}_{(p,q)}$$

is symmetrical and positive semidefinite.

A pattern of vectors of consumption of private goods and provision of public goods, $(c^1, \ldots, c^n; a)$ is *feasible* if an output vector of private goods $x = (x_j)$ exists such that

$$\sum_\nu c^\nu \leqq x, \quad c^\nu \geqq 0, \quad (x, a) \in T.$$

A feasible allocation $(c_*^1, \ldots, c_*^n; a_*)$ is a Pareto optimum if no other feasible allocation $(c^1, \ldots, c^n; a)$ exists such that

$$u^\nu(c^\nu, a) \geqq u^\nu(c_*^\nu, a_*), \quad \text{for all } \nu$$
$$u^\nu(c^\nu, a) > u^\nu(c_*^\nu, a_*), \quad \text{for some } \nu.$$

Proposition 1′. *Let assumptions* (U1′),(U2′),(U3′), *and* (T1′),(T2′) *be satisfied. Then, a feasible allocation* $(c_*^1, \ldots, c_*^n; a_*)$ *is a Pareto optimum if, and only if, a vector of positive utility weights* $\alpha = (\alpha^\nu) > 0$ *exists such that* $(c_*^1, \ldots, c_*^n; a_*)$ *is the optimum solution to the following maximum problem:*

Find an allocation $(c_*^1, \ldots, c_*^n; a_*)$ *that maximizes the social utility function*

$$W = \sum_\nu \alpha^\nu u^\nu(c^\nu, a)$$

among all feasible allocations.

The proof of Proposition 1′ is identical with that of Proposition 1, where $(c^1, \ldots, c^n)$ and $(c_*^1, \ldots, c_*^n)$ are replaced by $(c^1, \ldots, c^n; a)$ and $(c_*^1, \ldots, c_*^n; a_*)$.

The optimum solution $(c_*^1, \ldots, c_*^n; a_*)$ to the maximum problem above, together with the associated output vector of private goods x_*, is uniquely determined. They are denoted by

$$c_*^\nu = c^\nu(\alpha), \quad a_* = a(\alpha), \quad x_* = x(\alpha).$$

Then, applying the Kuhn–Tucker theorem on concave programming, one can find nonnegative vectors $p_* = (p_{j^*})$ and $q_* = (q_{k^*})$ such that $(c^1(\alpha), \ldots, c^n(\alpha), a(\alpha), x(\alpha); p_*, q_*)$ is a nonnegative saddlepoint of the Lagrangian form:

$$L(c^1, \ldots, c^n, a, x; p, q)$$
$$= \sum_\nu \alpha^\nu u^\nu(c^\nu, a) + p\left(x - \sum_\nu c^\nu\right) + qa, c^\nu \geqq 0, (x, a) \in T.$$

The vectors of imputed prices p_* and q_* are uniquely determined; they are denoted by $p(\alpha)$ and $q(\alpha)$, and satisfy the following conditions:

$$x(\alpha) = x(p(\alpha), q(\alpha)), \quad a(\alpha) = a(p(\alpha), q(\alpha))$$
$$\sum_\nu c^\nu(\alpha) = x(\alpha)$$
$$\alpha^\nu u^\nu_{c^\nu}(c^\nu(\alpha), a(\alpha)) \leqq p(\alpha) \quad (\text{mod. } c^\nu(\alpha))$$
$$\sum_\nu \alpha^\nu u^\nu_a(c^\nu(\alpha), a(\alpha)) = q(\alpha).$$

It is apparent that

$$p(\alpha) > 0, \quad q(\alpha) > 0, \quad \text{for all } \alpha = (\alpha^\nu) > 0.$$

Lindahl Equilibrium

We now assume that a certain fraction s^ν of total revenue $px + qa$, $(x, a) \in T$ is distributed to each consumer ν. It is assumed that

$$s^\nu > 0, \quad \text{for all } \nu, \text{ and } \sum_\nu s^\nu = 1.$$

A feasible allocation $(c^1_*, \ldots, c^n_*; a_*)$ is a Lindahl equilibrium if there exist nonzero, nonnegative vectors of prices $p_*, q_*, q^1_*, \ldots, q^n_*$ and an output vector of private goods x_* such that

(i) (x_*, a_*) maximizes $p_*x + q_*a$ subject to $(x, a) \in T$;
(ii) for each ν, (c^ν_*, a_*) maximizes $u^\nu(c^\nu, a^{(\nu)})$ subject to the constraints that

$$p_*c^\nu + q^\nu_* a^{(\nu)} \leqq s^\nu(p_*x_* + q_*a_*), \quad c^\nu, a^{(\nu)} \geqq 0;$$

(iii) $$\sum_\nu c^\nu \leqq x_*;$$

(iv) $$q_* = \sum_\nu q^\nu_*.$$

In other words, Lindahl equilibrium is obtained when the quantity of public goods actually provided, a_*, is precisely equal to the quantity of public goods $a^{(\nu)}$ that each consumer ν wishes to be provided under the given budgetary constraint on the assumption that he or she has to pay for the provisions of public goods at the virtual price q^ν_* assigned to that person.

The definition of Lindahl equilibrium easily implies that

$$q_* = \sum_\nu q_*^\nu, \quad q_*^\nu = \alpha^\nu u_a^\nu(c_*^\nu, a_*).$$

Any Lindahl equilibrium $(c_*^1, \ldots, c_*^n; a_*)$ is a Pareto optimum. Hence, in view of Proposition 1′, a positive vector of utility weights $\alpha_* = (\alpha_*^\nu) > 0$ always exists such that

$$c_*^\nu = c^\nu(\alpha_*),\ a_* = a(\alpha_*),\ x_* = x(\alpha_*),\ p_* = p(\alpha_*),\ q_* = q(\alpha_*).$$

We denote by $q_*^\nu = q^\nu(\alpha_*)$ the virtual price of public goods assigned to each consumer ν.

For any nonzero, nonnegative vector of utility weights $\alpha = (\alpha^\nu) \geqq 0$, we define

$$z^\nu(\alpha) = s^\nu[p(\alpha)x(\alpha) + q(\alpha)a(\alpha)] - [p(\alpha)c^\nu(\alpha) + q^\nu(\alpha)a(\alpha)]$$
$$\sum_\nu z^\nu(\alpha) = 0.$$

Then, a positive vector of utility weights $\alpha_* = (\alpha_*^\nu)$ is a Lindahl equilibrium if, and only if,

$$z^\nu(\alpha_*) = 0, \quad \text{for all } \nu.$$

Proposition 2′. *Let assumptions* (U1′),(U2′),(U3′) *and* (T1′),(T2′) *be satisfied. Then there always exists a Lindahl equilibrium.*

Proposition 3′. *Let assumptions* (U1′),(U2′),(U3′) *and* (T1′),(T2′) *be satisfied. Then, for any initial condition* $\alpha_0 > 0$, *the solution path* $\alpha(t;\alpha_0)$ *to the following system of differential equations* (A′) *uniquely exists and converges to a positive vector of utility weights* $\alpha_* > 0$ *associated with a Lindahl equilibrium.*

$$\text{(A}'\text{)} \qquad \dot{\alpha}^\nu(t) = \alpha^\nu(t)[u^\nu(\bar{c}^\nu(t), \bar{a}^{(\nu)}(t)) - u^\nu(c^\nu(t), a(t))], \quad \textit{for all } \nu,$$

where $\alpha(0;\alpha_0) = \alpha_0$, *and* $u^\nu(\bar{c}^\nu(t), \bar{a}^{(\nu)}(t))$ *maximizes* $u^\nu(c^\nu, a^{(\nu)})$ *subject to the budget constraints*

$$p(\alpha(t))c^\nu + q^\nu(\alpha(t))a^{(\nu)}$$
$$\leqq s^\nu[p(\alpha(t))x(\alpha(t)) + q(\alpha(t))a(\alpha(t))],\ c^\nu, a^{(\nu)} \geqq 0.$$

Proposition 4′. *Let assumptions* (U1′),(U2′),(U3′) *and* (T1′),(T2′) *be satisfied. Then the set* Γ_* *of all vectors of utility weights* $\alpha_* = (\alpha_*^\nu) > 0$ *associated with Lindahl equilibrium is nonempty, locally convex, and piecewise connected.*

6. GLOBAL WARMING AND LINDAHL EQUILIBRIUM

The foregoing analysis has been applied to examine the welfare effect of global warming and other climate changes due to the emission of carbon dioxide and other greenhouse gases.

In this section, we examine the conditions under which the resulting allocation of scarce resources is a Lindahl equilibrium and the adjustment processes converge asymptotically to a Lindahl equilibrium.

The analysis is developed within the framework recently introduced by Mäler and Uzawa (1994), Chichilnisky and Heal (1994), and others, although the formulation of the model slightly differs from those introduced by them. We postulate that, as in Chapter 1, each greenhouse gas is measured so as to equate the greenhouse effect with that of carbon dioxide. Hence, we may assume that carbon dioxide is the only chemical agent with a greenhouse effect.

The relations between the production of private goods and the emission of CO_2 are specified by the state of available technologies and organizational arrangements together with the quantities of productive factors endowed in the economy. We denote by T the set of all combinations (x, a) of vectors of production of private goods, $x = (x_j)$, and the emission of CO_2, a, that can be technologically produced from the given endowments of factors of production:

We assume that

(T1″) Production possibility set T is nonempty and closed. All vectors $(x, a) \in T$ are nonnegative: $(x, a) \geqq (0, 0)$, $(0, 0) \in T$, and, if $(x, a) \in T$, $0 \leqq x' \leqq x$, $0 \leqq a' \leqq a$, then $(x', a') \in T$;

(T2″) For any nonzero, nonnegative vector of prices $(p, q) \geq (0, 0)$, the production plan $(x(p, q), a(p, q))$ that maximizes

$$px - qa$$

among all feasible production plans $(x, a) \in T$ is uniquely determined, continuous, and continuously twice-differentiable.

Assumption (T2″) implies that the matrix of second-order partial derivatives

$$\begin{pmatrix} x_p & x_q \\ -a_p & -a_q \end{pmatrix}_{(p,q)}$$

is symmetrical and positive semidefinite.

The preference ordering of consumer ν ($\nu = 1, \ldots, n$) is assumed to be defined over the combinations of vectors of private goods consumed by ν, $c^\nu = (c_j^\nu)$, and of the quantity a of CO_2 emitted by economic activities, primarily by the combustion of fossil fuels. We assume that, for each consumer ν, the preference ordering may be represented by the utility function $u^\nu(c^\nu, a)$. The following conditions are assumed for utility functions $u^\nu(c^\nu, a)$.

(U1″) $u^\nu(c^\nu, a)$ is defined, continuous, and continuously twice-differentiable for all $(c^\nu, a) \geqq (0, 0)$.

(U2″) Marginal utilities are always positive for the consumption of private goods, $c^\nu = (c_j^\nu)$, but negative with respect to the emission of CO_2, a, that is,

$$u_{c^\nu}^\nu > 0, \quad u_a^\nu < 0 \quad \text{for all } (c^\nu, a) \geqq (0, 0).$$

(U3″) $u^\nu(c^\nu, a)$ is strictly concave with respect to (c^ν, a), that is,

$$u^\nu(c^\nu(t), a(t)) > (1-t)u^\nu(c_0^\nu, a_0) + tu^\nu(c_1^\nu, a_1)$$
$$\text{for all } (c_0^\nu, a_0) \neq (c_1^\nu, a_1),\ 0 < t < 1,$$

where

$$c^\nu(t) = (1-t)c_0^\nu + tc_1^\nu, \quad a(t) = (1-t)a_0 + ta_1.$$

A pattern of vectors of consumption of private goods $(c^1, \ldots, c^n)$ and CO_2 emissions a is a *feasible allocation* if there exists an output vector of private goods x such that

$$\sum_\nu c^\nu \leqq x, \quad c^\nu \geqq 0, \quad (x, a) \in T.$$

A feasible allocation $(c_*^1, \ldots, c_*^n; a_*)$ is a Pareto optimum if no other feasible allocation $(c^1, \ldots, c^n; a)$ exists such that

$$u^\nu(c^\nu, a) \geqq u^\nu(c_*^\nu, a_*), \quad \text{for all } \nu$$
$$u^\nu(c^\nu, a) > u^\nu(c_*^\nu, a_*), \quad \text{for some } \nu.$$

Proposition 1″. *Let assumptions* (U1″),(U2″),(U3″) *and* (T1″),(T2″) *be satisfied. Then a feasible allocation* $(c_*^1, \ldots, c_*^n; a_*)$ *is a Pareto optimum if, and only if, there exists a vector of positive utility weights* $\alpha_* = (\alpha_*^\nu)$ *such that* $(c_*^1, \ldots, c_*^n; a_*)$ *is the optimum solution to the following maximum problem:*

Find an allocation $(c_*^1, \ldots, c_*^n; a_*)$ *that maximizes the social utility function*

$$W = \sum_\nu \alpha^\nu u^\nu(c^\nu, a)$$

among all feasible allocations.

Proposition 2″. *Let assumptions* (U1″),(U2″),(U3″) *and* (T1″),(T2″) *be satisfied. Then a Lindahl equilibrium always exists.*

Proposition 3″. *Let assumptions* (U1″),(U2″),(U3″) *and* (T1″),(T2″) *be satisfied. Then, for any initial condition* $\alpha_0 > 0$, *the solution path* $\alpha(t;\alpha_0)$ *to the following system of differential equations* (A″) *with any initial condition* $\alpha(0;\alpha_0) = \alpha_0$ *uniquely exists and converges to a positive vector of utility weights* $\alpha_* > 0$ *associated with a Lindahl equilibrium.*

$$\text{(A}''\text{)} \qquad \dot{\alpha}^\nu(t) = \alpha^\nu(t)[u^\nu(\overline{c}^\nu(t), \overline{a}^{(\nu)}(t)) - u^\nu(c^\nu(t), a(t))], \quad \text{for all } \nu,$$

where $(\overline{c}^\nu(t), \overline{a}^{(\nu)}(t))$ is the solution to the following system of Euler–Lagrange equations corresponding to $\alpha(t) = \alpha(t;\alpha_0)$:

$$\overline{\alpha}^\nu(t) u_{c^\nu}^\nu(\overline{c}^\nu, \overline{a}^{(\nu)}) = p(\alpha(t))$$
$$-\overline{\alpha}^\nu(t) u_a^\nu(\overline{c}^\nu, \overline{a}^{(\nu)}) = q^\nu(\alpha(t))$$
$$p(\alpha(t))\overline{c}^\nu - q^\nu(\alpha(t))\overline{a}^{(\nu)} = s^\nu[p(\alpha(t))x(\alpha(t)) - q(\alpha(t))a(\alpha(t))].$$

Proposition 4″. *Let assumptions* (U1″),(U2″),(U3″) *and* (T1″),(T2″) *be satisfied. Then the set* Γ_* *of all vectors of utility weights* $\alpha_* = (\alpha_*^\nu) > 0$ *associated with Lindahl equilibria is a nonempty cone, locally convex, and piecewise connected.*

7. TRADABLE EMISSION PERMITS AND LINDAHL EQUILIBRIUM

To handle the existence and stability of market equilibrium for tradable emission permits, we consider an international economy involving many countries that are generically denoted by ν, $\nu = 1, \ldots, n$. For each country ν, the production plan is specified by (x^ν, a^ν), where $x^\nu = (x_j^\nu)$ and a^ν denote the vector of production of private goods and the emission of CO_2, respectively. For each country ν, the set of all production plans (x^ν, a^ν) that are technologically feasible from the given quantities of factors of production endowed within country ν is denoted by T^ν.

We assume that, for each country ν, the set of technologically feasible production plans T^ν satisfies conditions (T1″) and (T2″), where the production plan $(x^\nu, a^\nu) \in T^\nu$ that maximizes $px^\nu - qa^\nu$ is denoted by $(x^\nu(p, q), a^\nu(p, q))$.

Then the aggregate quantity of CO_2 emitted into the atmosphere a is given by

$$a = \sum_\nu a^\nu.$$

A pattern $(c^1, \ldots, c^n; a)$ of vectors of consumption of private goods for each country ν, $c^\nu = (c_j^\nu)$, and the aggregate quantity of CO_2 emissions, a, is a feasible allocation if production plans $(x^\nu, a^\nu) \in T^\nu$ exist for all ν such that

$$\sum_\nu c^\nu \leqq \sum_\nu x^\nu, \quad a = \sum_\nu a^\nu, \quad (x^\nu, a^\nu) \in T^\nu.$$

A feasible allocation $(c_*^1, \ldots, c_*^N; a_*)$ is a *Lindahl equilibrium* if conditions (i), (ii), (iii), and (iv) are satisfied, where

$$x_* = \sum_\nu x_*^\nu, \quad a_* = \sum_\nu a_*^\nu, \quad (x_*^\nu, a_*^\nu) \in T^\nu \quad \text{for all } \nu.$$

(i) (x_*, a_*) maximizes $p_*x - q_*a$ subject to $(x, a) \in T$;

(ii) for each ν, (c_*^ν, a_*) maximizes $u^\nu(c^\nu, a^{(\nu)})$ subject to the constraints that

$$p_*c^\nu - q_*^\nu a^{(\nu)} \leqq s^\nu(p_*x_* - q_*a_*), \; c^\nu, a^{(\nu)} \geqq 0;$$

(iii) $$\sum_\nu c^\nu \leqq x_*;$$

(iv) $$q_* = \sum_\nu q_*^\nu.$$

For any nonzero, nonnegative vector of utility weights, $\alpha = (\alpha^\nu) \geqq 0$, we define

$$z^\nu(\alpha) = [p(\alpha)x^\nu(\alpha) - q(\alpha)a^\nu(\alpha)] - [p(\alpha)c^\nu(\alpha) - q^\nu(\alpha)a(\alpha)],$$

where $x^\nu(\alpha) = x^\nu(p(\alpha), q(\alpha)), a^\nu(\alpha) = a^\nu(p(\alpha), q(\alpha))$.

Then, we have

$$\sum_\nu z^\nu(\alpha) = 0,$$

and a positive vector of utility weights $\alpha_* = (\alpha_*^\nu)$ is a Lindahl equilibrium if, and only if,

$$z^\nu(\alpha_*) = 0, \quad \text{for all } \nu.$$

It is straightforward to verify that Propositions 2″–4″ hold for our international model of global warming.

Let us now examine the equilibrium conditions for the international market where tradable emission permits are exchanged. Suppose that, for each country ν, the quantities of tradable emission permits initially allotted are given by b^ν, where $b^\nu \geqq 0$ for all ν, and $a = \sum_\nu b^\nu$ is the total quantity of emission permits initially allotted.

Exactly in the same manner as previously, an equilibrium for the international market for tradable emission permits is always a Pareto optimum with respect to the given total emission of CO_2, a, and, accordingly, a vector of positive utility weights $\alpha_* = (\alpha_*^\nu) > 0$ exists such that the given equilibrium is obtained as the optimum solution to the following maximum problem:

Find an allocation $(c_*^1, \ldots, c_*^n; a_*)$ that maximizes the social utility function

$$W = \sum_\nu a^\nu u^\nu(c^\nu, a)$$

subject to the constraints

$$\sum_\nu c^\nu \leqq \sum_\nu x^\nu, \; a = \sum_\nu a^\nu, \; (x^\nu, a^\nu) \in T^\nu \quad \text{for all } \nu,$$

where a is the total emission of CO_2 given as the aggregate of tradable emission permits allotted to the countries involved.

For the given total emission of CO_2, a, the optimum solution and other relevant variables for the maximum problem are all uniquely determined and are denoted by $c^\nu(\alpha)$, $a^\nu(\alpha)$, $x^\nu(\alpha)$, $p(\alpha)$, $q(\alpha)$.

Note that

$$\sum_\nu a^\nu(\alpha) = a = \sum_\nu b^\nu.$$

We define the z^ν functions as follows:

$$z^\nu(\alpha) = [p(\alpha)x^\nu(\alpha) - p(\alpha)c^\nu(\alpha)] + q(\alpha)[b^\nu - a^\nu(\alpha)].$$

Then, we have

$$\sum_\nu z^\nu(\alpha) = 0, \quad \text{for all } \alpha \in S,$$

and the international market for tradable emission permits is at equilibrium if, and only if,

$$z^\nu(\alpha) = 0, \quad \text{for all } \nu.$$

For each ν, let us define $\overline{\alpha}^\nu$ by the following conditions:

$$\overline{\alpha}^\nu u^\nu_{c^\nu}(\overline{c}^\nu, a) = p(\alpha)$$
$$p(\alpha)\overline{c}^\nu = p(\alpha)x^\nu(\alpha) + q(\alpha)[b^\nu - a^\nu(\alpha)].$$

Then, we have

$$\overline{\alpha}^\nu \geqq \alpha^\nu, \quad \text{or} \quad \overline{\alpha}^\nu \leqq \alpha^\nu \quad \text{according as} \quad z^\nu(\alpha) \geqq 0, \quad \text{or} \quad z^\nu(\alpha) \leqq 0.$$

Therefore, the approach we have introduced in the proof of Proposition 1 above may be applied to the international market for tradable emission permits to establish the following propositions:

- For any given initial allotment of tradable emission permits $(b^1, \ldots, b^n)$ with total emission of CO_2, a, an equilibrium of the international market for tradable emission permits always exists.
- For any given initial allotment of tradable emission permits $(b^1, \ldots, b^n)$ the set of all equilibria of the international market for tradable emission permits is a nonempty, closed, locally convex, and locally connected set.

Proposition 1″. *Let assumptions* (U1″),(U2″), (U3″) *and* (T1″),(T2″) *be satisfied. Then a feasible allocation* $(c^1_*, \ldots, c^n_*; a_*)$ *is a Pareto optimum if, and only if, there exists a vector of positive utility weights* $\alpha_* = (\alpha^\nu_*)$ *such that* $(c^1_*, \ldots, c^n_*; a_*)$ *is the optimum solution to the following maximum problem:*

Find an allocation $(c_*^1, \ldots, c_*^n; a_*)$ *that maximizes the social utility function*

$$W = \sum_\nu \alpha^\nu u^\nu(c^\nu, a)$$

among all feasible allocations.

The proof of Proposition 1″ is carried out exactly in the same manner as for Proposition 1′, and the notation introduced there may be used for the case of CO_2 emission.

We assume that a certain fraction θ^ν of total revenue $px - qa$, $(x, a) \in T$, is distributed to each consumer ν. A feasible allocation $(c_*^1, \ldots, c_*^n; a_*)$ is a Lindahl equilibrium if there exist nonzero, nonnegative vectors of prices $p_*, q_*, q_*^1, \ldots q_*^n$, and an output vector of private goods, x_*, such that

(i)′ (x_*, a_*) maximizes $p_* x - q_* a$ subject to $(x, a) \in T$;
(ii)′ for each ν, (c_*^ν, a_*) maximizes $u^\nu(c^\nu, a^{(\nu)})$ subject to

$$p_* c^\nu - q_*^\nu a^{(\nu)} \leqq \theta^\nu (p_* x_* - q_* a_*),\ c^\nu \geqq 0,\ a^{(\nu)} \geqq 0;$$

(iii)′ $$\sum_\nu x_*^\nu \leqq x_*;$$

(iv)′ $$q_* = \sum_\nu q_*^\nu.$$

Then

$$q_* = \sum_\nu q_*^\nu, \quad q_*^\nu = -u_a^\nu(c_*^\nu, a_*).$$

We define, for any nonzero, nonnegative vector of utility weights $\alpha = (\alpha^\nu)$, the following quantities:

$$z^\nu(\alpha) = \theta^\nu \left\{p(\alpha)x(\alpha) - q(\alpha)a(\alpha)\right\} - \left\{p(\alpha)c^\nu(\alpha) - q^\nu(\alpha)a(\alpha)\right\}.$$

Then we have

$$\sum_\nu z^\nu(\alpha) = 0, \quad \text{for all } \alpha \in S,$$

and $(c^1(\alpha), \ldots, c^N(\alpha); a(\alpha))$ is a Lindahl equilibrium if, and only if,

$$z^\nu(\alpha) = 0, \quad \text{for all } \nu.$$

For each $\alpha = (\alpha^\nu) \in S$, $(\overline{c}^\nu, \overline{a}^{(\nu)})$ is defined by the following conditions:

$$\overline{\alpha}^{\nu} u_{c^{\nu}}^{\nu}(\overline{c}^{\nu}, \overline{a}^{(\nu)}) = p(\alpha)$$
$$-\overline{\alpha}^{\nu} u_{a}^{\nu}(\overline{c}^{\nu}, \overline{a}^{(\nu)}) = q^{\nu}(\alpha)$$
$$p(\alpha)\overline{c}^{\nu} - q^{\nu}(\alpha)\overline{a}^{(\nu)} = \theta^{\nu}\{p(\alpha)x(\alpha) - q(\alpha)a(\alpha)\}.$$

Note that $\overline{a}^{(\nu)} \geqq a(\alpha)$, or $\overline{a}^{(\nu)} \leqq a(\alpha)$, according as $z^{(\nu)} \geqq 0$, or $z^{(\nu)} \leqq 0$.

The relations we have obtained above imply that the lines of argument used in proving Propositions 2, 3, and 4 are valid for our present case of global warming. That is, the following propositions hold true.

Proposition 2″. *Let assumptions* (U1″),(U2″),(U3″) *and* (T1″),(T2″) *be satisfied. Then a Lindahl equilibrium always exists.*

Proposition 3″. *Let assumptions* (U1″),(U2″),(U3″) *and* (T1″),(T2″) *be satisfied. Then, for any initial condition* $\alpha_0 > 0$, *the solution path* $\alpha(t;\alpha_0)$ *to the system of differential equations*

(A″) $$\dot{\alpha}^{\nu}(t) = \alpha^{\nu}(t)\{u^{\nu}(\overline{c}^{\nu}(t), \overline{a}^{\nu}(t)) - u^{\nu}(c^{\nu}(t), a(t))\} \text{ for all } \nu,$$

where $(\overline{c}^{\nu}(t), \overline{a}^{(\nu)})$ *is the solution to* (A″) *for* $\alpha = \alpha(t)$, *uniquely exists and asymptotically converges to a Lindahl equilibrium.*

Proposition 4″. *Let assumptions* (U1″),(U2″),(U3″) *and* (T1″),(T2″) *be satisfied. Then the set* Γ_* *of all vectors of utility weights* $\alpha_* = (\alpha_*^{\nu}) > 0$ *associated with Lindahl equilibrium is a nonempty cone and is piecewise connected.*

MATHEMATICAL NOTES

PROOF OF PROPOSITION 1

For the given Pareto optimal allocation $(c_*^1, \ldots, c_*^n; x_*^1, \ldots, x_*^n)$, we define the set B in the n-dimensional vector space by

$$B = \{\beta = (\beta^{\nu}) : (\beta^{\nu}) \leqq (u^{\nu}(c^{\nu}) - u^{\nu}(c_*^{\nu})) \text{ for some feasible } (c^1, \ldots, c^n; x^1, \ldots, x^n)\}.$$

In view of the assumptions (U1–3) and (T1–2), the set B thus defined is a nonempty, closed, convex set in the n-dimensional vector space. The Pareto optimality of allocation $(c_*^1, \ldots, c_*^n; x_*^1, \ldots, x_*^n)$ implies that set

B does not possess a common point with the following convex set C:

$$C = \{c = (c^\nu) : c^\nu > 0, \quad \text{for all } \nu\}.$$

Hence, there exists a nonzero vector $\alpha = (\alpha^\nu)$ that separates two convex sets B and C; that is,

$$\alpha\beta \leqq \alpha c, \text{ for all } \beta \in B \text{ and } c \in C.$$

The definition of set C implies that the separating vector $\alpha = (\alpha^\nu)$ is nonnegative and nonzero; that is,

$$\alpha^\nu \geqq 0; \quad \text{for all } \nu, \quad \text{and} \quad \alpha^\nu > 0, \quad \text{for some } \nu.$$

We can show that a separating vector $\alpha = (\alpha^\nu)$ actually exists whose components are all positive:

$$a > 0, \text{ that is, } \alpha^\nu > 0, \quad \text{for all } \nu. \tag{1}$$

Suppose, to the contrary, no separating vector α satisfying (1) exists. Then an ν^0, say $\nu^0 = 1$ must exist such that

$$B^- \subset E^1 = \{\alpha = (\alpha^\nu) : \alpha^1 = 0, \alpha^\nu \text{ arbitrary for } \nu \neq 1\}, \tag{2}$$

where B^- is the polar cone of set B:

$$B^- = \{\alpha = (\alpha^\nu) : \alpha\beta \leqq 0, \text{ for all } \beta \in \beta\}.$$

Taking the polar cones of both sides of (2), we obtain

$$(B^-)^- \supset (E^1)^- = \{\beta = (\beta^\nu) : \beta^1 \text{ arbitrary, and } \beta^\nu = 0, \text{ for } \nu \neq 1\}. \tag{3}$$

On the other hand,

$$(B^-)^- = \text{Closure of } [B] = \{t\beta : t \geqq 0, \beta \in B\},$$

which, in conjunction with (3), implies that a sequence of feasible allocations $\{(c_s^1, \ldots, c_s^n; x_s^1, \ldots, x_s^n)\}$ and a sequence of nonnegative numbers $\{t_s\}$ exist such that

$$\lim_{s\to\infty} t_s\{u^1(c_s^1) - u^1(c_*^1)\} > 0, \; \lim_{s\to\infty} t_s\{u^\nu(c_s^\nu) - u^\nu(c_*^\nu)\} = 0, \quad \text{for } \nu \neq 1.$$

Because the set of all feasible allocations is compact (bounded and closed), a subsequence $\{s_k\}$ exists such that $\lim_{k\to\infty} t_{s_k} = t_0 > 0$,

$\lim_{k\to\infty} c^{\nu}_{s_k} = c^{\nu}_0$, and $\lim_{k\to\infty} x^{\nu}_{s_k} = x^{\nu}_0$ all exist. Hence,

$$t_0\{u^1(c^1_0) - u^1(c^1_*)\} > 0,\ t_0\{u^{\nu}(c^{\nu}_0) - u^{\nu}(c^{\nu}_*)\} = 0 \quad \text{for } \nu \neq 1,$$

which, in view of (1), implies

$$u^1(c^1_0) > u^1(c^1_*); u^{\nu}(c^{\nu}_0) = u^{\nu}(c^{\nu}_*) \quad \text{for } \nu \neq 1,$$

contradicting the assumed Pareto-optimality of $(c^1_*, \ldots, c^n_*; x^1_*, \ldots, x^n_*)$.

Thus, we have shown the existence of a vector $\alpha = (\alpha^{\nu})$, $\alpha^{\nu} > 0$ for all ν, such that

$$\sum_{\nu} \alpha^{\nu} u^{\nu}(c^{\nu}_*) \geqq \sum_{\nu} \alpha^{\nu} u^{\nu}(c^{\nu}) \quad \text{for all feasible } (c^1, \ldots, c^n; x^1, \ldots, x^n).$$

Conversely, if a feasible allocation $(c^1_*, \ldots, c^n_*; x^1_*, \ldots, x^n_*)$ is optimum, then it is easily shown to be a Pareto optimum. Q. E. D.

PROOF OF PROPOSITION 2

Proposition 2 is proved in the same manner as Proposition 3 in Chapter 1.

Let us consider the n-dimensional simplex S defined by

$$S = \left\{\alpha = (\alpha^{\nu}) : \alpha^{\nu} \geqq 0, \sum_{\nu} \alpha^{\nu} = 1\right\}.$$

We denote by $c^{\nu}(\alpha)$, $x^{\nu}(\alpha)$, and $p(\alpha)$ the optimum vectors and the vector of imputed prices for the optimum problem with weight vector α. Then the following conditions are satisfied:

$$\sum_{\nu} c^{\nu}(\alpha) = \sum_{\nu} x^{\nu}(\alpha),\ x^{\nu}(\alpha) = x^{\nu}(p(\alpha))$$

$$\alpha^{\nu} u^{\nu}_{c^{\nu}} \leqq p(\alpha), \quad (\text{mod. } c^{\nu}(\alpha))$$

Let us define $z^{\nu}(\alpha)$ as follows:

$$z^{\nu}(\alpha) = p(\alpha)x^{\nu}(\alpha) - p(\alpha)c^{\nu}(\alpha).$$

Then we have

$$\sum_{\nu} z^{\nu}(\alpha) = 0, \quad \text{for all } \alpha \in S.$$

For each $\alpha \in S$ and each ν, we define $\overline{\alpha}^\nu$ and $\overline{c}^\nu$ by the following conditions:

$$\overline{\alpha}^\nu u^\nu_{c^\nu}(\overline{c}^\nu) = p(\alpha)$$
$$p(\alpha)\overline{c}^\nu = p(\alpha)x^\nu(\alpha).$$

It is apparent that, for each ν, such $\overline{c}^\nu$ is obtained as the optimum solution to the maximum problem:

Maximize $u^\nu(c^\nu)$ subject to the constraints

$$c^\nu \geqq 0, \;\; p(\alpha)c^\nu \leqq p(\alpha)x^\nu(\alpha).$$

The value of $\overline{\alpha}^\nu$ then is uniquely determined.

Note that $\overline{\alpha} = (\overline{\alpha}^\nu)$ is defined for all $\alpha \in S$, is continuous, and $\overline{\alpha} = (\overline{\alpha}^\nu) > 0$. We define $\beta(\alpha) = (\beta^\nu(\alpha))$ by

$$\beta^\nu(\alpha) = \frac{1}{\lambda(\alpha)}\overline{\alpha}^\nu, \text{ for all } \nu,$$

where

$$\lambda(\alpha) = \sum_\nu \overline{\alpha}^\nu > 0, \text{ for all } \alpha \in S.$$

Then $\beta(\alpha) \in S$, for all $\alpha \in S$, and $\alpha \to \beta(\alpha)$ is a continuous mapping from S onto itself. Hence, an application of Brouwer's fixed-point theorem ensures that an $\alpha \in S$ exists such that

$$\beta(\alpha) = \alpha; \quad \text{that is,} \quad \overline{\alpha}^\nu = \lambda(\alpha)\alpha^\nu \text{ for all } \nu.$$

We can now show that

$$\lambda(\alpha) = 1.$$

Suppose $\lambda(\alpha) > 1$. Then,

$$p(\alpha)c^\nu(\alpha) < p(\alpha)\overline{c}^\nu = p(\alpha)x^\nu(\alpha), \text{ for all } \nu.$$

Hence, $z^\nu(\alpha) > 0$ for all ν, and $\sum_\nu z^\nu(\alpha) > 0$, thus contradicting relation $\lambda(\alpha) > 1$.

Similarly, $\lambda(\alpha) < 1$ leads to a contradiction. Thus, $\lambda(\alpha) = 1$, implying that $\overline{\alpha}^\nu = \alpha^\nu$ for all ν and $z^\nu(\alpha) = 0$ for all ν. Q. E. D.

PROOF OF PROPOSITION 3

It may be first recalled that

$$\sum_{\nu} c^{\nu}(t) = \sum_{\nu} x^{\nu}(t)$$

$$\alpha^{\nu}(t) u^{\nu}_{c^{\nu}}(c^{\nu}(t)) \leqq p(t), \ (\text{mod.}\, c^{\nu}(t)),$$

where $c^{\nu}(t) = c^{\nu}(\alpha(t))$, $x^{\nu}(t) = x^{\nu}(\alpha(t))$, $p(t) = p(\alpha(t))$, and so on.

Then positive numbers $\overline{\alpha}^{\nu}(t)$ exist such that

$$\overline{\alpha}^{\nu}(t) u^{\nu}_{c^{\nu}}(\overline{c}^{\nu}(t)) = p(t)$$

$$p(t)\overline{c}^{\nu}(t) = p(t) x^{\nu}(t).$$

To prove Proposition 3, we show that the function

$$W(\alpha) = \sum_{\nu} \alpha^{\nu}, \ \alpha = (\alpha^{\nu})$$

is a Lyapunov function for the system of differential equations (A).

The assumptions (U1), as expressed by the inequality (U1)′, yield the following inequalities.

$$\alpha^{\nu}(t)\left\{u^{\nu}(\overline{c}^{\nu}(t)) - u^{\nu}(c^{\nu}(t))\right\} \leqq \alpha^{\nu}(t) u^{\nu}_{c^{\nu}}(c^{\nu}(t))\left\{\overline{c}^{\nu}(t) - c^{\nu}(t)\right\}$$

with strict inequality whenever $\overline{c}^{\nu}(t) \neq c^{\nu}(t)$, for some ν.

We obtain

$$\dot{\alpha}^{\nu}(t) \leqq p(t)\left\{\overline{c}^{\nu}(t) - c^{\nu}(t)\right\} = p(t)x^{\nu}(t) - p(t)c^{\nu}(t)$$

with strict inequality whenever $\overline{\alpha}^{\nu}(t) \neq \alpha^{\nu}(t)$, for some ν.

By differentiating $W(\alpha)$ with respect to time t, we obtain

$$\dot{W}(t) \leqq \sum_{\nu}\left\{p(t)x^{\nu}(t) - p(t)c^{\nu}(t)\right\} = 0$$

with strict inequality whenever $\overline{\alpha}^{\nu}(t) \neq \alpha^{\nu}(t)$, for some ν.

We now obtain the following Lyapunov inequality for the solution path $\alpha(t;\alpha_0)$ to the system of differential equations (A) with initial condition $\alpha_0 = (\alpha_0^{\nu})$:

(L) $$\dot{W}(t;\alpha_0) \leqq 0, \ \text{for all}\ t$$

with strict inequality whenever $\alpha(t;\alpha_0)$ is not an equilibrium vector.

Then the Lyapunov theorem (as proved, e.g., by Uzawa 1961) may be applied to show that the solution path $\alpha(t;\alpha_0)$ to the system of differential equations (A) uniquely exists, is continuous with respect to initial condition α_0, and, for any convergent sequence $\{\alpha(t_k;\alpha_0)\}$, $\lim_{k\to\infty}\alpha(t_k;\alpha_0)$, is an equilibrium vector. That is, the adjustment process defined by (A) is *quasi-stable* in the sense defined in Uzawa (1961).

As α^ν approaches 0, $c^\nu(\alpha)$ also approaches 0, and $U^\nu(\overline{c}^\nu) - U^\nu(c^\nu(\alpha))$ remains positive for small values of α^ν. Hence, the solution path $\alpha^\nu(t;\alpha_0)$ remains positive and bounded away from 0. The Lyapunov inequality (L) implies that, for any initial condition α_0, the solution path $\alpha(t;\alpha_0)$ to the system of differential equations (A) remains bounded and bounded away from 0. Hence, there must exist a convergent subsequence $\{\alpha(t_k;\alpha_0)\}$ denoted by

$$\lim_{k\to\infty}\alpha(t_k;\alpha_0) = \alpha_*,$$

such that α_* is an equilibrium vector whenever $\alpha_* \neq 0$; hence,

$$W(\alpha_*) = \sum_\nu \alpha_*^\nu = \lim_{t\to\infty} W(t:\alpha_0).$$

Thus, a small neighborhood V of equilibrium vector α_* exists such that, for any initial condition $\alpha_0 \in V$, the solution path $\alpha(t:\alpha_0)$ converges to an equilibrium vector; that is, $\lim_{t\to\infty}\alpha(t;\alpha_0)$ always exists and is an equilibrium vector.

The preceding proof, however, is not applicable when

$$\lim_{t\to\infty} W(\alpha(t)) = 0.$$

In this case, we define $\beta = (\beta^\nu)$:

$$\beta^\nu = \frac{\alpha^\nu}{W(\alpha)}.$$

Then, we have

$$\beta^\nu \geqq 0, \ \sum_\nu \beta^\nu = 1$$

$$\dot{\beta}^\nu = \beta^\nu\left\{u^\nu(\overline{c}^\nu) - u^\nu(c^\nu)\right\} - \beta^\nu\frac{\dot{W}(\alpha)}{W(\alpha)}$$

$$\dot{W}(\alpha) \leqq 0.$$

Let $\beta_* = (\beta_*^\nu)$ be any accumulating point of $\{\beta(t)\}$; that is,

$$\beta_* = \lim_{k\to\infty} \beta(t_k), \quad \lim_{k\to\infty} t_k = \infty.$$

Suppose β_* is not a competitive equilibrium. Then a ν must exist such that

$$z^\nu(\beta_*) > 0, \text{ or } u^\nu(\bar{c}_*^\nu) - u^\nu(c_*^\nu) > 0,$$

where $\bar{c}_*^\nu$, c_*^ν are the vectors associated with β_*.

Hence, a positive number ε exists such that

$$\dot{\beta}^\nu > 0, \text{ for all } \beta \text{ such that } \|\beta - \beta_*\| < \varepsilon,$$

contradicting the assumed condition that β_* is an accumulating point of $\{\beta(t)\}$.

The Lyapunov theorem also implies that, for any equilibrium vector α_*, two neighborhoods

$$V = \{\alpha : \|\alpha - \alpha_*\| < \varepsilon\}$$
$$V_0 = \{\alpha : \|\alpha - \alpha_*\| < \varepsilon_0\} \quad (0 < \varepsilon_0 < \varepsilon)$$

exist such that, for any initial condition $\alpha_0 \in V_0$, the solution path $\alpha(t; \alpha_0)$ always remains in V. Such a neighborhood V_0 is referred to as the core neighborhood associated with the neighborhood V. Let us denote by $\xi^\nu = (\xi^\nu)$ the vector of deviations from equilibrium α_*^ν:

$$\xi^\nu = \alpha^\nu - \alpha_*^\nu.$$

The right-hand quantities of the system of differential equations (A) may be denoted by

$$z^\nu = \alpha^\nu\{u^\nu(\bar{c}^\nu(\alpha)) - u^\nu(c^\nu(\alpha))\},$$

which may be regarded as functions of either α or ξ. The equilibrium conditions are characterized by

$$z^\nu(\alpha_*) = 0, \text{ for all } \nu.$$

Let us denote by $\Lambda(\alpha) = (\lambda^{\nu\eta}(\alpha))$ the Jacobian matrix of $z^\nu(\alpha) = (z^\nu(\alpha))$:

$$\lambda^{\nu\eta}(\alpha) = \left(\frac{\partial z^\nu}{\partial \alpha^\eta}\right).$$

In view of assumptions (U1), (U2), (U3) and (T1), (T2), each element of the Jacobian matrix $\Lambda(\alpha) = (\lambda^{\nu\eta}(\alpha))$ is a continuously differentiable function of α. Then there exists a small neighborhood V of equilibrium α_* such that the asymptotic behavior of the solution paths to (A) with initial condition $\alpha_0 \in V$ becomes identical with that of the solution paths to the following system of differential equations:

$$\dot{\xi}^\nu = \sum_\eta \lambda_*^{\nu\eta} \xi^\eta, \quad \text{or} \quad \dot{\xi} = \Lambda_* \xi,$$

where the Jacobian matrix $\Lambda_* = (\lambda_*^{\nu\eta})$ is evaluated $\alpha = \alpha_*$.

Because the system of differential equations (A) is quasi-stable, the characteristic roots of the Jacobian matrix $\Lambda_* = (\lambda_*^{\nu\eta})$ are either negative or 0. In particular, $\Lambda \mathbf{1} = 0$. Hence, for any initial condition $\alpha_0 \in V_0$, the solution path $\alpha(t; \alpha_0)$ approaches, as t goes to infinity, an equilibrium vector in the neighborhood V_0. Thus, we have shown that the system of differential equations (A) is locally stable.

It is also apparent that a vector α in the core neighborhood V_0 associated with V is an equilibrium vector if, and only if,

$$\alpha = \alpha_* + \xi, \ \Lambda_* \xi = 0.$$

Hence, the set of all equilibrium vectors in V_0 is convex. Thus, we have shown that the set Γ_* of all equilibrium vectors is locally convex.

The relation between initial conditions and convergent equilibrium vectors is straightforward. Let V_0 be the core neighborhood associated with V and let α_0 be any vector in V_0; then, α_0 can be expressed as

$$\alpha_0 = \alpha_* + \xi, \quad \xi = \xi_* + \xi_{**}, \quad \xi_* \in V \cap H_*, \quad \xi_{**} \in H_{**},$$

where H_* and H_{**} are, respectively, the spaces spanned by the characteristic vectors corresponding to zero and negative characteristic roots. Such a decomposition is uniquely determined, and ξ_* is a continuous, continuously differentiable functions of α_0.

Then, it is apparent that

$$\lim_{t \to \infty} \alpha(t; \alpha_0) = \alpha_* + \xi_*.$$

Because the system of differential equations (A) is quasi-stable, the solution path $\alpha(t; \alpha_0)$ for any initial condition α_0 has a convergent subsequence $\{\alpha(t_k;\alpha_0)\}$ such that

$$\lim_{t\to\infty} \alpha(t_k;\alpha_0) = \alpha_*$$

is an equilibrium vector. The local stability of the system of differential equations (A), as shown above, ensures that the solution path $\alpha(t;\alpha_0)$ itself converges to equilibrium α_*. Thus, we have shown that the system of differential equations (A) is globally stable. Q. E. D.

PROOF OF PROPOSITION 4

Assumptions (U1), (U2), (U3) and (T1), (T2), in view of Proposition 2, imply that the set Γ_* of all equilibrium vectors of utility weights is a nonempty cone. In the course of the proof of Proposition 3, we have shown that Γ_* is locally convex. To prove that Γ_* is piecewise connected, let us consider two equilibrium vectors, $\alpha_0, \alpha_1 \in \Gamma_*$ and denote by $\alpha(\theta)$ the line segment connecting α_0 and α_1; that is,

$$\alpha(\theta) = (1-\theta)\alpha_0 + \theta\alpha_1,\ 0 \leqq \theta \leqq 1.$$

In view of the global stability of the system of differential equations (A),

$$\alpha_*(\theta) = \lim_{t\to\infty} \alpha(t;\alpha(\theta))$$

exists for all $0 \leqq \theta \leqq 1$, $\alpha_*(0) = \alpha_0$, $\alpha_*(1) = \alpha_1$ and is continuous for all $0 < \theta < 1$. Because $\lim_{t\to\infty} \alpha(t;\alpha_0)$ is a continuously differentiable function of initial condition α_0, the path $\alpha_*(\theta)$ is a continuously differentiable curve connecting α_0 and α_1. Q. E. D.

PROOF OF PROPOSITION 2′

The proof of Proposition 2′ may be carried out in exactly the same manner as for Proposition 2 with the following modifications:

For each $\alpha = (\alpha^\nu) \in S$, $(\overline{c}^\nu, \overline{a}^{(\nu)})$ are defined by the following conditions:

$$\overline{\alpha}^\nu u^\nu_{c^\nu}(\overline{c}^\nu, \overline{a}^{(\nu)}) = p(\alpha)$$
$$\overline{\alpha}^\nu u^\nu_a(\overline{c}^\nu, \overline{a}^{(\nu)}) = q^\nu(\alpha)$$
$$p(\alpha)\overline{c}^\nu + q^\nu(\alpha)\overline{a}^{(\nu)} = s^\nu[p(\alpha)x(\alpha) + q(\alpha)a(\alpha)].$$

Note that $\overline{\alpha}^\nu \geqq \alpha^\nu$, or $\overline{\alpha}^\nu \leqq \alpha^\nu$ according to whether $z^\nu(\alpha) \geqq 0$ or $z^\nu(\alpha) \leqq 0$.

PROOF OF PROPOSITIONS 3′ AND 4′

Propositions 3′ and 4′ are proved in exactly the same manner as for Propositions 3 and 4. One only has to note the following relations:

$$\begin{aligned}
&\alpha^\nu(t)\left\{u^\nu(\overline{c}^\nu(t), \overline{a}^{(\nu)}(t)) - u^\nu(c^\nu(t), a(t))\right\} \\
&\quad \leqq \alpha^\nu(t)\left\{u^\nu_{c^\nu}(c^\nu(t), a(t))(\overline{c}^\nu(t) - c^\nu(t))\right. \\
&\qquad \left. + u^\nu_a(c^\nu(t), a(t))(\overline{a}^{(\nu)}(t) - a(t))\right\} \\
&\quad = p(t)[\overline{c}^\nu(t) - c^\nu(t)] + q^\nu(t)[\overline{a}^{(\nu)}(t) - a(t)] = z^\nu(\alpha^\nu(t))
\end{aligned}$$

with equality when $\overline{\alpha}^\nu(t) \neq \alpha^\nu(t)$.

$$\sum_\nu z^\nu(\alpha) = 0, \quad \text{for all } \alpha \in S.$$

PROOF OF PROPOSITION 1″

The proof of Proposition 1″ is carried out in exactly the same manner as for Proposition 1′, and the notation introduced there may be used for the case of CO_2 emission.

We define, for any nonzero, nonnegative vector of utility weights, $\alpha = (\alpha^\nu)$, the following quantities:

$$z^\nu(\alpha) = s^\nu[p(\alpha)x(\alpha) - q(\alpha)a(\alpha)] - [p(\alpha)c^\nu(\alpha) - q^\nu(\alpha)a(\alpha)].$$

Then we have

$$\sum_\nu z^\nu(\alpha) = 0, \quad \text{for all } \alpha \in S,$$

and $(c^1(\alpha), \ldots, c^N(\alpha); a(\alpha))$ is a Lindahl equilibrium if, and only if,

$$z^\nu(\alpha) = 0, \text{ for all } \nu.$$

For each $\alpha = (\alpha^\nu) \in S$, $(\overline{c}^\nu, \overline{a}^{(\nu)})$ is defined by the following conditions:

$$\begin{aligned} &\overline{\alpha}^{\nu} u^{\nu}_{c^{\nu}}(\overline{c}^{\nu}, \overline{a}^{(\nu)}) = p(\alpha) \\ &-\overline{\alpha}^{\nu} u^{\nu}_{a}(\overline{c}^{\nu}, \overline{a}^{(\nu)}) = q^{\nu}(\alpha) \\ &p(\alpha)\overline{c}^{\nu} - q^{\nu}(\alpha)\overline{a}^{(\nu)} = s^{\nu}[p(\alpha)x(\alpha) - q^{\nu}(\alpha)a(\alpha)]. \end{aligned}$$

Note that $\overline{a}^{(\nu)} \geqq a(\alpha)$, or $\overline{a}^{(\nu)} \geqq a(\alpha)$ according to whether $z^{(\nu)} \geqq 0$, or $z^{(\nu)} \leqq 0$.

3

Global Warming and Tradable Emission Permits

1. INTRODUCTION

Among the many institutional arrangements and policy measures proposed to control the emission of carbon dioxide and other greenhouse gases and effectively abate the processes of global warming, the institution of international markets for tradable emission permits is probably the one that has most attracted the attention of the economist, as typically argued by Tietenberg (1985, 1992), Bertram (1992), and Barrett et al. (1992), Barrett and Taylor (1995) and others.

Bertram, Stephens, and Wallace (1989) argued that a worldwide system of tradable emission permits could be an effective way of advancing the interests of developing countries in harmony with the global community's interest in protecting the atmosphere. This egalitarian view was expounded and reinforced further by Grubb (1989, 1990), Hoel (1991), Tietenberg (1992), Rose and Stevens (1993), and others.

The main advantages of markets for tradable emission permits are their ability to achieve environmental aims with a minimal bureaucratic apparatus. One of the central problems with most such schemes is the allocation of the initial allotments among the countries involved. The "license to pollute" tends to be granted to those countries that are already major polluters with the result that the rents associated with a growing scarcity of pollution entitlements fall into the hands of these countries. However, as argued by Grubb (1989), of all the instruments examined, the system of tradable emission permits is the most promising. It is flexible in operation and effectively and efficiently abates global warming. The costs of alternative permit allocations have been tentatively calculated by Larsen and Shah (1992, 1994), and others.

In this chapter, we would like to examine the patterns of resource allocation and income distribution and the resulting levels of world utility when the institution of markets for tradable emission permits is implemented and to introduce the criteria by which the welfare implications of the initial allotment of tradable emission permits may systematically be examined.

2. MARKET EQUILIBRIUM FOR TRADABLE EMISSION PERMITS

We will use the premises set up in Chapter 1 to discuss the welfare implications of the institutional arrangements of markets for tradable emission permits and associated problems. We suppose that an international market exists in which permits to emit CO_2 are freely traded between the countries involved. We denote by b^ν the amount of emission permits initially allotted to each country ν. When the amount of CO_2 emissions in country ν is a^ν, then country ν has to purchase emission permits by the amount $a^\nu - b^\nu$ or to sell emission permits by the amount $b^\nu - a^\nu$.

With respect to the institutional arrangements of the market for tradable emission permits, when countries get together to implement the working of the market, the most crucial issue is how to agree on the initial allotments of tradable emission permits among the countries involved, as argued, for example, by Rose and Stevens (1993), Bertram (1992), and Larson and Shah (1992, 1994), among others. However, we begin our discussion of tradable emission permits with the presumption that the quantity of total emission permits a and the initial allotments of emission permits (b^ν) among the countries are somehow predetermined to be agreeable to all the countries involved:

$$a = \sum_\nu b^\nu.$$

Produced goods are assumed to be internationally traded at competitive markets, whereas no trade takes place for factors of production.

The balance-of-payments conditions for country ν are given by

$$pc^{\nu} = px^{\nu} - q(a^{\nu} - b^{\nu}),$$

where $p = (p_j)$ is the vector of prices of produced goods and q is the price of emission permits on the international market, and the vectors of consumption and production are respectively denoted by c^{ν}, x^{ν}.

An equilibrium of the international market for tradable emission permits $(c^1, \ldots, c^n, x^1, \ldots, x^n, a^1, \ldots, a^n; p, q)$ is obtained if one finds the prices of produced goods and tradable emission permits, denoted respectively by p and q, and the pattern of consumption vector c^{ν}, production vector x^{ν}, and CO_2 emissions a^{ν} of individual countries ν such that the following conditions are satisfied:

(i) For each country ν, the consumption vector c^{ν} is so determined that country ν's utility

$$u^{\nu}(c^{\nu}, a) = \varphi(a)u^{\nu}(c^{\nu})$$

is maximized subject to the balance-of-payments conditions

$$pc^{\nu} = px^{\nu} - q(a^{\nu} - b^{\nu}). \tag{1}$$

(ii) For each country ν, the employment of each factor of production ℓ is within the availability K^{ν}_{ℓ}:

$$f^{\nu}(x^{\nu}, a^{\nu}) \leqq K^{\nu}. \tag{2}$$

(iii) The world markets for produced goods are in equilibrium:

$$\sum_{\nu} c^{\nu} = \sum_{\nu} x^{\nu}.$$

(iv) The sum of CO_2 emissions of all countries in the world is equal to the sum of initial allotments of tradable emission permits; that is,

$$\sum_{\nu} a^{\nu} = a.$$

Exactly as in the case of deferential equilibrium, the maximum problem for each country ν is solved by introducing the Lagrangian unknowns associated with constraints (1) and (2) to be denoted, respectively, by λ^ν, $\lambda^\nu r^\nu$. The Lagrangian form is given by

$$L^\nu(c^\nu, x^\nu, a^\nu; \lambda^\nu, \lambda^\nu r^\nu) = \varphi(a)u^\nu(c^\nu) + \lambda^\nu[px^\nu - pc^\nu - q(a^\nu - b^\nu)] \\ + \lambda^\nu r^\nu[K^\nu - f^\nu(x^\nu, a^\nu)].$$

When expressed in units of world prices, the optimum conditions are

$$\alpha^\nu \varphi(a) u^\nu_{c^\nu}(c^\nu) = p \tag{3}$$

$$p = r^\nu f^\nu_{x^\nu}(x^\nu, a^\nu) \tag{4}$$

$$q = r^\nu[- f^\nu_{a^\nu}(x^\nu, a^\nu)], \tag{5}$$

where

$$\alpha^\nu = \frac{1}{\lambda^\nu} > 0.$$

As in the case discussed in Chapter 1, relations (4) and (5) put together mean that the combination (x^ν, a^ν) of production vector x^ν and CO_2 emissions a^ν at the optimum is obtained by maximizing

$$px^\nu - qa^\nu$$

over the technological possibility set $(x^\nu, a^\nu) \in T^\nu$.

By multiplying both sides of Equations (4) and (5), respectively, by x^ν, a^ν and by noting the Euler identity, we obtain

$$px^\nu - qa^\nu = r^\nu[f^\nu_{x^\nu}(x^\nu, a^\nu)x^\nu + f^\nu_{a^\nu}(x^\nu, a^\nu)a^\nu] \\ = r^\nu f^\nu(x^\nu, a^\nu) = r^\nu K^\nu.$$

That is, the net evaluation of output is equal to the sum of the rental payments to all factors of production.

On the assumption that all factors of production are owned by individual members of the country ν, national income y^ν is equal to the sum of the rental payments, $r^\nu K^\nu = \sum_\ell r^\nu_\ell K^\nu_\ell$, and the value measured in market prices of the allotment of emission permits qb^ν; that is,

$$y^\nu = r^\nu K^\nu + qb^\nu = (px^\nu - qa^\nu) + qb^\nu \\ = px^\nu - q(a^\nu - b^\nu) = pc^\nu.$$

Multiply both sides of Equation (3) by c^ν and note the Euler identity to obtain

$$\alpha^\nu \varphi(a) u^\nu(c^\nu) = \alpha^\nu \varphi(a) u^\nu_{c^\nu}(c^\nu) c^\nu = pc^\nu.$$

Hence, we have the following basic relation:

$$\alpha^\nu \varphi(a) u^\nu(c^\nu) = y^\nu. \tag{6}$$

Given the initial allotment of tradable emission permits to individual countries (b^ν), market equilibrium for the world economy under the tradable emission permits regime is obtained if we find a vector of prices p and the price of tradable emission permits q for which conditions (iii) and (iv) are satisfied.

The discussion carried out so far shows that market equilibrium for the world economy under the tradable emission permits regime may be obtained as the standard market equilibrium for the world economy when, in each country ν, carbon taxes are levied with a rate equal to the market price q of tradable emission permits and balance-of-payments condition (1) is satisfied.

On the other hand, it is straightforward to see that any standard market equilibrium for the world economy, when in each country ν uniform carbon taxes are levied with the rate equal to q, may be regarded as the market equilibrium under the tradable emission permits regime with a suitable initial allotment of tradable emission permits among individual countries. Thus, we have established the following proposition.

Proposition 1. *Market equilibrium for the world economy under the tradable emission permits regime corresponds precisely to the standard market equilibrium under uniform carbon taxes with the rate equal to the market price q of tradable emission permits, where the initial allotment of tradable emission permits among individual countries is suitably chosen.*

3. WELFARE IMPLICATIONS OF TOTAL ALLOTMENT OF TRADABLE EMISSION PERMITS

We would like first to examine the relationships between the total quantity of the initial allotments of tradable emission permits and the ensuing level of the world aggregate utility.

Let us assume that the quantity of the total emission permits a and the initial allotments of emission permits (b^ν) among countries are given as follows:

$$a = \sum_\nu b^\nu.$$

An equilibrium of the market for tradable emission permits is represented by $(c^1, \ldots, c^n, x^1, \ldots, x^n, a^1, \ldots, a^n; p, q)$, where p and q are the prices of produced goods and tradable emission permits, respectively, and c^ν, x^ν, a^ν are the vector of consumption, the vector of production, and CO_2 emissions at the equilibrium, respectively.

We now consider the weighted world utility

$$W = \sum_\nu \alpha^\nu \varphi(a) u^\nu(c^\nu), \tag{7}$$

where, for each country ν, α^ν is the inverse of the marginal utility of income λ^ν introduced in the previous section:

$$\alpha^\nu = \frac{1}{\lambda^\nu} > 0.$$

We examine the effect on the weighted world utility W of the marginal increase in the total quantity a of tradable emission permits, assuming that the utility weights α^ν are not affected by such a marginal increase.

By taking total differentials of both sides of (7) and by noting relations (3) and (6), we obtain

$$\begin{aligned} dW &= \sum_\nu \alpha^\nu \varphi(a) u^\nu_{c^\nu}(c^\nu) dc^\nu + \sum_\nu \alpha^\nu \varphi'(a) u^\nu(c^\nu) da \\ &= \sum_\nu p dc^\nu - \tau(a) \sum_\nu \alpha^\nu \varphi(a) u^\nu(c^\nu) da \\ &= \sum_\nu p dc^\nu - \tau(a) \sum_\nu y^\nu da \\ &= \sum_\nu p dc^\nu - \tau(a) y da, \end{aligned} \tag{8}$$

where $\tau(a)$ is the impact coefficient of global warming, and y is the sum of national incomes of all countries:

$$\tau(a) = -\frac{\varphi'(a)}{\varphi(a)}, \quad y = \sum_\nu y^\nu.$$

By taking total differentials of both sides of equilibrium conditions for produced goods, we obtain

$$\sum_{\nu} dc^{\nu} = \sum_{\nu} dx^{\nu}. \tag{9}$$

On the other hand, the conditions of the producer optimum for the combination (x^{ν}, a^{ν}) of production vector x^{ν} and CO_2 emissions a^{ν} imply that

$$p\, dx^{\nu} = q\, da^{\nu}. \tag{10}$$

Substituting (9) and (10) into relations (8), we obtain

$$\begin{aligned} dW &= \sum_{\nu} pdx^{\nu} - \tau(a)yda = \sum_{\nu} qda^{\nu} - \tau(a)yda \\ &= [q - \tau(a)y]da. \end{aligned}$$

In other words, we have

$$\frac{dW}{da} = q - \theta, \tag{11}$$

where

$$\theta = \tau(a)y. \tag{12}$$

The quantity θ defined by (12) is nothing but the marginal disutility of total CO_2 emissions a with respect to world utility W, as defined by (7). To elucidate what is meant by this statement, let us consider the following maximum problem:

Social Optimum Problem

For the given total CO_2 emissions a, find the pattern of consumption and production of goods for individual countries and CO_2 emissions by individual countries $(c_*^1, \ldots, c_*^n, x_*^1, \ldots, x_*^n, a_*^1, \ldots, a_*^n)$ that maximizes the world utility

$$W = \sum_{\nu} \alpha^{\nu} \varphi(a) u^{\nu}(c^{\nu})$$

among all feasible patterns of allocations $(c^1, \ldots, c^n, x^1, \ldots, x^n, a^1, \ldots, a^n)$:

$$\sum_\nu c^\nu = \sum_\nu x^\nu \tag{13}$$

$$f^\nu(x^\nu, a^\nu) \leqq K^\nu \tag{14}$$

$$a = \sum_\nu a^\nu. \tag{15}$$

The social optimum problem is solved by introducing the Lagrangian unknowns associated with constraints (13), (14), and (15) to be denoted, respectively, by p, r^ν, θ. The Lagrangian form is given by

$$L(c^\nu, x^\nu, a^\nu; p, r^\nu, \theta) = \sum_\nu \alpha^\nu \varphi(a) u^\nu(c^\nu) + p\left(\sum_\nu x^\nu - \sum_\nu c^\nu\right) + \sum_\nu r^\nu [K^\nu - f^\nu(x^\nu, a^\nu)] + \theta\left(a - \sum_\nu a^\nu\right)$$

with given total CO_2 emissions a.

The marginality conditions for the optimum combination (c^ν, x^ν, a^ν) of consumption vector c^ν, production vector x^ν, and CO_2 emissions a^ν are

$$\alpha^\nu \varphi(a) u^\nu_{c^\nu}(c^\nu) = p$$

$$p = r^\nu f^\nu_{x^\nu}(x^\nu, a^\nu)$$

$$\theta = r^\nu[-f^\nu_{a^\nu}(x^\nu, a^\nu)]$$

together with feasibility conditions (13), (14), and (15).

Differentiating the world utility W totally with respect to a, we obtain

$$\begin{aligned}
\frac{dW}{da} &= \sum_\nu \alpha^\nu \varphi(a) u^\nu_{c^\nu}(c^\nu) \frac{dc^\nu}{da} + \sum_\nu \alpha^\nu \varphi'(a) u^\nu(c^\nu) \\
&= \sum_\nu p \frac{dc^\nu}{da} - \tau(a) \sum_\nu \alpha^\nu \varphi(a) u^\nu(c^\nu) \\
&= \sum_\nu p \frac{dx^\nu}{da} - \tau(a) \sum_\nu y^\nu \\
&= \sum_\nu \theta \frac{da^\nu}{da} - \tau(a) \sum_\nu y^\nu \\
&= \theta - \tau(a) y.
\end{aligned}$$

That is, we have

$$\frac{dW}{da} = \theta - \tau(a)y, \tag{16}$$

where

$$\tau(a)y = \sum_{\nu} \alpha^{\nu}[-\varphi'(a)]u^{\nu}(c^{\nu}) \tag{17}$$

is nothing but the marginal social disutility, or the imputed price, of atmospheric concentrations of CO_2.

The imputed price of atmospheric concentrations of CO_2, θ, being the Lagrangian unknown associated with constraint (15), is decreased as total CO_2 emissions a are increased. We can demonstrate that $\tau(a)y$ is increased as total CO_2 emissions a are increased. This can be shown by differentiating both sides of (17) with respect to a

$$\frac{d}{da}[\tau(a)y] = \sum_{\nu} \alpha^{\nu}[-\varphi'(a)]u^{\nu}_{c^{\nu}}(c^{\nu})\frac{dc^{\nu}}{da} + \sum_{\nu} \alpha^{\nu}[-\varphi''(a)]u^{\nu}(c^{\nu}).$$

By noting that

$$\sum_{\nu} \alpha^{\nu}[-\varphi'(a)]u^{\nu}_{c^{\nu}}(c^{\nu})\frac{dc^{\nu}}{da} = \tau(a)\sum_{\nu} p\frac{dc^{\nu}}{da} = \tau(a)\sum_{\nu} p\frac{dx^{\nu}}{da}$$
$$= \tau(a)\sum_{\nu} \theta\frac{da^{\nu}}{da} = \tau(a)\theta,$$

we have

$$\frac{d}{da}[\tau(a)y] = \tau(a)\theta + \sum_{\nu} \alpha^{\nu}[-\varphi''(a)]u^{\nu}(c^{\nu}) > 0.$$

The forgoing discussion leads us to the following proposition.

Proposition 2. *Market equilibrium* $(c^1, \ldots, c^n, x^1, \ldots, x^n, a^1, \ldots, a^n; p, q)$ *in the world market for tradable emission permits with the given total allotment of tradable emission permits emissions,* $a = \sum_{\nu} b^{\nu}$, *is a social optimum if, and only if, market price* q *of tradable emission permits is equal to the imputed price* θ *of atmospheric concentrations of* CO_2 *to be given by*

$$\theta = \tau(b)y,$$

thus precisely coinciding with the market equilibrium under the uniform carbon tax scheme, as introduced in Chapter 1.

If market price q of tradable emission permits is higher (lower) than the imputed price θ of atmospheric concentrations of CO_2, then an increase in the total allotment a of tradable emission permits will increase (decrease) the world utility

$$W = \sum_{\nu} \alpha^{\nu} \varphi(a) u^{\nu}(c^{\nu}).$$

4. WELFARE IMPLICATIONS OF THE INITIAL ALLOTMENT OF TRADABLE EMISSION PERMITS

We next examine the relationships between the initial allotment of tradable emission permits and the ensuing distribution of real incomes between countries when the market for tradable emission permits is at equilibrium.

Let us assume that the quantity of the total emission permits a is so chosen that the market price of tradable emission permits q is equal to the imputed price θ of atmospheric concentrations of CO_2

$$q = \theta,$$

where

$$\theta = \tau(a) y,$$

and the initial allotment of emission permits (b^{ν}) among countries is given by

$$a = \sum_{\nu} b^{\nu}.$$

Suppose that the initial allotment b^{ν} to a particular country ν is marginally increased. We would like to see if the utility, or real national income of country ν

$$\varphi(a) u^{\nu}(c^{\nu}) = y^{\nu}$$

may be increased accordingly. To see this, we would like first to consider the relationships between the weight α^{ν} given to country ν's utility and the real national income y^{ν} of country ν.

Let us recall that, in view of the balance-of-the payments conditions, the following relations hold:

$$y^{\nu} = pc^{\nu} = px^{\nu} - q(a^{\nu} - b^{\nu}).$$

Then, we may have, as an approximation of the first order, that

$$dy^\nu = pdx^\nu - qda^\nu + qdb^\nu = qdb^\nu.$$

Hence,

$$\frac{dy^\nu}{db^\nu} = q > 0. \tag{18}$$

The relation (18), together with some cumbersome calculations, implies that an increase in the initial allotment b^ν to country ν induces a decrease in marginal utility of country ν's national income λ^ν and an increase in the utility weight $\alpha^\nu = \frac{1}{\lambda^\nu}$ of country ν; that is,

$$\frac{d\alpha^\nu}{db^\nu} > 0.$$

Conversely, the larger the utility weight α^ν of country ν, the larger is the level of national income y^ν, and, accordingly, the larger is the initial allotment to country ν, b^ν. This is easily seen from the following lemma.

Lemma. *Consider the following maximization problem:*

Find $x = (x_j)$ that maximizes

$$pf(x) = \sum_i p_i f_i(x)$$

subject to the constraints

$$x \leqq 0, \quad g(x) = (g_l(x)) \geqq 0,$$

where $f(x) = (f_i(x))$ and $g(x) = (g_l(x))$ are vector-valued functions of $x = (x_j)$, and $p = (p_i)$ is a given vector.

Let x^0 and x^1 be the optimum solutions to the maximum problem with p^0 and p^1, respectively, and

$$\Delta p - p^1 - p^0, \Lambda x = x^1 - x^0, \Delta f(x) = f(x^1) - f(x^0).$$

Then, the following inequality holds:

$$\Delta p \, \Delta f(x) \geqq 0.$$

Proof. Because x^0 is optimum for the maximum problem with respect to p^0 and x^1 is feasible, we have

$$p^0 f(x^0) \geqq p^0 f(x^1) \Rightarrow -p^0 \Delta f(x) \geqq 0.$$

Similarly,

$$p^1 f(x^1) \geqq p^1 f(x^0) \Rightarrow (p^0 + \Delta p)\Delta f(x) \geqq 0.$$

By adding these two inequalities, we obtain the desired inequality.

Q. E. D.

We have now established the following proposition.

Proposition 3. *Suppose total allotment of tradable emission permits, $a = \sum_\nu b^\nu$, is chosen so that market price q of tradable emission permits is equal to the imputed price θ of atmospheric concentrations of CO_2*

$$q = \theta,$$

where

$$\theta = \tau(a)y,$$

thus implying that the resulting state of allocation at the market equilibrium of the market for tradable emission permits is a social optimum.

Then a one-to-one correspondence exists between the pattern of initial allotment of tradable emission permits (b^ν) and the system of weights for the utilities of individual countries (α^ν) except for the proportionality.

The larger the initial allotment to country ν, b^ν, the larger is the utility weight α^ν of country ν. Conversely, the larger the utility weight α^ν of country ν, the larger is the initial allotment to country ν, b^ν.

5. LINDAHL EQUILIBRIUM AND TRADABLE EMISSION PERMITS

In Chapter 2, we emphasized the importance of Lindahl equilibrium for economies involving public goods in the Samuelsonian sense in general and global warming in particular. In this section, we examine the welfare implications of Lindahl equilibrium in the international market for tradable emission permits and derive propositions concerning the stability of adjustment processes for the initial allotment of tradable emission permits.

Conditions for Lindahl Equilibrium

Let us briefly recapitulate the definition of Lindahl equilibrium in the international market for tradable emission permits. The quantity of the total emission permits is given by a, and the initial allotments of emission permits among countries are given by (b^ν), where

$$a = \sum_\nu b^\nu.$$

An equilibrium of the market for tradable emission permits is obtained at $(c^1, \ldots, c^n, x^1, \ldots, x^n, a^1, \ldots, a^n; p, q)$, where the following conditions are satisfied:

(i) For each country ν, the balance-of-payments conditions are satisfied as denoted by

$$pc^\nu = px^\nu - q(a^\nu - b^\nu), \tag{19}$$

and when expressed in units of world prices, marginal utilities are equal to market prices p:

$$\alpha^\nu \varphi(a) u^\nu_{c^\nu}(c^\nu) = p. \tag{20}$$

(ii) For each country ν, the combination (x^ν, a^ν) of production vector x^ν and CO_2 emissions a^ν at the optimum is obtained by maximizing

$$px^\nu - qa^\nu$$

over the technological possibility set $(x^\nu, a^\nu) \in T^\nu$.

(iii) Total demand for produced goods is equal to total supply:

$$\sum_\nu c^\nu = \sum_\nu x^\nu.$$

(iv) The sum of CO_2 emissions of all countries in the world is equal to the sum of initial allotments of tradable emission permits; that is,

$$\sum_\nu a^\nu = a.$$

An equilibrium $(c^1, \ldots, c^n, x^1, \ldots, x^n, a^1, \ldots, a^n; p, q)$ of the market for tradable emission permits is a Lindahl equilibrium if a set of individual prices $q^1, \ldots, q^n$ exists such that, for each country ν

$$q = \sum_{\nu} q^{\nu}, q^{\nu} > 0, \tag{21}$$

and the following conditions are satisfied.

(v) For each country ν, (c^{ν}, a) maximizes $\varphi(a^{(\nu)})u^{\nu}(c^{\nu})$ subject to the constraints that

$$pc^{\nu} - q^{\nu}a^{(\nu)} = px^{\nu} - qa^{\nu}, \quad c^{\nu}, a^{(\nu)} \geqq 0.$$

In other words, Lindahl equilibrium is obtained when the level a of total CO_2 emissions of all countries in the world is precisely equal to the level that each country ν wishes on the assumption that country ν is paid at the individual price q^{ν} assigned to it.

The conditions (v) mean that

$$pc^{\nu} - q^{\nu}a = px^{\nu} - qa^{\nu} \tag{22}$$

and that individual price q^{ν} assigned to each country ν is equal to the marginal disutility, for country ν, of atmospheric concentrations of CO_2 when expressed in units of world prices, that is,

$$q^{\nu} = \alpha^{\nu}[-\varphi'(a)]u^{\nu}(c^{\nu}). \tag{23}$$

In view of the balance-of-payments condition (19), Equation (22) implies that

$$qb^{\nu} = q^{\nu}a, \quad \text{or} \quad \frac{q^{\nu}}{q} = \frac{b^{\nu}}{a}. \tag{24}$$

On the other hand, we have from (20) and the Euler identity for utility function $u^{\nu}(c^{\nu})$ that

$$\alpha^{\nu}\varphi(a)u^{\nu}(c^{\nu}) = pc^{\nu} = y^{\nu},$$

which, together with (23), implies

$$q^{\nu} = \tau(a)y^{\nu}, \tag{25}$$

where

$$\tau(a) = -\frac{\varphi'(a)}{\varphi(a)}$$

is the impact coefficient of global warming.

By summing both sides of Equation (25) over all countries and noting condition (21), we obtain

$$q = \tau(a)y, \tag{26}$$

where $y = \sum_\nu y^\nu$ is the world income.

Relation (26) in particular implies the proposition that Lindahl equilibrium is a Pareto optimum, which was shown previously.

In view of (25) and (26), relation (24) implies

$$\frac{y^\nu}{y} = \frac{b^\nu}{a}. \tag{27}$$

Relation (27) means that, at the Lindahl equilibrium, the initial allotments of tradable emission permits to individual countries are proportional to the national incomes of individual countries.

On the other hand, let us suppose that the initial allotments of tradable emission permits to individual countries are proportional to the national incomes of individual countries; that is, relation (27) is satisfied. Then we have

$$\frac{q^\nu}{q} = \frac{\tau(a)y^\nu}{\tau(a)y} = \frac{y^\nu}{y} = \frac{b^\nu}{a}.$$

Hence,

$$q = \sum_\nu q^\nu, q^\nu > 0$$

$$pc^\nu - q^\nu a = px^\nu - qa^\nu, \text{ for all } \nu$$

$$q^\nu = \tau(a)y^\nu = \tau(a)\alpha^\nu\varphi(a)u^\nu(c^\nu) = \alpha^\nu[-\varphi'(a)]u^\nu(c^\nu), \text{ for all } \nu.$$

That is, Lindahl conditions are satisfied.

Thus we have established the following proposition.

Proposition 4. *Equilibrium* $(c^1, \ldots, c^n, x^1, \ldots, x^n, a^1, \ldots, a^n; p, q)$ *of the world market for tradable emission permits is a Lindahl equilibrium if, and only if, the initial allotments of tradable emission permits to individual countries* (b^ν) *are proportional to the national incomes of individual countries* (y^ν)*:*

$$\frac{b^\nu}{a} = \frac{y^\nu}{y}, \text{ for all } \nu.$$

6. ADJUSTMENT PROCESSES FOR THE ALLOTMENTS OF TRADABLE EMISSION PERMITS

According to Proposition 4, Lindahl equilibrium is obtained when the initial allotments of tradable emission permits to individual countries (b^ν) are so chosen that they are proportional to the national incomes of individual countries (y^ν).

However, the initial allotments of tradable emission permits to individual countries (b^ν) are to be determined prior to the opening of the world market for tradable emission permits. Hence, we need some sort of adjustment processes concerning initial allotments of tradable emission permits to individual countries to reach the initial allotments of tradable emission permits that satisfy the proportionality conditions stipulated in Proposition 4:

$$\frac{b^\nu}{a} = \frac{y^\nu}{y}, \quad \text{for all } \nu.$$

The adjustment process concerning allotments of tradable emission permits introduced in this section will be divided into two stages. The first stage is concerned with the adjustment in the total quantity a of allotments of tradable emission permits, whereas the second stage concerns allotments of tradable emission permits to individual countries (b^ν).

Let us denote by t the time variable during the process of adjustment, and the total quantity a and the allotments of tradable emission permits to individual countries b^ν at time t are denoted respectively by $a(t), b^\nu(t)$, where

$$a(t) = \sum_\nu b^\nu(t).$$

The relevant variables at the corresponding market equilibrium are denoted by $c^\nu(t), x^\nu(t), \alpha^\nu(t), p(t), q(t), q^\nu(t), y^\nu(t), y(t)$, where

$$\sum_\nu a^\nu(t) = a(t)$$

$$y^\nu(t) = p(t)c^\nu(t) = p(t)x^\nu(t) - q(t)[a^\nu(t) - b^\nu(t)], \qquad \text{for all } \nu$$

$$y(t) = \sum_\nu y^\nu(t)$$

$$q^\nu(t) = \tau(a(t))y^\nu(t), \qquad \text{for all } \nu.$$

Lindahl equilibrium is characterized by the following conditions:

$$q(t) = \tau(a(t))y(t)$$

$$\frac{y^\nu(t)}{y(t)} = \frac{b^\nu(t)}{b(t)} \quad \text{for all } \nu.$$

The First Stage of the Adjustment Process

The first stage of the adjustment process concerns the adjustment in the total quantity of allotments of tradable emission permits. It is defined by the dynamic equation

$$\text{(B)} \qquad \dot{a}(t) = k[q(t) - \tau(a(t))y(t)],$$

with the given initial condition $a(0) = a_0 > 0$, where $k > 0$ is the speed of adjustment, which is assumed to be a positive constant.

As was shown in Section 2, an increase in $a(t)$ results in a lowering of the market price $q(t)$ of tradable emission permits and an increase in $\tau(a(t))y(t)$. Hence, dynamic equation (B) is globally stable.

Proposition 5. *Let us consider the adjustment process with respect to individual allotments of tradable emission permits defined by the dynamic equation*

$$\text{(B)} \qquad \dot{a}(t) = k[q(t) - \tau(a(t))y(t)],$$

with the given initial condition $a(0) = a_0 > 0$, where $k > 0$ is the speed of adjustment assumed to be a positive constant, $a(t)$ is the quantity of total CO_2 emissions, $q(t)$ is the market price of tradable emission permits, and $y(t)$ is the world national income:

$$a(t) = \sum_\nu a^\nu(t), \quad y(t) = \sum_\nu y^\nu(t).$$

Then the adjustment process with respect to the total quantity of allotments of tradable emission permits defined by the dynamic equation (B) *is globally stable, always approaching the level associated with a Lindahl equilibrium. That is, for any initial condition $a(0) = a_0 > 0$, the solution path $a(t)$ to the dynamic equation* (B) *uniquely exists and converges to the level a_* at which*

$$q_* = \tau(a_*)y_*,$$

where q_*, y_* are, respectively, the market price of tradable emission permits and the level of world income, which both correspond to the total quantity of allotments of tradable emission permits a_*.

The Second Stage of the Adjustment Process

The second stage of the adjustment process consists of the adjustment in individual allotments of tradable emission permits. We suppose that the first stage of the adjustment process is completed so that the second stage of the adjustment process may begin with the total quantity a_* of allotments of tradable emission permits corresponding to a social optimum

$$q_* = \tau(a_*)y_*.$$

The second stage of the adjustment process is defined by the following system of dynamic equations:

$$\text{(C)} \qquad \dot{b}^\nu(t) = k[a(t)y^\nu(t) - b^\nu(t)y(t)] \quad (\nu = 1, \ldots, n),$$

where k is the speed of adjustment, assumed to be a positive constant, with the initial conditions $a(0) = a_*$, $(b^\nu(0)) = (b_0^\nu) > 0$ satisfying

$$\sum_\nu b_0^\nu = a_*, \quad b_0^\nu > 0 \quad (\nu = 1, \ldots, n). \tag{28}$$

We may, without loss of generality, assume that $k = 1$. Because

$$\begin{aligned}\sum_\nu \dot{b}^\nu(t) &= \sum_\nu [(a(t)y^\nu(t) - b^\nu(t)y(t)] \\ &= a(t)\sum_\nu y^\nu(t) - \sum_\nu b^\nu(t)y(t) \\ &= a(t)y(t) - a(t)y(t) = 0, \qquad \text{for all } t,\end{aligned}$$

conditions (28) imply that

$$a(t) = \sum_\nu b^\nu(t) = a_*, \qquad \text{for all } t.$$

Hence, $(c^\nu(t), x^\nu(t), a^\nu(t))$ is always a social optimum, and

$$q(t) = \tau(a_*)y(t), \quad q^\nu(t) = \tau(a_*)y^\nu(t).$$

Let us now define the vector $(\alpha^\nu(t))$ of utility weights at time t by the following marginality conditions:

$$\alpha^\nu(t)\varphi(a(t))u^\nu_{c^\nu}(c^\nu(t)) = p(t).$$

Then, $(c^\nu(t), x^\nu(t), a^\nu(t))$ is a social optimum with respect to the world utility

$$W = \sum_\nu \alpha^\nu(t)\varphi(a)u^\nu(c^\nu).$$

That is, $(c^\nu(t), x^\nu(t), a^\nu(t))$ maximizes W among all feasible allocations.

In view of Proposition 3, the larger the initial allotment $b^\nu(t)$ to country ν, the larger is the utility weight $\alpha^\nu(t)$ of country ν. Conversely, the larger the utility weight $\alpha^\nu(t)$ of country ν, the larger is the initial allotment $b^\nu(t)$ to country ν. Hence, the system of dynamic equations (**) may be transformed from one with respect to the pattern of individual allotments $(b^\nu(t))$ to one with respect to utility weights $(\alpha^\nu(t))$.

To find such a system of dynamic equations in terms of $(\alpha^\nu(t))$, we consider the following maximization problem:

Find $(\overline{c}^\nu(t), \overline{a}^{(\nu)}(t))$ that maximizes

$$\varphi(\overline{a}^{(\nu)})u^\nu(\overline{c}^\nu)$$

subject to the budgetary constraints

$$p(t)\overline{c}^\nu - q^\nu(t)\overline{a}^\nu = p(t)x^\nu(t) - q(t)a^\nu(t). \tag{29}$$

Let us first recall that the marginality conditions for the maximization problem are

$$\overline{\alpha}^\nu(t)\varphi(\overline{a}^{(\nu)}(t))u^\nu_{c^\nu}(\overline{c}^\nu(t)) = p(t) \tag{30}$$

$$\overline{\alpha}^\nu(t)\tau(\overline{a}^{(\nu)}(t))\varphi(\overline{a}^{(\nu)}(t))u^\nu(\overline{c}^\nu(t)) = q^\nu(t), \tag{31}$$

where

$$\tau(\overline{a}^{(\nu)}(t)) = -\frac{\varphi'(\overline{a}^{(\nu)}(t))}{\varphi(\overline{a}^{(\nu)}(t))}.$$

Let us also note the following relations:

$$q(t) = \tau(a(t))y(t), \;\; q^\nu(t) = \tau(a(t))y^\nu(t), \tag{32}$$

where

$$\tau(a(t)) = -\frac{\varphi'(a(t))}{\varphi(a(t))}.$$

From relations (30) and (31), by noting the Euler identity for utility functions $u^\nu(c^\nu)$ and (32), we obtain

$$\tau(\overline{a}^{(\nu)}(t))p(t)\overline{c}^\nu(t) = \tau(a(t))y^\nu(t).$$

Hence,

$$p(t)\overline{c}^{\nu}(t) = \frac{\tau(a(t))}{\tau(\overline{a}^{(\nu)}(t))} y^{\nu}(t). \tag{33}$$

We would like first to show that

$$\overline{a}^{(\nu)}(t) > a(t) \Leftrightarrow q(t)b^{\nu}(t) > q^{\nu}(t)a(t). \tag{34}$$

Suppose $\overline{a}^{(\nu)}(t) > a(t)$. We note that

$$\overline{a}^{(\nu)}(t) > a(t) \Rightarrow \tau(\overline{a}^{(\nu)}(t)) > \tau(a(t)).$$

Hence, in view of relations (33), we have

$$p(t)\overline{c}^{\nu}(t) < y^{\nu}(t). \tag{35}$$

On the the hand, we have

$$\begin{aligned} p(t)\overline{c}^{\nu}(t) &= p(t)x^{\nu}(t) - q(t)a^{\nu}(t) + q^{\nu}(t)\overline{a}^{(\nu)}(t) \\ &> p(t)x^{\nu}(t) - q(t)a^{\nu}(t) + q^{\nu}(t)a(t). \end{aligned}$$

Because

$$y^{\nu}(t) = p(t)x^{\nu}(t) - q(t)a^{\nu}(t) + q(t)b^{\nu}(t),$$

inequality (35) implies

$$q(t)b^{\nu}(t) > q^{\nu}(t)a(t).$$

Similarly, we can show that

$$\overline{a}^{(\nu)}(t) < a(t) \Rightarrow q(t)b^{\nu}(t) < q^{\nu}(t)a(t),$$

thus proving the validity of relation (34).

We next show that

$$\overline{a}^{(\nu)}(t) > a(t) \Leftrightarrow \varphi(\overline{a}^{(\nu)}(t))u^{\nu}(\overline{c}^{\nu}(t)) < \varphi(a(t))u^{\nu}(c^{\nu}(t)). \tag{36}$$

Suppose $\overline{a}^{(\nu)}(t) > a(t)$. Then we have

$$\begin{aligned} &\overline{a}^{(\nu)}(t) > a(t) \Rightarrow \varphi(\overline{a}^{(\nu)}(t)) < \varphi(a(t)) \\ &p(t)\overline{c}^{\nu}(t) < y^{\nu}(t) = p(t)c^{\nu}(t) \Rightarrow u^{\nu}(\overline{c}^{\nu}(t)) < u^{\nu}(c^{\nu}(t)). \end{aligned}$$

Hence,

$$\varphi(\overline{a}^{(\nu)}(t))u^{\nu}(\overline{c}^{\nu}(t)) < \varphi(a(t))u^{\nu}(c^{\nu}(t)).$$

Similarly, we can show that

$$\overline{a}^{(\nu)}(t) < a(t) \Rightarrow \varphi(\overline{a}^{(\nu)}(t))u^\nu(\overline{c}^\nu(t)) > \varphi(a(t))u^\nu(c^\nu(t)),$$

thus proving the validity of relations (36).

From two relations (34) and (36),we obtain

$$q^\nu(t)a(t) < q(t)b^\nu(t) \Rightarrow \varphi(\overline{a}^{(\nu)}(t))u^\nu(\overline{c}^\nu(t)) < \varphi(a(t))u^\nu(c^\nu(t)).$$

Hence, the system of dynamic equations (C) with respect to the pattern of individual allotments $(b^\nu(t))$ may be transformed to the following system of dynamic equations (C′) with respect to utility weights $(\alpha^\nu(t))$:

$$(\text{C}') \qquad \dot{\alpha}^\nu(t) \sim \left[\varphi(\overline{a}^{(\nu)}(t))u^\nu(\overline{c}^\nu(t)) - \varphi(a(t))u^\nu(c^\nu(t))\right] \quad (\nu = 1, \ldots, n),$$

where the sign $\sim$ indicates that both side of the equation have the same plus or minus sign.

The local structure of the adjustment process may be reduced to the dynamic system (A′), as introduced in Chapter 2 as follows:

$$(\text{A}') \qquad \dot{\alpha}^\nu(t) = \alpha^\nu(t)\left[u^\nu(\overline{c}^\nu(t), \overline{a}^{(\nu)}(t)) - u^\nu(c^\nu(t), a(t))\right] \quad (\nu = 1, \ldots, n).$$

Proposition 3′ in Chapter 2 may be applied to show that the adjustment process (A′) is globally stable. Hence, the adjustment process (C′) is quasi-stable in the sense introduced by Uzawa (1961). Because the set of all Lindahl equilibria is locally convex and locally connected, as proved in Chapter 2, quasi-stability of the adjustment process (C′) implies global stability. We have thus established the following proposition.

Proposition 6. *Let us consider the adjustment process with respect to individual allotments of tradable emission permits defined by the following system of dynamic equations*

$$(\text{C}) \qquad b^\nu(t) = k[a(t)y^\nu(t) - b^\nu(t)y(t)] \quad (\nu = 1, \ldots, n),$$

where k is the speed of adjustment assumed to be a positive constant, with the initial conditions $a(0) = a_*$, $(b^\nu(0)) = (b_0^\nu) > 0$, satisfying

$$\sum_\nu b_0^\nu = a_* \quad b_0^\nu > 0, \quad (\nu = 1, \ldots, n).$$

Then the system of dynamic equations (C) *is globally stable, approaching the level associated with a Lindahl equilibrium. That is, for any initial conditions* $a(0) = a_*$, $(b^\nu(0)) = (b_0^\nu) > 0$, *the solution path* $(b^\nu(t))$ *to the system of dynamic equations* (C) *uniquely exists and converges to the initial allotments of tradable emission permits associated with a Lindahl equilibrium as t goes to infinity.*

7. EGALITARIAN INDEX FOR THE INITIAL ALLOTMENT OF EMISSION PERMITS

The initial allotments of emission permits to individual countries (b^ν) are generally given in the following form:

$$b^\nu = \left[(1+\varepsilon)\frac{N^\nu}{N} - \varepsilon\frac{y^\nu}{y}\right]a,$$

where N^ν is the population of country ν, N is the world population $(N = \sum_\nu N^\nu)$, and the egalitarian index ε takes the value not less than -1: $\varepsilon \geqq -1$.

A simple calculation shows that

$$\sum_\nu b^\nu = a.$$

The first coefficient $(1+\varepsilon)\frac{N^\nu}{N}$ expresses the basic principle of humanitarianism that all people on the earth are treated equally. The reason the second coefficient $\varepsilon\frac{y^\nu}{y}$ has a minus sign is as follows. The atmospheric concentrations of CO_2 and other greenhouse gases today are the result of past industrial activities, and the stock of factors of productive capital endowed in each country expresses the extent of the effect of past accumulation of greenhouse gases that remains today, of which national income y^ν is a proxy variable.

The larger the egalitarian index ε, the more the outcome is egalitarian. There are two cases of reference:

The neutral case	$\varepsilon = 0,$	$b^\nu = \frac{N^\nu}{N}a.$
The anti-egalitarian case	$\varepsilon = -1,$	$b^\nu = \frac{y^\nu}{y}a.$

Proposition 7. *The equilibrium of the market for tradable emission permits satisfying the Lindahl conditions corresponds precisely to the anti-egalitarian case*

$$\varepsilon = -1 \quad b^{\nu} = \frac{y^{\nu}}{y} a.$$

Proof. The balance-of-payments conditions are

$$pc^{\nu} - qb^{\nu} = px^{\nu} - qa^{\nu}.$$

The Lindahl conditions are expressed as

$$\begin{aligned} & pc^{\nu} - q^{\nu}a = px^{\nu} - qa^{\nu} \\ & q^{\nu} = \tau(a)y^{\nu} \\ & q = \tau(a)y. \end{aligned}$$

Hence,

$$qb^{\nu} = q^{\nu}b \Rightarrow \frac{b^{\nu}}{b} = \frac{q^{\nu}}{q} = \frac{\tau(a)y^{\nu}}{\tau(a)y} = \frac{y^{\nu}}{y}. \qquad \text{Q. E. D.}$$

One may be somewhat puzzled by Proposition 7. We have been working on the Lindahl solution, particularly within the context of global warming, with the understanding that it gives us a solution that is fair and equitable, as the title of Lindahl's 1919 article suggests.

4

Dynamic Analysis of Global Warming

1. INTRODUCTION

The problems of global warming are genuinely dynamic. From past human activities we inherit an excess concentration of atmospheric carbon dioxide, and the choices we make today concerning the use of fossil fuels and related activities significantly affect all future generations through the phenomenon of global warming, which is brought about by the atmospheric concentrations of carbon dioxide due to the combustion of fossil fuels today. Thus, we have to take into account explicitly the changes in the welfare levels of all future generations caused by the increases in the atmospheric accumulations of carbon dioxide. The degree of uncertainty involved with these phenomena is too great to be subject to any objective analysis. We take instead a simplistic approach that all future paths are known for certain and derive several propositions concerning policy and institutional arrangements to bring about dynamically optimal patterns of intertemporal resource allocation. We need further analysis to see if the basic nature of our conclusions will apply to the more general circumstances governed by a high degree of uncertainty and unpredictability.

In this chapter, we examine the dynamic analysis of global warming and, as in the previous chapters, various carbon tax schemes, focusing on the implications for the processes of capital accumulation and the welfare of future generations.

The dynamic analysis of global warming in this chapter and the next few chapters will be developed primarily along the lines suggested by numerous contributions to the dynamic theory of optimal capital accumulation and the scientific analysis of global warming. We cite only a few among them that have had pertinent influences on the analysis developed in this chapter: Ramsey (1928), Arrow (1962a,b), Arrow and Kurz (1970), Keeler, Spence, and Zeckhauser (1971), Stiglitz and Dasgupta (1971), Forster (1973), Dasgupta and Heal (1974, 1979), Mäler (1974), Solow (1974), Uzawa (1974a,b, 1975, 1991, 1992a,b), Nordhaus (1980, 1982, 1993a), Dasgupta (1982a), Stockfish (1982), Krautkraemer (1985), Musu (1990), (Norgaard, 1990b), IPCC (1991b, 2001, 2002), Pearce (1991), Poterba (1991), Grossman and Helpman (1991), Hoel (1992, 1994), Howarth and Norgaard (1992), Gradus and Smulders (1993), Tahvonen and Kuuluvainen (1993), and Huan and Cai (1994).

2. CARBON DIOXIDE ACCUMULATION IN THE ATMOSPHERE: A SIMPLE DYNAMIC MODEL

We denote by V_t the amount of carbon dioxide accumulated in the atmosphere at time t. The quantity V_t is measured in actual tons (in weights of carbon content) or in terms of the density of carbon dioxide in the atmosphere. We also adopt as the origin of the measurement the stable pre-Industrial Revolution level of 600 GtC (approximately corresponding to the density of 280 ppm). The current level of 750 GtC (approximately 360 ppm) is expressed as $V_t = 150$ GtC.

The premises of the dynamic model introduced in this chapter are primarily based on the scientific findings on global warming and related subjects reported by Keeling (1968, 1983), Dyson and Marland (1979), Takahashi et al. (1980), Marland (1988), Myers (1988), Ramanathan et al. (1985), and IPCC (1991b, 2000), among others.

Changes of CO_2 Accumulations due to Natural Causes

The atmospheric accumulations of CO_2 change over time due to natural and anthropogenic activities. Let us first consider changes in the atmospheric level of CO_2 due to natural activities.

A certain portion of atmospheric concentrations of CO_2 is absorbed by the oceans (roughly estimated at 50%) and to a lesser extent by living land plants. In the simple dynamic model postulated in this section, the exchange of carbon dioxide between the atmosphere and the terrestrial biosphere is not taken into consideration. It will be explicitly addressed in the more general model introduced in Chapter 6.

As mentioned previously, roughly 75–90 GtC of carbon are annually exchanged between the atmosphere and the surface oceans. The mechanisms by which atmospheric carbon dioxide is absorbed into the surface oceans are rather complicated. They partly depend on the extent to which the surface waters of the oceans are saturated with CO_2, on the one hand, and the extent to which CO_2 is accumulated in the atmosphere in excess of the equilibrium level. The studies made by several meteorologists and oceanologists – in particular by Keeling (1968, 1983), Takahashi et al. (1980), and others – suggest that the rate of ocean uptake is closely related to the atmospheric accumulations of CO_2 in excess of the stable, pre-Industrial Revolution level of 280 ppm.

As an approximation of the first order, we assume that the amount of atmospheric carbon dioxide annually absorbed by the oceans is given by μV_t, where V_t is the atmospheric concentrations of CO_2 measured in actual tons of CO_2 with the pre-Industrial Revolution level of 600 GtC as the origin of measurement, and the rate of absorption μ is a certain constant. The studies made by Takahashi et al. (1980) and others indicate that the rate of absorption μ would have a magnitude of 2–4 percent. Indeed, according to the estimates made by Ramanathan et al. (1985) and others, CO_2 remains airborne 7 to 17 years, and about half of it is absorbed by the surface ocean, again resulting in the magnitude of $\mu = 2$–4 percent. In what follows, we assume that $\mu = 0.04$.

In the simple dynamic model, we assume that the anthropogenic change in atmospheric carbon dioxide is exclusively caused by the combustion of fossil fuels in connection with industrial, agricultural, and urban activities. We denote by a_t the annual rate of increase in the atmospheric level of CO_2 due to anthropogenic activities. The magnitude of a_t is currently estimated around 6 GtC per annum; that is, $a_t = 6$ GtC.

The dynamic equation for the atmospheric level of CO_2 is now formally written as

$$\dot{V}_t = a_t - \mu V_t,$$

where $\dot{V}_t = \frac{dV_t}{dt}$ denotes the rate of change in V_t over time.

The rate of anthropogenic change in the atmospheric level of CO_2, a_t, is primarily determined by the combustion of fossil fuels and is closely related to the levels of production and consumption activities conducted during the year observed.

Specifications for Utility Functions

Our analysis will be developed on the premises that are similar but different with regard to certain crucial aspects such as those introduced in Chapter 1. At the risk of repetition, they will be described in detail before we proceed with the dynamic analysis of global warming.

There exist n countries in the world. Each country is generically denoted by ν ($\nu = 1, \ldots, n$). We are concerned with the processes by which various relevant economic variables are determined at a particular moment in time t. For the present, all variables are denoted without explicit reference to t.

We assume that the level of the utility u^ν of each country ν depends on the amount of atmospheric concentrations of CO_2 at time t, V, rather than the amount of the annual CO_2 emissions, a, as was the case with the static analysis developed in Chapter 1. That is, the utility function for each country ν is expressed in the following manner:

$$u^\nu = u^\nu(c^\nu, V),$$

where $c^\nu = (c_j^\nu)$ is the vector of goods consumed in country ν and V is the atmospheric concentrations of CO_2 measured in tons of CO_2 accumulated in the atmosphere, both at time t.

As in Chapter 1, we assume that, for each country ν, utility function $u^\nu(c^\nu, V)$ satisfies the following neoclassical conditions:

(U1) $u^\nu(c^\nu, V)$ is defined, continuous, and continuously twice-differentiable for all $(c^\nu, V) \geqq (0, 0)$.

(U2) Marginal utilities are positive for the consumption of private goods $c^\nu = (c_j^\nu)$, but the atmospheric concentrations of carbon dioxide have a negative marginal utility; that is,

$$u^{\nu}_{c^{\nu}}(c^{\nu}, V) > 0, u^{\nu}_{V}(c^{\nu}, V) < 0, \quad \text{for all } (c^{\nu}, V) \geqq (0, 0).$$

(U3) Marginal rates of substitution between any pair of consumption goods are diminishing; or more specifically, $u^{\nu}(c^{\nu}, V)$ is strictly quasi-concave with respect to c^{ν} for any given $V \geqq 0$.

For each country ν, we also assume that utility function $u^{\nu}(c^{\nu}, V)$ is strongly separable with respect to c^{ν} and V in the sense originally introduced by Goldman and Uzawa (1964), as discussed in detail in Chapter 1; that is,

$$u^{\nu}(c^{\nu}, V) = \varphi(V)u^{\nu}(c^{\nu}).$$

As with the static case, the function $\varphi(V)$ expresses the extent to which people are adversely affected by global warming, which is referred to as the *impact index* of global warming.

We assume that the impact index $\varphi(V)$ of global warming is identical for all countries. We may assume that the impact index function $\varphi(V)$ satisfies the following conditions:

$$\varphi(V) > 0, \quad \varphi'(V) < 0, \quad \varphi''(V) < 0, \quad \text{for all } t.$$

As in the static case, the impact index function $\varphi(V)$ of the following form is often postulated:

$$\varphi(V) = (\hat{V} - V)^{\beta}, \quad 0 \leqq V < \hat{V}, \tag{1}$$

where $\hat{V}$ is the critical level of the atmospheric accumulation of CO_2 and β is the sensitivity parameter, $0 < \beta < 1$. If the level of the atmospheric accumulation of CO_2 were higher than the critical level $\hat{V}$, irrevocable damage would be inflicted on the global environment. The critical level of the atmospheric accumulation of CO_2 is usually assumed to be twice the level prevailing before the Industrial Revolution; that is, $\hat{V} = 600$ GtC.

The relative rate of the marginal change in the impact index due to the marginal increase in the atmospheric accumulation of CO_2 is defined by

$$\tau(V) = -\frac{\varphi'(V)}{\varphi(V)},$$

which is again referred to as the *impact coefficient* of global warming. The impact coefficient $\tau(V)$ satisfies the following conditions:

$$\tau(V) > 0, \tau'(V) - [\tau(V)]^2 > 0.$$

For the impact index function $\varphi(V)$ of the form (1), the impact coefficient $\tau(V)$ is given by

$$\tau(V) = \frac{\beta}{\hat{V} - V}.$$

We retain the neoclassical assumptions for utility functions $u^\nu(c^\nu)$ as introduced in Chapter 1.

(U1′) $u^\nu(c^\nu)$ is defined, positive, continuous, and continuously twice-differentiable, respectively, for all $c^\nu \geqq 0$.

(U2′) Marginal utilities are positive for the consumption of private goods $c^\nu = (c_j^\nu)$:

$$u_{c^\nu}^\nu(c^\nu) > 0, \quad \text{for all } c^\nu \geqq 0.$$

(U3′) $u^\nu(c^\nu)$ is strictly quasi-concave with respect to $c^\nu \geqq 0$; that is, for any pair of vectors of consumption, c_0^ν, c_1^ν, such that $u^\nu(c_0^\nu) = u^\nu(c_1^\nu)$ and $c_0^\nu \neq c_1^\nu$,

$$u^\nu((1-t)c_0^\nu + tc_1^\nu) < (1-t)u^\nu(c_0^\nu) + tu^\nu(c_1^\nu), \quad \text{for all } 0 < t < 1.$$

(U4′) $u^\nu(c^\nu)$ is homogeneous of order 1 with respect to c^ν:

$$u^\nu(tc^\nu) = tu^\nu(c^\nu), \quad \text{for all } t \geqq 0, c^\nu \geqq 0.$$

The Euler identity will play a crucial role in the dynamic context, too.

$$u^\nu(c^\nu) = u_{c^\nu}^\nu(c^\nu)c^\nu, \quad \text{for all } c^\nu \geqq 0.$$

Specifications for Production Possibility Sets

The conditions concerning the production of goods in each country ν are specified by the production possibility set T^ν in exactly the same manner as in the static case. We briefly recapitulate the discussion concerning the production possibility set T^ν.

Those factors of production that are essential in the production of goods are generically denoted by ℓ $(\ell = 1, \ldots, L)$. The endowments of factors of production available in each country ν are expressed by an L-dimensional vector $K^\nu = (K_1^\nu, \ldots, K_L^\nu)$.

In the static case, the endowments of factors of production available in each country ν are assumed to be given exogenously and to remain constant throughout the discussion. In the dynamic situation, however, the endowments of factors of production available in each country ν at each time are endogenously determined in the sense that they are the outcomes of the choices made in the past by the members of the economy. In this chapter, however, the endowments of factors of production are regarded as given. In Chapter 5, the processes of capital accumulation will be discussed.

The conditions concerning the production of goods in each country ν are specified by the production possibility set T^ν, which summarizes the technological possibilities and organizational arrangements for country ν as well as the quantities of factors of production available in country ν.

In each country ν, the minimum quantities of factors of production needed to produce goods by the production vector $x^\nu = (x_j^\nu)$ with the CO_2 emission at the level a^ν are specified by an L-dimensional vector-valued function

$$f^\nu(x^\nu, a^\nu) = \left(f_1^\nu(x^\nu, a^\nu), \ldots, f_L^\nu(x^\nu, a^\nu)\right).$$

The production possibility set T^ν is defined by

$$T^\nu = \{(x^\nu, a^\nu)\colon (x^\nu, a^\nu) \geqq 0,\ f^\nu(x^\nu, a^\nu) \leqq K^\nu\}.$$

Postulates (T1–3), as specified in Chapter 1, imply that the production possibility set T^ν is a closed, convex set of $J+1$-dimensional vectors (x^ν, a^ν).

3. MARKET EQUILIBRIUM AND GLOBAL WARMING

We consider the situation in which carbon taxes at the rate of θ^ν are levied on the emission of CO_2 in each country ν.

Market equilibrium for the world economy is obtained if we find the prices of goods p at which total demand is equal to total supply:

$$\sum_\nu c^\nu = \sum_\nu x^\nu.$$

Total CO_2 emissions a are given by

$$a = \sum_{\nu} a^{\nu}.$$

Supply and demand conditions are specified in the same manner as in the static model.

(i) Supply conditions in each country are obtained by maximizing net profits

$$px^{\nu} - \theta^{\nu} a^{\nu}$$

over $(x^{\nu}, a^{\nu}) \in T^{\nu}$, that is, subject to the constraints that

$$f^{\nu}(x^{\nu}, a^{\nu}) \leqq K^{\nu}.$$

(ii) Demand conditions in each country ν are obtained by maximizing utility function

$$u^{\nu}(c^{\nu}, V) = \varphi(V) u^{\nu}(c^{\nu})$$

subject to budget constraints

$$pc^{\nu} = y^{\nu}, c^{\nu} \geqq 0,$$

where y^{ν} is national income of country ν.

The optimum levels of production and CO_2 emissions in country ν are determined by the following marginality conditions, which are exactly identical with those in Chapter 1:

$$p = r^{\nu} f^{\nu}_{a^{\nu}}(x^{\nu}, a^{\nu})$$
$$\theta^{\nu} = r^{\nu}[-f^{\nu}_{a^{\nu}}(x^{\nu}, a^{\nu})],$$

where r^{ν} is the vector of rental prices of factors of production in country ν.

Because the technologies are assumed to be subject to constant returns to scale, (T4), we have that

$$px^{\nu} - \theta^{\nu} a^{\nu} = r^{\nu}[f^{\nu}_{x^{\nu}}(x^{\nu}, a^{\nu})x^{\nu} + f^{\nu}_{a^{\nu}}(x^{\nu}, a^{\nu})a^{\nu}]$$
$$= r^{\nu} f^{\nu}(x^{\nu}, a^{\nu}) = r^{\nu} K^{\nu}.$$

That is, the net evaluation of output is equal to the sum of the rental payments to all factors of production.

As in Chapter 1, when all factors of production are owned by individual members of the country ν, then national income y^ν of country ν is equal to the sum of the rental payments $r^\nu K^\nu$ and the tax payments $\theta^n a^\nu$ made by the producers for the emission of CO_2 in country ν; hence,

$$y^\nu = r^\nu K^\nu + \theta^\nu a^\nu = (px^\nu - \theta^\nu a^\nu) + \theta^\nu a^\nu = px^\nu.$$

That is, national income y^ν of country ν is equal to the value px^ν of outputs in units of market prices.

The optimum vector of consumption c^ν is obtained by solving the following marginality conditions:

$$\varphi(V)u^\nu_{c^\nu}(c^\nu) = \lambda^\nu p,$$

where λ^ν is the Lagrangian unknown associated with the budgetary constraints.

One of the basic problems we face in the dynamic analysis of global warming is to see how the carbon tax rate θ^ν in each country ν is determined. We extend to the dynamic context the concept of deferential equilibrium as introduced in Chapter 1 for the static context.

Deferential Equilibrium in the Dynamic Context

Deferential equilibrium is obtained if, when each country chooses the levels of production activities today, it takes into account the negative impact on the future levels of its own utilities brought about by the CO_2 emissions of that country today.

Consider the situation in which a combination (x^ν, a^ν) of production vector and CO_2 emissions is chosen in country ν. Suppose CO_2 emissions in country ν are increased by a marginal amount. This would induce a marginal increase in the aggregate amount of CO_2 emissions in the world, effecting a marginal increase in the atmospheric level of CO_2. The resulting marginal increase in the degree of future global warming would cause a marginal decrease in country ν's utility. Deferential equilibrium is obtained if this marginal decrease in country ν's future utility due to the marginal increase in CO_2 emissions today in country ν is taken into consideration in determining the levels of consumption, production, and CO_2 emissions today.

The marginal decrease in country ν's utility due to the marginal increase in CO_2 emissions today in country ν is given by the partial derivative, with minus sign, of utility function $u^\nu(c^\nu, V)$ of country ν with respect to atmospheric accumulations of CO_2, V; that is,

$$-\frac{\partial u^\nu}{\partial V} = -\varphi'(V)u^\nu(c^\nu) = \tau(V)\varphi(V)u^\nu(c^\nu),$$

where $\tau(V)$ is the impact coefficient of global warming

$$\tau(V) = -\frac{\varphi'(V)}{\varphi(V)}.$$

We assume that future utilities of country ν are discounted at a rate δ that is exogenously given. We also assume that the rate of utility discount δ is a positive constant and is identical for all countries in the world. We have assumed in the preceding section that the rate at which atmospheric carbon dioxide is annually absorbed by the oceans is a certain constant μ with a value of around 4 percent. Hence, for each country ν, the *imputed price* ψ^ν of the atmospheric accumulations of CO_2 is given by the discounted present value of the marginal decrease in country ν's utility due to the marginal increase in CO_2 emissions at time t in country ν:

$$\psi^\nu = \frac{1}{\delta + \mu}\left[-\frac{\partial u^\nu}{\partial V}\right] = \frac{1}{\delta + \mu}\tau(V)\varphi(V)u^\nu(c^\nu). \tag{2}$$

Deferential equilibrium is obtained if the marginal decrease in country ν's future utilities due to the marginal increase in CO_2 emissions today in country ν is balanced with the marginal increase in country ν's future utilities due to the resulting marginal increase in the level of production.

If the level of CO_2 emissions in country ν is a^ν, then the net level of country ν's utility is given by

$$\varphi(V)u^\nu(c^\nu) - \psi^\nu a^\nu.$$

The choice of the levels of consumption, production, and CO_2 emissions for each country ν under the deferential behavioristic postulates then may be viewed as the optimum solution to the following maximum problem:

Find the combination (c^ν, x^ν, a^ν) of consumption vector, production vector, and CO_2 emissions that maximizes the net level of country ν's utility

$$\varphi(V)u^{\nu}(c^{\nu}) - \psi^{\nu}a^{\nu}$$

subject to the constraints that

$$pc^{\nu} = px^{\nu},\, c^{\nu} \geqq 0 \tag{3}$$

$$f^{\nu}(x^{\nu}, a^{\nu}) \leqq K^{\nu}. \tag{4}$$

The maximum problem is solved in terms of the Lagrangian form

$$L^{\nu}(c^{\nu}, x^{\nu}, a^{\nu}; \lambda^{\nu}r^{\nu})$$
$$= [\varphi(V)u^{\nu}(c^{\nu}) - \psi^{\nu}a^{\nu}] + \lambda^{\nu}(px^{\nu} - pc^{\nu}) + \lambda^{\nu}r^{\nu}[K^{\nu} - f^{\nu}(x^{\nu}, a^{\nu})],$$

where V and ψ^{ν} are given. The variables λ^{ν}, $\lambda^{\nu}r^{\nu}$ are the Lagrangian unknowns associated with constraints (3) and (4), respectively.

The optimum conditions are

$$\varphi(V)u^{\nu}_{c^{\nu}}(c^{\nu}) = \lambda^{\nu}p$$
$$\lambda^{\nu}p = \lambda^{\nu}r^{\nu}f^{\nu}_{x^{\nu}}(x^{\nu}, a^{\nu})$$
$$\psi^{\nu} = \lambda^{\nu}r^{\nu}[-f^{\nu}_{a^{\nu}}(x^{\nu}, a^{\nu})].$$

When expressed in units of market prices, the optimum conditions are

$$\alpha^{\nu}\varphi(V)u^{\nu}_{c^{\nu}}(c^{\nu}) = p \tag{5}$$

$$p = r^{\nu}f^{\nu}_{x^{\nu}}(x^{\nu}, a^{\nu}) \tag{6}$$

$$\theta^{\nu} = r^{\nu}[-f^{\nu}_{a^{\nu}}(x^{\nu}, a^{\nu})], \tag{7}$$

where

$$\alpha^{\nu} = \frac{1}{\lambda^{\nu}} > 0,$$

and θ^{ν} is the imputed price of atmospheric concentrations of CO_2 in units of market prices

$$\theta^{\nu} = \frac{\psi^{\nu}}{\lambda^{\nu}},$$

which, by substitution into (2), implies

$$\theta^{\nu} = \frac{1}{\delta + \mu}\tau(V)\alpha^{\nu}\varphi(V)u^{\nu}(c^{\nu}). \tag{8}$$

By multiplying both sides of relation (5) by c^ν, we find that

$$\alpha^\nu \varphi(V) u^\nu_{c^\nu}(c^\nu) c^\nu = p c^\nu.$$

By making use of the Euler identity and noting the budget constraint (3), we obtain

$$\alpha^\nu \varphi(V) u^\nu(c^\nu) c^\nu = p x^\nu = y^\nu, \tag{10}$$

where y^ν is national income of country ν expressed as

$$y^\nu = p x^\nu.$$

Hence, in view of (8), we obtain

$$\theta^\nu = \frac{\tau(V)}{\delta + \mu} y^\nu. \tag{11}$$

Marginality conditions (6) and (7) imply that net profits

$$p x^\nu - \theta^\nu a^\nu$$

are maximized over the technological possibility set $(x^\nu, a^\nu) \in T^\nu$, where carbon tax rate θ^ν is determined by (11).

Hence, the conditions for deferential equilibrium in the dynamic context are identical with those for a standard market equilibrium when carbon taxes with rate θ^ν given by (11) are levied; that is,

(i) For each country ν, the consumption vector c^ν maximizes country ν's utility function

$$u^\nu(c^\nu, V) = \varphi(V) u^\nu(c^\nu)$$

subject to the budgetary constraints

$$p c^\nu = y^\nu, \; c^\nu \geqq 0,$$

where $y^\nu = p x^\nu$ is national income of country ν, and the level of atmospheric CO_2 accumulations, V, is assumed to be given.

(ii) For each country ν, the combination (x^ν, a^ν) of production vector x^ν and CO_2 emissions a^ν maximizes net profits

$$p x^\nu - \theta^\nu a^\nu$$

over the technological possibility set $(x^\nu, a^\nu) \in T^\nu$.

Deferential equilibrium for the world economy in the dynamic context then is obtained if we find the prices of goods p at which total demand is equal to total supply:

$$\sum_{\nu} c^{\nu} = \sum_{\nu} x^{\nu}.$$

Total CO_2 emissions a are given by

$$a = \sum_{\nu} a^{\nu}.$$

The preceding discussion may be summarized by the following proposition:

Proposition 1. *Deferential equilibrium corresponds precisely to the standard market equilibrium under the system of carbon taxes, where, in each country ν, the carbon taxes are levied with the tax rate θ^{ν} that is proportional to the national income y^{ν} of each country ν with the discounted present value $\frac{\tau(V)}{\delta+\mu}$ of the impact coefficient of global warming $\tau(V)$ as the coefficient of proportion; that is,*

$$\theta^{\nu} = \frac{\tau(V)}{\delta+\mu} y^{\nu},$$

where $\tau(V)$ is the impact coefficient of global warming,

$$\tau(V) = -\frac{\varphi'(V)}{\varphi(V)},$$

δ is the rate of utility discount, and μ is the rate at which atmospheric carbon dioxide is annually absorbed by the oceans.

4. UNIFORM CARBON TAXES AND SOCIAL OPTIMUM

In the previous section, we have seen that deferential equilibrium may be obtained as the standard market equilibrium, provided the carbon tax rate θ^{ν} in each country ν is equal to

$$\theta^{\nu} = \frac{\tau(V)}{\delta+\mu} y^{\nu},$$

where y^{ν} is national income of country ν and $\tau(V)$ is the impact coefficient of global warming. Exactly as in Chapter 1, we now would like to examine the implications of market equilibrium when the uniform carbon taxes with the rate θ given by

$$\theta = \frac{\tau(V)}{\delta + \mu} y, \quad y = \sum_{\nu} y^{\nu} \tag{12}$$

are levied.

The conditions for market equilibrium under the uniform carbon tax scheme in the dynamic context are obtained in exactly the same manner as in the static context.

(i) For each country ν, the consumption vector c^{ν} maximizes country ν's utility function

$$u^{\nu}(c^{\nu}, V) = \varphi(V) u^{\nu}(c^{\nu})$$

subject to budget constraints

$$pc^{\nu} = y^{\nu}, \quad c^{\nu} \geqq 0,$$

where $y^{\nu} = px^{\nu}$ is national income of country ν.

(ii) For each country ν, the combination (x^{ν}, a^{ν}) of production vector x^{ν} and CO_2 emissions a^{ν} maximizes net profits

$$px^{\nu} - \theta a^{\nu}$$

over the technological possibility set $(x^{\nu}, a^{\nu}) \in T^{\nu}$.

(iii) Prices of goods p are determined so that total demand is equal to total supply:

$$\sum_{\nu} c^{\nu} = \sum_{\nu} x^{\nu}.$$

(iv) Total CO_2 emissions a are given by

$$a = \sum_{\nu} a^{\nu}.$$

The optimum vector of consumption c^{ν} is obtained by the following marginality condition expressed in units of market prices:

$$\alpha^{\nu} \varphi(V) u^{\nu}_{c^{\nu}}(c^{\nu}) = p, \tag{13}$$

where

$$\alpha^{\nu} = \frac{1}{\lambda^{\nu}} > 0.$$

The producer optimum is obtained by the following marginality conditions:

$$p = r^{\nu} f_{x^{\nu}}^{\nu}(x^{\nu}, a^{\nu}) \tag{14}$$

$$\theta = r^{\nu}[-f_{a^{\nu}}^{\nu}(x^{\nu}, a^{\nu})]. \tag{15}$$

As before, because of the linear homogeneity hypothesis for utility functions, marginality condition (13) for the consumer optimum yields the following basic relation:

$$\alpha^{\nu}\varphi(V)u^{\nu}(c^{\nu}) = pc^{\nu} = px^{\nu} = y^{\nu}. \tag{16}$$

We now define the world utility W by

$$W = \sum_{\nu} \alpha^{\nu}\varphi(V)u^{\nu}(c^{\nu}), \tag{17}$$

which, in view of (16), may be written as

$$W = \sum_{\nu} y^{\nu} = y.$$

The imputed price ψ of the atmospheric concentrations of CO_2 with respect to the world utility W is given by

$$\psi = \frac{1}{\delta + \mu}\left[-\frac{\partial W}{\partial V}\right] = \frac{1}{\delta + \mu}\sum_{\nu} \alpha^{\nu}[-\varphi'(V)]u^{\nu}(c^{\nu}), \tag{18}$$

which, in view of relation (16), may be written as

$$\psi = \frac{\tau(V)}{\delta + \mu}\sum_{\nu} \alpha^{\nu}\varphi(V)u^{\nu}(c^{\nu}) = \frac{\tau(V)}{\delta + \mu}\sum_{\nu} y^{\nu} = \frac{\tau(V)}{\delta + \mu}y.$$

That is, the imputed price ψ of the atmospheric concentrations of CO_2 with respect to the world utility W defined by (17) is equal to the uniform carbon tax rate given by (12):

$$\psi = \theta. \tag{19}$$

If we take into account the loss in the level of world utility due to total CO_2 emissions a to be evaluated at the imputed price ψ of the atmospheric concentrations of CO_2, the net level of world utility may be defined by

$$W - \psi a = \sum_{\nu} \alpha^{\nu}\varphi(V)u^{\nu}(c^{\nu}) - \psi a. \tag{20}$$

Social Optimum in the Dynamic Context

We consider the following social optimum problem:
Find the pattern of consumption and production of goods for individual countries, the pattern of CO_2 emissions by individual countries, and total CO_2 emissions of the world $(c_*^1, \ldots, c_*^n, x_*^1, \ldots, x_*^n, a_*^1, \ldots, a_*^n, a_*)$ that maximize the net level of world utility (20) among all feasible patterns of allocation $(c^1, \ldots, c^n, x^1, \ldots, x^n, a^1, \ldots, a^n, a)$:

$$\sum_\nu c^\nu = \sum_\nu x^\nu, \quad a = \sum_\nu a^\nu, \quad (x^\nu, a^\nu) \in T^\nu,$$

where V and ψ are, respectively, the atmospheric concentrations of CO_2 and the imputed price of the atmospheric concentrations of CO_2 with respect to world utility W.

The social optimum problem may be solved in terms of the Lagrangian form:

$$L(c^1, \ldots, c^n, x^1, \ldots, x^n, a^1, \ldots, a^n a; p, \theta, r^1, \ldots, r^L)$$

$$= \left[\sum_\nu \alpha^\nu \varphi(V) u^\nu(c^\nu) - \psi a\right] + p\left[\sum_\nu x^\nu - \sum_\nu c^\nu\right] + \theta\left[a - \sum_\nu a^\nu\right]$$
$$+ \sum_\nu r^\nu [K^\nu - f^\nu(x^\nu, a^\nu)].$$

It is apparent that marginal conditions (13), (14), (15), and (19) are the Euler–Lagrange conditions. Thus, we have established the following proposition.

Proposition 2. *Consider the uniform carbon tax scheme, where the rate θ is proportional to the aggregate income of the world y with the discounted present value $\frac{\tau(V)}{\delta + \mu}$ of the impact coefficient of global warming $\tau(V)$ as the coefficient of proportion:*

$$\theta = \frac{\tau(V)}{\delta + \mu} y,$$

where

$$\tau(V) = -\frac{\varphi'(V)}{\varphi(V)}, \quad y = \sum_\nu y^\nu.$$

Then the market equilibrium obtained under such a uniform carbon tax scheme is a social optimum in the sense that a set of positive weights exists for the utilities of individual countries $(\alpha^1, \ldots, \alpha^n)$, $[\alpha^\nu > 0]$ *such that the net level of the world utility*

$$W - \theta a = \sum_\nu \alpha^\nu \varphi(V) u^\nu(c^\nu) - \theta a$$

is maximized among all feasible patterns of allocation $(c^1, \ldots, c^n, x^1, \ldots, x^n, a^1, \ldots, a^n, a)$

$$\sum_\nu c^\nu = \sum_\nu x^\nu, \quad a = \sum_\nu a^\nu, \quad (x^\nu, a^\nu) \in T^\nu.$$

Then world utility W is equal to the aggregate national income of the world:

$$W = y,$$

and the imputed price ψ *of the atmospheric concentrations of* CO_2, *defined by (18), is equal to carbon tax rate* θ:

$$\psi = \theta.$$

NOTES. Proposition 2 contains certain ambiguities in the way it is stated. When the uniform carbon tax rate

$$\theta = \frac{\tau(V)}{\delta + \mu} y$$

is announced, the level of the world national income y is not exactly known. Hence, we need some sort of adjustment processes concerning the uniform carbon tax rate θ.

Suppose the uniform carbon tax rate is announced at an arbitrarily given level $\theta > 0$, and let the relevant variables at the market equilibrium under the carbon tax scheme with the rate θ be denoted by $p, c^\nu, x^\nu, a^\nu, y^\nu, y$. Then the imputed price ψ of atmospheric concentrations of CO_2 with respect to world utility W is given by

$$\psi = \frac{\tau(V)}{\delta + \mu} y,$$

where

$$y = \sum_\nu y^\nu, \quad y^\nu = px^\nu, \quad \nu = 1, \ldots, n.$$

Suppose tax rate θ is increased by the marginal amount $\Delta\theta$. Because (x^ν, a^ν) maximizes net profits

$$px^\nu - \theta a^\nu = y^\nu - \theta a^\nu$$

over the technological possibility set $(x^\nu, a^\nu) \in T^\nu$, the lemma in Chapter 2 may be applied to obtain

$$\Delta y^\nu \Delta\theta < 0.$$

Hence,

$$\Delta y \Delta\theta < 0,$$

which implies

$$\Delta\psi\Delta\theta < 0.$$

Thus, the imputed price ψ of atmospheric concentrations of CO_2 is a decreasing function of tax rate θ, and, as θ approaches infinity, ψ approaches zero. Hence, a tax rate θ uniquely exists such that

$$\psi = \theta.$$

The preceding discussion may be illustrated by Figure 4.1, where carbon tax rate θ is measured along the abscissa, whereas imputed price ψ of the atmospheric concentrations of CO_2 is measured along the ordinate. The downward-sloping curve *AA* depicts the relationships between carbon tax rate θ and imputed price ψ. The uniquely determined intersection *E* of curve *AA* and 45° line *OB* corresponds to the market equilibrium.

Then, it is straightforward to see that the following adjustment process with respect to tax rate θ is globally stable:

$$\frac{d\theta}{dt} = k(\psi - \theta),$$

where the speed of adjustment *k* is positive.

Similarly, as in the static context, the concept of social optimum in the dynamic context may be defined for any arbitrarily given set of positive weights for the utilities of individual countries $(\alpha^1, \ldots, \alpha^n)$, $[\alpha^\nu > 0]$. A pattern of allocation $(c_*^1, \ldots, c_*^n, x_*^1, \ldots, x_*^n, a_*^1, \ldots, a_*^n, a_*)$ is a social optimum if the net level of world utility (20) is maximized among all feasible patterns of allocation $(c^1, \ldots, c^n, x^1, \ldots, x^n, a^1, \ldots, a^n, a)$.

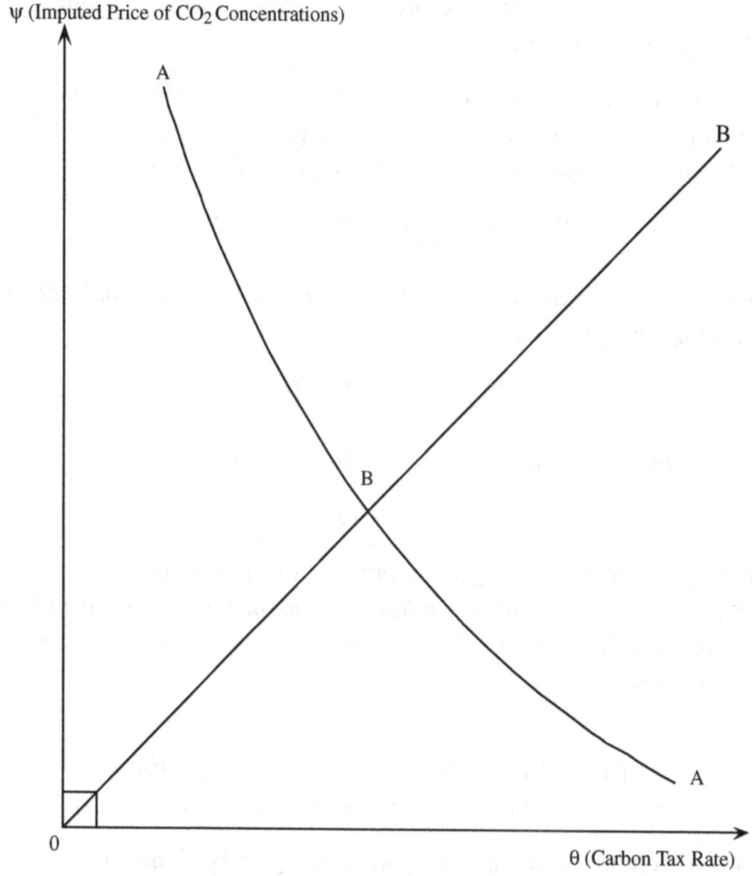

Figure 4.1. Determination of Proportional Carbon Taxes.

A social optimum in the dynamic context necessarily implies the existence of the uniform carbon tax scheme with the rate $\theta = \frac{\tau(V)}{\delta + \mu} y$. However, the balance-of-payments requirements

$$pc^{\nu} = px^{\nu}$$

are generally not satisfied.

It is apparent that, if a social optimum in the dynamic context satisfies the balance-of-payments requirements, then it corresponds to the market equilibrium under the uniform carbon tax scheme. The existence of such a social optimum is ensured by the following

Proposition 3, which may be proved in exactly the same manner as Proposition 3 in Chapter 1.

Proposition 3. *There always exists a set of positive weights for the utilities of individual countries* $(\alpha^1, \ldots, \alpha^n)$, $[\alpha^\nu > 0]$ *such that the social optimum in the dynamic sense with respect to the world utility*

$$W - \psi a = \sum_\nu \alpha^\nu \varphi(V) u^\nu(c^\nu) - \psi a,$$

where ψ *is the imputed price of the atmospheric concentrations of* CO_2 *with respect to world utility*

$$W = \sum_\nu \alpha^\nu \varphi(V) u^\nu(c^\nu),$$

satisfies the balance-of-payments requirements

$$pc^\nu = px^\nu$$

and, accordingly, the corresponding pattern of allocation $(c^1, \ldots, c^n, x^1, \ldots, x^n, a^1, \ldots, a^n, a)$, *in conjunction with prices of goods p and the carbon tax scheme with the uniform rate* $\theta = \tau(a)y$, *constitutes a market equilibrium for the world.*

5. THE DYNAMIC STABILITY OF THE ATMOSPHERIC CONCENTRATION OF CO_2

In this section, we would like to see if the process of the atmospheric accumulation of CO_2 under the uniform carbon tax scheme is dynamically stable. The dynamic equation for the process of the atmospheric accumulation of CO_2 is given by

$$\dot{V} = a - \mu V, \tag{21}$$

where a is the level of total emissions of CO_2 at time t and μ is the rate at which atmospheric concentrations of CO_2 are annually absorbed by the oceans. The time suffix t will be omitted.

Let us slightly modify the way by which the market equilibrium under the uniform carbon tax scheme is obtained, as described in the preceding Notes.

Suppose the assumed level of the world national income is specified at an arbitrarily given level $y_0 > 0$, and let the relevant variables at the market equilibrium under the carbon tax scheme with the rate θ be denoted by $p, c^\nu, x^\nu, a^\nu, y^\nu, y$, where

$$\theta = \frac{\tau(V)}{\delta + \mu} y_0.$$

The imputed price ψ of atmospheric concentrations of CO_2 with respect to world utility W is given by

$$\psi = \frac{\tau(V)}{\delta + \mu} y,$$

where

$$y = \sum_\nu y^\nu, \quad y^\nu = px^\nu, \quad \nu = 1, \ldots, n.$$

Suppose the assumed level of the world national income y_0 is increased by the marginal amount Δy_0. Then the carbon tax rate is increased by $\Delta\theta$, where

$$\Delta\theta = \frac{\tau(V)}{\delta + \mu} \Delta y_0.$$

Hence, relationships between the assumed level y_0 of the world income and the actual world income y at the market equilibrium under the uniform carbon tax scheme are depicted by the downward-sloping curve AA in Figure 4.2, where the abscissa measures the assumed level of the world income y_0 and the actual world income y is measured along the ordinate. The unique intersection E of curve AA and 45° line OB corresponds to the market equilibrium.

Because (x^ν, a^ν) maximizes net profits

$$px^\nu - \theta a^\nu = y^\nu - \frac{\tau(V)}{\delta + \mu} y_0 a^\nu$$

over the technological possibility set $(x^\nu, a^\nu) \in T^\nu$, the lemma in Chapter 2 may again be applied to obtain

$$\Delta y^\nu \Delta V < 0, \quad \Delta a^\nu \Delta V < 0,$$

which imply

$$\Delta y \Delta V < 0, \quad \Delta a \Delta V < 0.$$

Therefore, an increase in the level V of the atmospheric accumulation of CO_2 implies a downward shift of the AA curve in Figure 4.2,

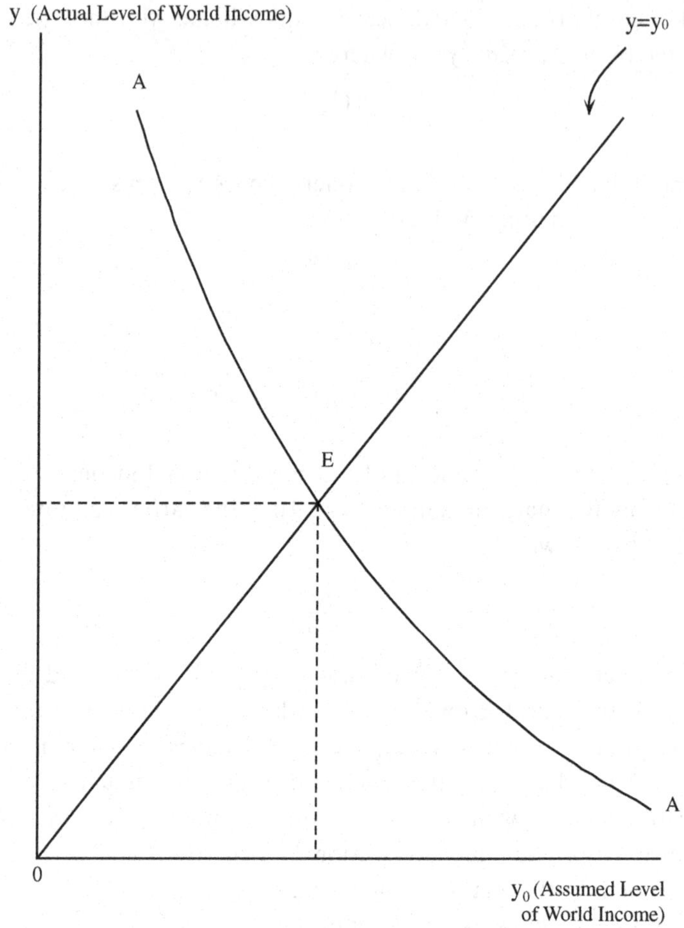

Figure 4.2. Determination of World Income.

resulting in a decrease in the equilibrium of world national income y and the total CO_2 emissions a. Thus, the right-hand side of the dynamic equation (21) is a decreasing function of V, implying that the process of the atmospheric accumulation of CO_2 under the uniform carbon tax scheme is dynamically stable and always approaches the stationary level V_*

$$a_* = \mu V_*,$$

where a_* is the total CO_2 emissions at the market equilibrium under the uniform carbon tax scheme. We have now established the following stability theorem.

Proposition 4. *The process of the atmospheric accumulation of CO_2 under the uniform carbon tax scheme is dynamically stable. That is, solution paths for the dynamic equation*

$$\dot{V} = a - \mu V,$$

where a is the level of total emissions of CO_2 at time t and μ is the rate at which atmospheric concentrations of CO_2 are annually absorbed by the oceans, always converge to the stationary level V_* to be given by the stationarity condition

$$a_* = \mu V_*,$$

where a_* is the total CO_2 emissions at the market equilibrium under the uniform carbon tax scheme.

5

Dynamic Optimality and Sustainability

1. INTRODUCTION

Global warming involves international and intergenerational equity and justice. Although global warming is largely caused by the emission of carbon dioxide and other greenhouse gases associated with economic activities mostly in developed countries and by the disruption of forests – particularly tropical rain forests – again mostly resulting from the industrial activities of the developed countries, it is the people in developing countries who have to bear the burden. The current generation may enjoy the fruits of the economic activities that cause global warming, but it is the people in all future generations who will have to suffer from a significant increase in atmospheric instability as a consequence.

In this chapter, we examine the problems of global warming and other global environmental issues primarily from the viewpoint of the international and intergenerational distribution of utility. We introduce the concept of sustainability, which may capture some aspects of international and intergenerational equity, and derive the conditions under which processes of capital accumulation and changes in environmental quality over time are sustainable. The conceptual framework for the dynamic analysis of environmental quality developed in previous chapters will be extended to deal with the problems of the irreversibility of processes of capital accumulation due to the Penrose effect. The concept of the Penrose effect was originally introduced by Uzawa (1968, 1969) in the context of macroeconomic analysis.

The analysis focuses on the formula for the system of imputed prices associated with the time-path of consumption that is dynamically optimum with respect to the intertemporal preference relation, where the presence of the Penrose effect implies the diminishing marginal rate of investment in private capital and social overhead capital upon the rate at which capital is accumulated. The dynamically optimum time-path of consumption is characterized by the proportionality of two systems of imputed prices, one associated with the given intertemporal preference ordering and another with the processes of accumulation of private and social overhead capital.

The analysis is based on the dynamic duality principles developed by Epstein and Haynes (1983), Lucas and Stokey (1984), Epstein (1987), and Uzawa (1996) in which the concept of imputed prices of both private capital and social overhead capital plays a pivotal role.

A time-path of consumption and capital accumulation is sustainable when the imputed price of each kind of capital, either private or social overhead capital, remains identical over time. In other words, a time-path of consumption is sustainable if all future generations will face the same imputed prices of various kinds of capital as those faced by the current generation. The existence of the sustainable time-path of consumption and capital accumulation starting with an arbitrarily given stock of capital is ensured when the processes of accumulation of various kinds of capital are subject to the Penrose effect, which exhibits the law of diminishing marginal rates of investment.

2. REVIEW OF THE OPTIMUM THEORY OF CAPITAL ACCUMULATION

In this section, we give a brief review of the theory of optimum capital accumulation. The basic premises of the dynamic analysis of capital accumulation and changes in environmental quality are that the intertemporal preference ordering prevailing in society is independent of the technological conditions and processes of capital accumulation, as typically illustrated by the Ramsey–Koopmans–Cass utility integral originally introduced by Ramsey (1928) and later expounded by Uzawa (1964), Koopmans (1965), Cass (1965), Srinivasan (1965), Arrow and Kurz (1970), and others. The Ramsey theory of dynamic optimum was further elaborated by Epstein and Haynes (1983), Lucas and Stokey

(1984), Roemer (1986), Epstein (1987), Rebelo (1993), and Uzawa (1996).

The problems of optimum economic growth and environmental quality were examined by several economists. Among them, we may cite those contributions having implications pertinent to the analysis to be developed in this chapter: Arrow (1962a, 1968), d'Arge (1971), Keeler, Spence, and Zeckhauser (1971), Forster (1973), Mäler (1974), Solow (1974b), Dasgupta and Heal (1974, 1979), Krautkraemer (1985), Musu (1990, 1994), Grossman and Helpman (1991), Uzawa (1991, 1992a,b), Aghion and Howitt (1992), Gradus and Smulders (1993), Huan and Cai (1994), Bovenberg and Smulders (1995), Smulders (1995), and Smulders and Gradus (1996).

We consider an economy whose behavioral characteristics are described by those of the representative consumer. To begin with, we consider the simple case in which only one kind of goods serve both for consumption and investment. The instantaneous level of the utility u_t at each time t is represented by a utility function

$$u_t = u(c_t),$$

where c_t is the quantity of goods consumed by the representative consumer at time t.

We assume that the utility function $u = u(c)$ remains identical over time, is defined for all nonnegative $c \geqq 0$, is continuous and continuously twice-differentiable, and satisfies the following conditions:

$$u(c) > 0, \quad u'(c) > 0, \quad u''(c) < 0, \quad \text{for all } c > 0$$
$$u(0) = 0, \quad u(+\infty) = +\infty.$$

We assume that the intertemporal preference ordering over the set of conceivable time-paths of consumption $(c_t : t \geqq 0)$ may be expressed by the Ramsey–Koopmans–Cass utility integral

$$U(c) = \int_0^\infty u(c_t)e^{-\delta t}\,dt, \quad c = (c_t),$$

where $u_t = u(c_t)$ is the utility function expressing the instantaneous level of utility at time t and δ is the utility rate of discount ($\delta > 0$).

The conceptual basis of the discount rate has been intensively examined in the literature by Koopmans (1965), Arrow (1965), Arrow and Kurz (1970), Bradford (1975), Dasgupta (1982a),

Lind (1982a,b), Sen (1982), Stiglitz (1982), Stockfish (1982), d'Arge (1989), Cropper and Portney (1992), Wallace (1993), Weitzman (1993), and Uzawa (1998).

We first consider the case in which only one kind of private capital exists. We denote by K_t the stock of capital at time t and by c_t, z_t, respectively, consumption and investment at time t. Then, we have

$$c_t + z_t = f(K_t),$$

where $f(K)$ is the production function, which is assumed to be independent of time t.

The production function $f(K)$ expresses the net national product produced from the given stock of capital K. We assume that production function $f(K)$ is defined, continuous, and continuously twice-differentiable for all $K \geqq 0$, that marginal products of capital are always positive, and that production processes are subject to the law of diminishing marginal returns:

$$f'(K) > 0, \quad f''(K) < 0, \quad \text{for all } K > 0.$$

The rate of capital accumulation at time t, $\dot{K}_t$, is given by the dynamic equation

$$\dot{K}_t = \alpha(z_t, K_t), \quad K_0 = K^0,$$

where K^0 is the initial stock of capital and $\alpha(z_t, K_t)$ is the Penrose function relating the rate of capital accumulation $\dot{K}_t$ to investment z_t and the stock of capital K_t at time t.

The Penrose function $\alpha(z, K)$ expresses the net rate of capital accumulation; thus, we may assume that the partial derivative of $\alpha(z, K)$ with respect to z is always positive, whereas with respect K it is always negative:

$$\alpha_z = \alpha_z(z, K) > 0, \quad \alpha_K = \alpha_K(z, K) < 0. \tag{1}$$

The Penrose Effect

The Penrose effect is expressed by the conditions that the Penrose function $\alpha(z, K)$ is concave and strictly quasi-concave with respect to (z, K):

$$\alpha_{zz} < 0, \alpha_{KK} < 0, \quad \alpha_{zz}\alpha_{KK} - \alpha_{KK}^2 \geqq 0. \tag{2}$$

The following condition is usually assumed for the Penrose function $\alpha(z, K)$:

$$\alpha_{zK}(z, K) = \alpha_{Kz}(z, K) < 0. \tag{3}$$

Note that all variables are assumed to be positive:

$$K^0, K_t, c_t, z_t > 0, \quad \text{for all } t \geqq 0.$$

The concept of the Penrose effect was originally introduced by Penrose (1959) to describe the growth processes of a firm. It was later formalized by Uzawa (1969) in the context of a Keynesian analysis of macroeconomic processes of dynamic equilibrium to elucidate the effect of investment activities on the processes of capital accumulation. It plays a crucial role in the following discussion.

Because the concept of the Penrose effect is not widely recognized, one may wonder if conditions (1)–(3) postulated above are consistent. Two examples of the Penrose function $\alpha(z, K)$ that satisfy conditions (1)–(3) are given, although the ranges of definition in both examples are constrained to the intervals.

Example 1. $\alpha(z, K) = z^p(\hat{K} - K)^q \quad [z > 0, 0 < K < \hat{K}]$, where $p, q, \hat{K} > 0$ are given, and $p + q < 1$.

$$\begin{aligned}
\alpha_z &= pz^{p-1}(\hat{K} - K)^q > 0 \\
\alpha_K &= -qz^p(\hat{K} - K)^{q-1} < 0 \\
\alpha_{zz} &= -p(1-p)z^{p-2}(\hat{K} - K)^q < 0 \\
\alpha_{KK} &= -q(1-q)z^p(\hat{K} - K)^{q-2} < 0 \\
\alpha_{zK} &= \alpha_{Kz} = -pqz^{p-1}(\hat{K} - K)^{q-1} < 0
\end{aligned}$$

$$\begin{vmatrix} \alpha_{zz} & \alpha_{zK} \\ \alpha_{Kz} & \alpha_{KK} \end{vmatrix} = \begin{vmatrix} -p(1-p)z^{p-2}(\hat{K} - K)^q & -pqz^{p-1}(\hat{K} - K)^{q-1} \\ -pqz^{p-1}(\hat{K} - K)^{q-1} & -q(1-q)z^p(\hat{K} - K)^{q-2} \end{vmatrix}$$

$$= pq(1 - p - q)z^{2p-2}(\hat{K} - K)^{2q-2} > 0.$$

Example 2. $\alpha(z, K) = (\hat{z} - z)^{-p}(\hat{K} - K)^{q} \quad [0 < z < \hat{z}, 0 < K < \hat{K}]$, where $p, q, \hat{z}, \hat{K} > 0$ are given and $0 < p < 1, 0 < q < \dfrac{1+p}{1+2p}$.

$$\alpha_z = pq(\hat{z} - z)^{-p-1}(\hat{K} - K)^{q} > 0$$
$$\alpha_K = -q(\hat{z} - z)^{-p}(\hat{K} - K)^{q-1} < 0$$
$$\alpha_{KK} = -q(1 - q(\hat{z} - z)^{-p}(\hat{K} - K)^{q-2} < 0$$
$$\alpha_{zK} = \alpha_{Kz} = -pq(\hat{z} - z)^{-p-1}(\hat{K} - K)^{q-1} < 0$$

$$\begin{vmatrix} \alpha_{zz} & \alpha_{zK} \\ \alpha_{Kz} & \alpha_{KK} \end{vmatrix} = \begin{vmatrix} -p(1+p)(\hat{z} - z)^{-p-2}(\hat{K} - K)^{q} & -pq(\hat{z} - z)^{-p-1}(\hat{K} - K)^{q-1} \\ -pq(\hat{z} - z)^{-p-1}(\hat{K} - K)^{q-1} & -q(1-q)(\hat{z} - z)^{-p}(\hat{K} - K)^{q-2} \end{vmatrix}$$
$$= pq\{1 + p - q(1+2p)\}(\hat{z} - z)^{-2p-2}(\hat{K} - K)^{2q-2} > 0.$$

Marginal Efficiency of Investment

A particularly important concept associated with the Penrose function $\alpha(z, K)$ is marginal efficiency of investment. This concept expresses the extent to which the marginal increase in investment z induces the marginal increase in net national product $f(K)$ in the future. The marginal efficiency of investment is composed of two components.

The first component is the marginal increase in net national product $f(K)$ directly induced by the marginal increase $\alpha_z(z, K)$ in the stock of capital due to the marginal increase in investment z; that is,

$$r(K)\alpha_z(z, K),$$

where $r(K) = f'(K)$ is the marginal product of capital.

The second component measures the extent of the marginal effect on future processes of capital accumulation due to the marginal increase in the stock of capital K; that is,

$$\alpha_K(z, K).$$

Thus, the marginal efficiency of investment $m = m(z, K)$ may be expressed as

$$m = m(z, K) = r(K)\alpha_z(z, K) + \alpha_K(z, K).$$

The marginal efficiency of investment $m = m(z, K)$ is a decreasing function of both investment z and the stock of capital K

$$m_z(z, K) = \frac{\partial m}{\partial z} = r\alpha_{zz} + \alpha_{Kz} < 0$$
$$m_K(z, K) = \frac{\partial m}{\partial K} = r'\alpha_z + (\alpha_{zK} + \alpha_{KK}) < 0,$$

where $r' = r'(K) = f''(K) < 0$.

In the standard neoclassical theory of investment, the Penrose effect is not recognized; that is,

$$\alpha(z, K) = z, \quad \text{for all } z \geqq 0,\ K \geqq 0.$$

Then,

$$m(z, K) = r$$
$$m_z(z, K) = 0, \quad m_K(z, K) = r' < 0, \quad \text{for all } z \geqq 0,\ K \geqq 0.$$

Dynamic Optimality and Imputed Price of Capital

A time-path of consumption and capital accumulation, $(c, K) = ((c_t, K_t))$, is dynamically optimum if it maximizes the Ramsey–Koopmans–Cass utility integral

$$U(c) = \int_0^\infty u(c_t)e^{-\delta t}\,dt, \quad c = (c_t)$$

subject to the constraints that

$$c_t + z_t = f(K_t) \tag{4}$$
$$\dot{K}_t = \alpha(z_t, K_t), \tag{5}$$

where the initial stock of capital $K_0 = K^0(K^0 \leq 0)$ is given.

To solve the problem of dynamic optimum, a crucial role is played by the concept of imputed price of capital. The imputed price of capital at time t, π_t, is the discounted present value of the marginal increases in outputs in the future measured in units of the utility due to the marginal increase in investment at time t; that is,

$$\pi_t = \int_t^\infty \pi_\tau m_\tau e^{-\delta(\tau - t)}\,d\tau, \tag{6}$$

where m_τ is marginal efficiency of investment at future time τ:

$$m_\tau = m(z_\tau, K_\tau) = r_\tau \alpha_z(z_\tau, K_\tau) + \alpha_K(z_\tau, K_\tau), \quad r_\tau = f'(K_\tau).$$

Note that, because m_τ is the marginal efficiency of investment at future time τ measured in units of the output, it has to be multiplied by imputed price π_τ to put it in units of the utility.

By differentiating both sides of (6) with respect to time t, we obtain the following differential equation:

$$\dot{\pi}_t = \delta \pi_t - m_t \pi_t. \tag{7}$$

Differential equation (7) is nothing but the Euler–Lagrange differential equation in the calculus of variations or the Ramsey–Keynes equation in the theory of optimum economic growth. The meaning of the Ramsey–Keynes equation (7) may better be brought out if we rewrite it as

$$\dot{\pi}_t + m_t \pi_t = \delta \pi_t. \tag{8}$$

Suppose capital is transacted as an asset on a perfectly competitive capital market and the imputed price π_τ is identified with the asset price. Consider the situation in which the unit of such an asset is held for the short time period $[t, t + \Delta t]$, $(\Delta t > 0)$. The gains obtained by holding such an asset are composed of capital gains $\Delta \pi_t = \pi_{t+\Delta t} - \pi_t$ and "earnings" $m_t \pi_t \Delta t$; that is,

$$\Delta \pi_t + m_t \pi_t \Delta t.$$

On other hand, the costs in holding such an asset for the time period $[t, t + \Delta t]$ consist of "interest" payment $\delta \pi_t \Delta t$. Hence, on a perfectly competitive capital market, these two amounts become equal; that is,

$$\Delta \pi_t + m_t \pi_t \Delta t = \delta \pi_t \Delta t,$$

which, after both sides are divided by Δt and the limit is taken as $\Delta t \to 0$, yields relation (8).

By dividing both sides of relation (7) by π_t, we obtain the following familiar equation:

$$\frac{\dot{\pi}_t}{\pi_t} = \delta - m_t. \tag{9}$$

The imputed real national income at time t, H_t, is given by

$$H_t = u(x_t) + \pi_t \alpha(z_t, K_t).$$

The optimum levels of consumption and investment at each time t, (c_t, z_t), are obtained if imputed real national income H_t at time t is maximized subject to the feasibility constraint (4). These levels may be obtained in terms of the Lagrangian unknown p_t associated with constraint (4). The Lagrangian form is then

$$L_t = u(c_t) + \pi_t \alpha(z_t, K_t) + p_t[f(K_t) - c_t - z_t],$$

and the first-order conditions are

$$u'(c_t) = p_t \tag{10}$$

$$\pi_t \alpha_z(z_t, K_t) = p_t, \tag{11}$$

where the value of p_t is so chosen that feasibility condition (4) is satisfied.

Lagrangian unknown p_t may be interpreted as the imputed price of the output at time t. Equation (10) means that the optimum level of consumption c_t at time t is obtained when marginal utility $u'(c_t)$ is equated with imputed price p_t at time t. Equation (11) means that the optimum level of investment z_t at time t is obtained when the value of the marginal product of investment z_t evaluated at the imputed price π_t of capital is equated with the imputed price p_t of the output at time t.

The dynamically optimum time-path of consumption and capital accumulation, $(c, K) = ((c_t, K_t))$, is obtained if the time-path of the imputed price of capital (π_t) satisfies the transversality conditions:

$$\lim_{t \to +\infty} \pi_t K_t e^{-\delta t} = 0.$$

Under the constraints qualifications imposed on the utility function, the production function, and the Penrose function, it is easily seen that, given any initial stock of capital K^0, $[K^0 > 0]$, the dynamically optimum time-path of consumption and capital accumulation, $(c^0, K^0) = ((c_t^0, K_t^0))$, generally exists and is uniquely determined.

Thus, the duality principle in the theory of the dynamic optimum may be obtained.

Dynamic Duality Principle
A time-path of consumption and capital accumulation, $(c^0, K^0) = ((c_t^0, K_t^0))$, is dynamically optimum if, and only if, a time-path of positive prices $p = (p_t)$ exists such that the following properties are satisfied.

(I) $c^0 = (c_t^0)$ maximizes the discounted present value of the expenditures

$$\int_0^\infty p_t c_t e^{-\delta t} dt$$

among all feasible time-paths of consumption $c = (c_t)$, and

(II) $c^0 = (c_t^0)$ minimizes the discounted present value of the expenditures

$$\int_0^\infty p_t c_t e^{-\delta t} dt$$

among all time-paths of consumption $c = (c_t)$ satisfying

$$\int_0^\infty u(c_t) e^{-\delta t} dt \geqq \int_0^\infty u(c_t^0) e^{-\delta t} dt.$$

Proof. It is apparent that the time-path of the imputed price of output, $p_t = u'(c_t^0) = \pi_t \alpha_z(z_t^0, K_t^0)$, satisfies properties (I) and (II). Q. E. D.

3. GLOBAL WARMING AND THE DYNAMIC OPTIMALITY OF CAPITAL ACCUMULATION

The optimum theory of capital accumulation, as briefly reviewed in the previous section, may be applied to global warming. The discussion will be carried out basically in terms of the simple dynamic model introduced in Chapter 4.

At the risk of repetition, basic premises of the model will briefly be described. We consider the world economy consisting of n countries, where each country is generically denoted by $\nu (\nu = 1, \ldots, n)$. The utility function for each country ν is expressed by

$$u^\nu(c^\nu, V) = \varphi(V) u^\nu(c^\nu),$$

where $u^\nu(c^\nu)$ is a function of the vector of goods consumed in country ν, $c^\nu = (c_j^\nu)$, and V is the atmospheric concentrations of CO_2.

The function $u^\nu(c^\nu)$ is continuous, continuously twice-differentiable, concave, strictly quasi-concave, and homogeneous of order 1 with respect to c^ν, whereas the impact index of global warming $\varphi(V)$ satisfies the following conditions:

$$\varphi(V) > 0, \varphi'(V) < 0, \varphi''(V) < 0.$$

The impact coefficient of global warming; $\tau(V)$, is given by

$$\tau(V) = -\frac{\varphi'(V)}{\varphi(V)},$$

where the following conditions are satisfied:

$$\tau(V) > 0, \tau'(V) - [\tau(V)]^2 > 0.$$

When the impact index function $\varphi(V)$ is of the form

$$\varphi(V) = (\hat{V} - V)^\beta, \quad 0 \leqq V < \hat{V},$$

where $\hat{V}$ is the critical level of the atmospheric accumulation of CO_2 and β is the sensitivity parameter, $0 < \beta < 1$, the impact coefficient $\tau(V)$ is given by

$$\tau(V) = \frac{\beta}{\hat{V} - V}.$$

We consider the case in which only one kind of capital exists. In each country ν, the minimum quantity of capital required to produce goods by $x^\nu = (x_j^\nu)$ with CO_2 emissions at the level a^ν is specified by a function $f^\nu(x^\nu, a^\nu)$. The production possibility set T^ν of country ν is given by

$$T^\nu = \{(x^\nu, a^\nu) : (x^\nu, a^\nu) \geqq 0, \quad f^\nu(x^\nu, a^\nu) \leqq K^\nu\}.$$

The neoclassical conditions, as specified in Chapter 4, imply that the production possibility set T^ν is a closed, convex set of $J+1$-dimensional vectors (x^ν, a^ν).

The stock of capital existing at time t in each country ν is denoted by K_t^ν. The rate of capital accumulation at time t, $\dot{K}_t^\nu$, is given by

$$\dot{K}_t^\nu = \alpha^\nu\big(\varphi(V_t) z_t^\nu, K_t^\nu\big),$$

where $K_0^\nu = K^{\nu 0}$ is the initial stock of capital in country ν, and $\alpha^\nu(z_t^\nu, K_t^\nu)$ is the Penrose function relating the rate of capital accumulation $\dot{K}_t^\nu$ to investment z_t^ν and the stock of capital K_t^ν at time t in country ν.

The partial derivative of $\alpha^\nu(z^\nu, K^\nu)$ with respect to z^ν is always positive, whereas with respect to K it is always negative:

$$\alpha_{z^\nu}^\nu = \alpha_{z^\nu}^\nu(z^\nu, K^\nu) > 0, \quad \alpha_{K^\nu}^\nu = \alpha_{K^\nu}^\nu(z^\nu, K^\nu) < 0.$$

The Penrose effect is expressed by the conditions that the Penrose function $\alpha^\nu(z^\nu, K^\nu)$ is concave and strictly quasi-concave with respect to (z^ν, K^ν).

The processes of capital accumulation in the presence of global warming exhibit complicated features that require careful consideration. We assume that the effects of global warming on the productive capacity of capital are similar in magnitude to the effects of global warming on the welfare of consumers. As an approximation of the first order, we assume that the rate of capital accumulation obtained as the result of the investment by the quantity z^ν may be expressed by $\alpha^\nu(\varphi(V_t)z_t^\nu, K_t^\nu)$; that is,

$$\dot{K}_t^\nu = \alpha^\nu\left(\varphi(V_t)z_t^\nu, K_t^\nu\right)$$

with the initial condition $K_0^\nu = K^{\nu 0}$.

Global Warming and Dynamic Optimum in the World Economy

The problems of the dynamic optimum for individual countries may be solved when produced goods are freely traded between countries, but once they are invested as productive capital no trade will take place between the countries.

For each country ν, the problem of dynamic optimality involving atmospheric concentrations of CO_2 is formulated as follows.

A time-path of consumption and capital accumulation, $(c^\nu, K^\nu) = ((c_t^\nu, K_t^\nu))$, is dynamically optimum when the control variables $x_t^\nu, a_t^\nu, c_t^\nu, z_t^\nu$ at all times t are so chosen that the Ramsey–Koopmans–Cass utility integral for country ν

$$U^\nu(c^\nu, V) = \int_0^\infty \varphi(V_t)u^\nu(c_t^\nu)e^{-\delta t}dt$$

is maximized subject to the constraints

$$\dot{K}_t^\nu = \alpha^\nu(\varphi(V_t)z_t^\nu, K_t^\nu), \tag{12}$$

where $K_0^\nu = K^{\nu 0}$ is the initial stock of capital in country ν;

$$p_t c_t^\nu + p_t z_t^\nu = p_t x_t^\nu, \tag{13}$$

where p_t is the vector of prices on the world market at time t; and

$$f^\nu(x_t^\nu, a_t^\nu) \leqq K_t^\nu. \tag{14}$$

The vector of prices on the world market at time t, p_t, will be so determined that produced goods are in equilibrium on the world market as denoted by

$$\sum_\nu c_t^\nu + \sum_\nu z_t^\nu = \sum_\nu x_t^\nu, \tag{15}$$

where $c_t^\nu, z_t^\nu, x_t^\nu$ are, respectively, the vectors of consumption, investment, and production for country ν at time t.

Note that the change in atmospheric concentrations of CO_2 at time t, V_t, is determined by the dynamic equation

$$\dot{V}_t = a_t - \mu V_t, \tag{16}$$

where a_t is the sum of CO_2 emissions of all countries in the world at time t,

$$a_t = \sum_\nu a_t^\nu, \tag{17}$$

and μ is the rate at which atmospheric concentrations of CO_2 are absorbed by the oceans.

Thus, the problem of the dynamic optimum for country ν depends on what other countries plan to do concerning the emission of CO_2, not only for today ($t = 0$) but also for the entire future ($0 < t < \infty$). We suppose that all countries do plan to choose the dynamically optimum time-paths of economic activities and that the future time-path of the atmospheric concentrations of CO_2, V_t, is obtained by assuming that CO_2 emissions of all countries, a_t, are at the dynamically optimum levels for the entire future. Such an esoteric problem setting would only be of academic interest without any practical importance whatsoever. However, we try to solve it if only to gain some insight into the intricate nature of the problems of global warming that concern us.

The problem of dynamic optimum for global warming, as posited here, may be solved in terms of imputed prices of the atmospheric concentrations of CO_2 and capital for individual countries. Concentrating on the dynamic optimum for country ν, we denote by ψ_t^ν the imputed price of atmospheric concentrations of CO_2 and by π_t^ν the imputed price of capital, both at time t. For country ν, the imputed real national income at time t, H_t^ν, is defined by

$$H_t^\nu = \varphi(V_t)u^\nu(c_t^\nu) + \pi_t^\nu\alpha^\nu(\varphi(V_t)z_t^\nu, K_t^\nu) - \psi_t^\nu a_t^\nu.$$

Note that the imputed price of the atmospheric concentrations of CO_2 may differ between the countries.

The combination $(x_t^\nu, a_t^\nu, c_t^\nu, z_t^\nu)$ of the optimum levels of production, CO_2 emissions, consumption, and investment for country ν at time t is obtained if imputed real national income H_t is maximized subject to the feasibility constraints (13) and (14). The values of control variables at each time t, $(x_t^\nu, a_t^\nu, c_t^\nu, z_t^\nu)$, may be obtained in terms of the Lagrangian unknowns λ_t^ν and $\lambda_t^\nu r_t^\nu$ associated, respectively, with constraints (13) and (14). The Lagrangian form then is

$$\begin{aligned} L_t^\nu = {} & \varphi(V_t)u^\nu(c_t^\nu) + \pi_t^\nu\alpha^\nu(\varphi(V_t)z_t^\nu, K_t^\nu) - \psi_t^\nu a_t^\nu \\ & + \lambda_t^\nu p_t[x_t^\nu - c_t^\nu - z_t^\nu] + \lambda_t^\nu r_t^\nu[K_t^\nu - f^\nu(x_t^\nu, a_t^\nu)]. \end{aligned}$$

The first-order conditions are

$$\varphi(V_t)u_{c^\nu}^\nu(c_t^\nu) = \lambda_t^\nu p_t \tag{18}$$

$$\pi_t^\nu\varphi(V_t)\alpha_{z^\nu}^\nu(\varphi(V_t)z_t^\nu, K_t^\nu) = \lambda_t^\nu p_t \tag{19}$$

$$\lambda_t^\nu p_t = \lambda_t^\nu r_t^\nu f_{x^\nu}^\nu(x_t^\nu, a_t^\nu) \tag{20}$$

$$\psi_t^\nu = \lambda_t^\nu r_t^\nu[-f_{a^\nu}^\nu(x_t^\nu, a_t^\nu)], \tag{21}$$

where the values of Lagrangian unknowns λ_t^ν and $\lambda_t^\nu r_t^\nu$ are so chosen that feasibility conditions (13) and (14) are satisfied.

The imputed price ψ_t^ν of the atmospheric concentrations of CO_2 at time t for country ν is the discounted present value of the marginal increases in the outputs in the future, measured in units of the utility, due to the marginal decrease in the atmospheric concentrations of CO_2 at time t; that is,

$$\psi_t^\nu = \int_t^\infty \omega_\tau^\nu e^{-(\delta+\mu)(\tau-t)}d\tau, \tag{22}$$

where ω_t^ν is the marginal decrease in country ν's utility at time t given by

$$\omega_t^\nu = [-\varphi'(V_t)]u^\nu(c_t^\nu) + [-\varphi'(V_t)]\alpha_{z^\nu}^\nu(\varphi(V_t)z_t^\nu, K_t^\nu)z_t^\nu.$$

Equation (22) is obtained if we note that the marginal decrease in country ν's utility at time t is expressed by ω_t^ν and the depletion rate of the atmospheric concentrations CO_2 of is μ.

By differentiating both sides of (22) with respect to time t, we obtain the following differential equation:

$$\dot{\psi}_t^\nu = (\delta + \mu)\psi_t^\nu - \omega_t^\nu. \tag{23}$$

Similar calculations may be made for the imputed price of capital for country ν at time t, π_t^ν, which is defined as the discounted present value of the marginal increases in the outputs in the future, measured in units of the utility, due to the marginal increase in investment at time t; that is,

$$\pi_t^\nu = \int_t^\infty \pi_\tau^\nu m_\tau^\nu e^{-\delta(\tau - t)} d\tau, \tag{24}$$

where m_t^ν is the marginal efficiency of investment for country ν at future time τ:

$$m_\tau^\nu = m^\nu(z_\tau^\nu, K_\tau^\nu) = \frac{r_\tau^\nu}{p_\tau}\varphi(V_t)\alpha_{z^\nu}^\nu,(\varphi(V_t)z_t^\nu, K_t^\nu) + \alpha_{K^\nu}^\nu(z_\tau^\nu, K_\tau^\nu).$$

Note that, because r_t^ν is measured in units of prices, r_τ^ν must be divided by p_τ in the calculations of the marginal efficiency of investment.

By differentiating both sides of (24) with respect to time t and rearranging, we obtain the following differential equation:

$$\frac{\dot{\pi}_t^\nu}{\pi_t^\nu} = \delta - m_t^\nu. \tag{25}$$

For each country ν, the dynamically optimum time-path of consumption and capital accumulation, $(c^\nu, K^\nu) = ((c_t^\nu, K_t^\nu))$, is obtained when the control variables $x_t^\nu, a_t^\nu, c_t^\nu, z_t^\nu$ at all times t are so chosen that the marginality conditions (18–21), together with feasibility conditions (13) and (14), are all satisfied and the imputed prices of capital and the atmospheric concentrations of CO_2, π_t^ν and ψ_t^ν, satisfy differential equations (25) and (23) together with the transversality conditions

$$\lim_{t \to +\infty} \pi_t^\nu K_t^\nu e^{-\delta t} = 0, \qquad \lim_{t \to +\infty} \psi_t^\nu V_t e^{-\delta t} = 0.$$

The prices on the world market at time t, p_t, are so determined that equilibrium condition (15) is satisfied, whereas the change in atmospheric concentrations V_t of CO_2 is determined by the dynamic equation (16), where a_t is given by (17).

Thus, we have derived the conditions for the dynamic optimality for individual countries. However, the existence of the dynamically optimum time-paths for individual countries is generally not guaranteed. Indeed, the problems of finding dynamic optima are extremely difficult when more than one state variable is involved. Besides the mathematical problems concerning the existence of dynamic optima for the problems of global warming as posited here, we need to be genuinely concerned with the more fundamental issues concerning intergenerational equity and justice.

4. SUSTAINABLE TIME-PATHS OF CONSUMPTION AND CAPITAL ACCUMULATION

As described in the Introduction, the many scientific studies made concerning global climate during the twentieth century convincingly tell us that the generations of our grandchildren will face calamitous climatic conditions as the result of the economic and other activities of the current generation, as particularly well documented in the series of IPCC Reports published by Cambridge University Press (IPCC 1991a,b,c,d; 1996a,b,c; and 2001a,b,c,d).

We wonder if we are justified in regarding the welfare of the generations of our grandchildren in terms of the discounted present value of the utilities inferred by the current generation as the utilities of future generations and in consigning their fate to the problems of the dynamic optimum conceived of purely from the viewpoint of the current generation.

When applied to the problems of the natural environment, commonsense interpretation of sustainability means that future generations will enjoy the same state of affairs concerning the natural environment as the current generation does. However, circumstances do not stay the same. The economic and social conditions surrounding us continuously evolve, new technologies are developed, and new products are introduced; above all, the social infrastructure is continuously being built and renovated, and the institutional arrangements concerning education, medicine, culture, and other fields are constantly changing. In the face of these complications, it seems almost impossible to reach a consensus about the intrinsic meaning of sustainabiliy with respect to the natural environment. We prefer instead to stay within the purified world of neoclassical economic theory and come out with certain propositions concerning the abatement of global warming that may serve as guidelines for devising an effective way to abate global warming and to leave the generation of our grandchildren a healthy and sane environment on natural, social, cultural, and other levels.

In what follows, we present a way of formulating the concept of sustainability within the theoretical framework of the economic analysis of global warming and derive propositions that may be consulted in devising institutional arrangements and policy measures likely to be effective in abating global warming and stabilizing atmospheric disequilibrium.

The problems of intergenerational equity and justice have been studied by a large number of economists and philosophers. Our formulation of the concept of sustainability is largely based on the contributions by Rawls (1971), Solow (1974a,b), Sen (1982), Norton (1989), Norgaard (1990a,b), Howarth and Norgaard (1990, 1992, 1995), Uzawa (1991, 1992a, 1998), Howarth and Monahan (1992), and Pezzey (1992).

Introducing the Concept of Sustainability

In this section, we formulate the concept of sustainability within the theoretical framework of the economic analysis of global warming presented in the previous chapters.

In the analysis of dynamic optimality, a crucial role is played by the concept of the imputed price of capital – either privately owned means of production or social overhead capital such as forests, oceans, and the atmosphere. The imputed price of a particular kind of capital expresses the extent to which the unit quantity of the stock of capital contributes to the welfare of the future generations of the society under consideration. At the same time, it is the legacy inherited from past generations that serves the welfare of the current generation. We define the concept of sustainability in terms of imputed price. That is, dynamic processes involving social overhead capital such as forests, the oceans, and the atmosphere are sustainable when each member of the society tries to ensure that the imputed prices of the various kinds of social overhead capital remain constant over time.

With regard to private capital, imputed prices may be identified with market prices provided that the conditions of perfect competitiveness prevail on the market. However, with regard to social overhead capital, the magnitude of the imputed price is regarded as the outcome of the calculations made by state authorities or economists whose professional expertise it is to make such calculations. Hence, when we try to introduce the concept of sustainability with reference to the imputed price of the natural environment, we have to be aware of the intrinsic difficulties involved in making calculations of its magnitude. However, in the analysis of the dynamic optimum of global warming, as developed in the previous chapters, it is possible to find ways by which the processes of economic activities, capital accumulation, and the abatement of the emissions of greenhouse gases are so harmonized within the market institutions that the ensuing time-paths of consumption and the atmospheric concentrations of greenhouse gases are sustainable.

Sustainability in the Simple Case

To begin, we introduce the concept of sustainability for the simple case in which the same kind of goods serve for both consumption and investment. As before, the instantaneous level of the utility u_t at each time t is represented by the utility function

$$u_t = u(c_t),$$

where c_t is the quantity of goods consumed by the representative consumer at time t.

The utility function $u = u(c)$ remains identical over time, is defined for all nonnegative $c \geqq 0$, is continuous and continuously twice-differentiable, and satisfies the following conditions:

$$u(c) > 0, \quad u'(c) > 0, \quad u''(c) < 0, \quad \text{for all } c > 0.$$

We first consider the case in which only one kind of private capital exists. We denote by K_t the stock of capital at time t and by c_t, z_t, respectively, consumption and investment at time t. Then, we have

$$c_t + z_t = f(K_t),$$

where $f(K)$ is the production function, which is assumed to be given independently of time t.

Production function $f(K)$ is defined, continuous, and continuously twice-differentiable for all $K \geqq 0$ and satisfies the following conditions:

$$f'(K) > 0,\ f''(K) < 0, \quad \text{for all } K > 0.$$

The rate of capital accumulation at time t, $\dot{K}_t$, is given by

$$\dot{K}_t = \alpha(z_t, K_t), \ \ K_0 = K^0,$$

where K^0 is the initial stock of capital, and $\alpha(z_t, K_t)$ is the Penrose function relating the rate of capital accumulation $\dot{K}_t$ with investment z_t and the stock of capital K_t, at time t.

The imputed price of capital at time t, π_t, is defined by the discounted present value of the marginal increases in the outputs in the future, measured in units of the utility, due to the marginal increase in investment at time t; that is,

$$\pi_t = \int_t^\infty \pi_\tau m_\tau e^{-\delta(\tau - t)} d\tau,$$

where m_τ is marginal efficiency of investment at future time τ:

$$m_\tau = m(z_\tau, K_\tau) = r_\tau \alpha_z(z_\tau, K_\tau) + \alpha_K(z_\tau, K_\tau),\ r_\tau = f'(K_\tau).$$

A feasible time-path of consumption and capital accumulation, $(c, K) = ((c_t, K_t))$, is sustainable when the imputed price of capital π_t remains constant at a certain level π; that is,

$$\pi_t = \pi, \quad \text{for all } t \geqq 0.$$

Thus, if a time-path of consumption is sustainable, then all future generations face the same imputed price of capital as the current generation does. Because the imputed price of capital at each time t expresses the discounted present value of the marginal increases of all future utilities due to the marginal increase in the stock of capital at time t, the concept of sustainability thus defined may capture certain aspects of intergenerational equity. In the following sections, we would like to see how the level of the imputed price π for sustainable time-paths is determined.

Under conditions of sustainability, we have, from the definition of imputed prices, that

$$m(z_t, K_t) = r_t\alpha_z(z_t, K_t) + \alpha_K(z_t, K_t) = \delta.$$

Sustainable Levels of Consumption and Investment

For a given stock of capital $K > 0$, the levels (c, z) of consumption and investment at the sustainable time-path are always uniquely determined. To prove this, the conditions for sustainability are put together as follows:

$$\dot{K} = \alpha(z, K) \tag{26}$$

$$c + z = f(K) \tag{27}$$

$$m = r\alpha_z + \alpha_K = \delta, \tag{28}$$

where the time suffix t is omitted.

By taking a differential of both sides of relations (27) and (28), we obtain

$$\begin{pmatrix} 1 & 1 \\ 0 & m_z \end{pmatrix} \begin{pmatrix} dc \\ dz \end{pmatrix} = \begin{pmatrix} r & 0 \\ -m_K & 1 \end{pmatrix} \begin{pmatrix} dK \\ d\delta \end{pmatrix},$$

where

$$m_z = r\alpha_{zz} + \alpha_{Kz} < 0, \quad m_K = r'\alpha_z + (r\alpha_{zK} + \alpha_{KK}) < 0$$
$$[r' = f''(K) < 0].$$

Hence,

$$\begin{pmatrix} dc \\ dz \end{pmatrix} = \begin{pmatrix} 1 & 1 \\ 0 & m_z \end{pmatrix}^{-1} \begin{pmatrix} r & 0 \\ -m_K & 1 \end{pmatrix} \begin{pmatrix} dK \\ d\delta \end{pmatrix}$$
$$= \frac{1}{m_z} \begin{pmatrix} rm_z + m_K & -1 \\ -m_K & 1 \end{pmatrix} \begin{pmatrix} dK \\ d\delta \end{pmatrix}$$

$$\frac{\partial c}{\partial K} = r + \frac{m_K}{m_z} > 0, \quad \frac{\partial z}{\partial K} = -\frac{m_K}{m_z} < 0,$$

$$\frac{\partial c}{\partial \delta} = -\frac{1}{m_z} > 0, \quad \frac{\partial z}{\partial \delta} = \frac{1}{m_z} < 0.$$

Thus, the levels of consumption and investment (c, z) at the sustainable time-path are uniquely determined. In addition, we have

$$\left.\frac{\partial \alpha}{\partial K}\right|_{\dot{K}=0} = \alpha_z \frac{dz}{dK} + \alpha_K = -\alpha_z \frac{m_K}{m_z} + \alpha_K < 0 \quad [\alpha_z > 0,\ \alpha_K < 0].$$

Hence, the differential equation (26) has a uniquely determined stationary state, and it is globally stable.

Thus, we have established the following proposition.

Proposition 1. *Suppose there is only one kind of capital. For any given stock of capital $K > 0$, the levels of consumption and investment at the sustainable time-path (c, z) are uniquely determined.*

The larger the stock of private capital K, the higher is the level of consumption c along the sustainable time-path and the lower is the level of investment z. The higher the rate of discount δ, the higher is the level of consumption c along the sustainable time-path, and the lower is the level of investment z.

At the sustainable time-path, the levels (c, z) of consumption and investment approach the long-run stationary state as time t goes to infinity.

Note that, for the standard case of the neoclassical world, we have

$$\alpha(z, K) = z, \ \text{ for all } z,\ K \geqq 0$$
$$m(z, K) = f'(K), \ \text{ for all } z,\ K \geqq 0.$$

Hence, a z that satisfies (28) does not generally exist.

The Case in Which Several Kinds of Private Capital Exist

For the case in which there are several kinds of private capital, the existence of a sustainable time-path of consumption and investment is guaranteed provided that processes of capital accumulation are subject to the Penrose effect, which exhibits the law of diminishing marginal rates of investment.

We denote by $K = (K_\ell)$ the vector of the stock of capital of various kinds, where $\ell(\ell = 1, \dots, L)$ generically refers to the type of private capital. The production function is represented by $f(K)$, where all the neoclassical conditions postulated in the previous chapters are satisfied. That is, $f(K)$ is given independently of time t, is defined for all nonnegative $K \geqq 0$, is continuous and continuously twice differentiable, concave, and strictly quasi-concave with respect to K, and marginal products are always positive.

The stock of capital $K(t) = (K_\ell(t))$ at time t is then determined by the following system of differentiable equations:

$$\dot{K}_\ell(t) = \alpha_\ell(z_\ell(t), K_\ell(t)), \quad (\ell = 1, \ldots, L)$$

with initial condition $K(0) = K^0 = (K_\ell^0)$, where $K^0 = (K_\ell^0) > 0$ is the vector of the initial stock of private capital, and $\alpha_\ell(z_\ell, K_\ell)$ is the Penrose function with regard to the capital of type ℓ expressing the relation between the rate of accumulation of the capital of type ℓ, $\dot{K}_\ell$, on the one hand, and investment z_ℓ in capital of type ℓ and the stock of the capital of type ℓ, K_ℓ, on the other. In what follows, the time variable t is occasionally omitted.

The Penrose effect is expressed by the conditions that, for the capital of each type ℓ, $\alpha_\ell(z_\ell, K_\ell)$ is a concave and strictly quasi-concave function of (z_ℓ, K_ℓ), and

$$\frac{\partial \alpha_\ell}{\partial z_\ell} > 0, \quad \frac{\partial \alpha_\ell}{\partial K_\ell} < 0, \quad (\ell = 1, \ldots, L).$$

Marginal products of investment in various kinds of private capital are given by

$$m = (m_\ell), \quad m_\ell = \frac{\partial f}{\partial K_\ell}\frac{\partial \alpha_\ell}{\partial z_\ell} + \frac{\partial \alpha_\ell}{\partial K_\ell} > 0, \quad (\ell = 1, \ldots, L).$$

Exactly as in the simple case, the imputed price of the capital of type ℓ at time t, $\pi_\ell(t)$, is defined as the discounted present value of the marginal increases in the output in the future, measured in units of the utility, due to the marginal increase in investment in the capital of type ℓ at time t; that is,

$$\pi_\ell(t) = \int_t^\infty \pi_\ell(\tau) m_\ell(\tau) e^{-\delta(\tau - t)} d\tau,$$

where $m_\ell(\tau)$ is marginal efficiency of investment at future time τ:

$$\begin{aligned} m_\ell(\tau) &= m(z_\ell(\tau), K_\ell(\tau)) \\ &= r_\ell(\tau)\alpha_{\ell z_\ell}(z_\ell(\tau), K_\ell(\tau)) + \alpha_{\ell K_\ell}(z_\ell(\tau), K_\ell(\tau)). \end{aligned}$$

A feasible time-path of consumption and capital accumulation, $(c(t), K(t))$, is sustainable, when, for each type ℓ of capital, the imputed price of capital $\pi_\ell(t)$ remains constant at a certain level π_ℓ; that is,

$$\pi_\ell(t) = \pi_\ell, \quad \text{for all } t \geqq 0.$$

A feasible time-path of consumption and capital accumulation, $(c(t), K(t)), K(t) = (K_\ell(t))$, is sustainable if a system of imputed prices of various kinds of private capital (π_ℓ) exists such that the following conditions are satisfied:

$$\begin{aligned}
&\dot{K}_\ell(t) = \alpha_\ell(z_\ell(t), K_\ell(t)) \\
&c(t) + \sum_\ell z_\ell(t) = f(K(t)), \ K(t) = (K_\ell(t)) \\
&m(z_\ell(t), K_\ell(t)) = \delta \\
&m(z_\ell(t), K_\ell(t)) = r_\ell(t)\alpha_{\ell z_\ell}(z_\ell(t), K_\ell(t)) + \alpha_{\ell K_\ell}(z_\ell(t), K_\ell(t)) \\
&\qquad\qquad\qquad\quad = f_{K_\ell}(K(t)).
\end{aligned}$$

The following proposition may easily be established:

Proposition 2. *Suppose there are several kinds of private capital. For any vector of given stock of private capital,* $K = (K_\ell) > 0$, *the levels of consumption and investment* (c, z) *with the vector of investment* $z = (z_\ell)$ *at the sustainable time-path are uniquely determined.*

The sustainable time-path of consumption and capital accumulation, $(c, K) = (c(t), K(t))$, *approaches the long-run stationary state as* t *goes to infinity.*

5. GLOBAL WARMING AND SUSTAINABILITY

The concept of sustainability as introduced in the previous sections may easily be extended to the case in which global warming affects the level of welfare of all countries in the world.

With regard to global warming, the concept of the proportional carbon tax scheme was introduced by Uzawa (1991, 1992a, 1993, 1995), as described in detail in Chapters 1, 3, and 4, primarily to serve as an effective policy measure for arresting the atmospheric disequilibrium caused by the emission of carbon dioxide and other greenhouse gases, where a particular burden would not be placed on developing countries.

For each country ν, a time-path of consumption and capital accumulation, $(c^\nu, K^\nu) = ((c_t^\nu, K_t^\nu))$, is feasible when the following equations hold:

$$\dot{K}_t^\nu = \alpha^\nu(\varphi(V_t)z_t^\nu, K_t^\nu),$$

where $K_0^\nu = K^{\nu 0}$ is the initial stock of capital in country ν,

$$p_t c_t^\nu + p_t z_t^\nu = p_t x_t^\nu, \tag{29}$$

where p_t is the vector of prices on the world market at time t, and

$$f^\nu(x_t^\nu, a_t^\nu) \leqq K_t^\nu. \tag{30}$$

The vector of prices at time t, p_t, is so determined that produced goods are in equilibrium on the world market.

The change in atmospheric concentrations of CO_2 at time t, V_t, is determined by the dynamic equation

$$\dot{V}_t = a_t - \mu V_t, \tag{31}$$

where a_t is the sum of CO_2 emissions of all countries in the world at time t,

$$a_t = \sum_\nu a_t^\nu,$$

and μ is the rate at which atmospheric concentrations of CO_2 are absorbed by the oceans.

For each country ν, a feasible time-path of consumption and capital accumulation, $(c^\nu, K^\nu) = ((c_t^\nu, K_t^\nu))$, is sustainable when the imputed prices of atmospheric concentrations of CO_2 and capital for country ν both remain constant at certain levels:

$$\pi_t^\nu = \pi^\nu, \; \psi_t^\nu = \psi^\nu, \quad \text{for all } t \geqq 0.$$

The imputed prices of capital and atmospheric concentrations of CO_2 for country ν satisfy the following differential equations:

$$\dot{\psi}_t^\nu = (\delta + \mu)\psi_t^\nu - \omega_t^\nu$$

$$\frac{\dot{\pi}_t^\nu}{\pi_t^\nu} = \delta - m_t^\nu,$$

where

$$\omega_t^\nu = [-\varphi'(V_t)][u^\nu(c_t^\nu) + \alpha_{z^\nu}^\nu(\varphi(V_t)z_t^\nu, K_t^\nu)z_t^\nu]$$

$$m_t^\nu = m^\nu(z_t^\nu, K_t^\nu) = \frac{r_t^\nu}{p_t}\varphi(V_t)\alpha_{z^\nu}^\nu(\varphi(V_t)z_t^\nu, K_t^\nu) + \alpha_{K^\nu}^\nu(z_t^\nu, K_t^\nu). \quad (32)$$

Hence, we have

$$\psi^\nu = \frac{1}{\delta + \mu}\omega_t^\nu \quad (33)$$

$$m^\nu(z_t^\nu, K_t^\nu) = \delta.$$

The optimum production, CO_2 emissions, consumption, and investment at time t for country ν $(x_t^\nu, a_t^\nu, c_t^\nu, z_t^\nu)$, are so determined that the imputed real national income H_t^ν is maximized subject to the feasibility constraints (29) and (30):

$$H_t^\nu = \varphi(V_t)u^\nu(c_t^\nu) + \pi^\nu\alpha^\nu(\varphi(V_t)z_t^\nu, K_t^\nu) - \psi^\nu a_t^\nu.$$

Such an $(x_t^\nu, a_t^\nu, c_t^\nu, z_t^\nu)$ may be obtained in terms of the Lagrangian unknowns λ_t^ν and $\lambda_t^\nu r_t^\nu$, respectively, associated with constraints (29) and (30). The marginality conditions are

$$\varphi(V_t)u_{c^\nu}^\nu(c_t^\nu) = \lambda_t^\nu p_t \quad (34)$$

$$\pi^\nu\varphi(V_t)\alpha_{z^\nu}^\nu(\varphi(V_t)z_t^\nu, K_t^\nu) = \lambda_t^\nu p_t \quad (35)$$

$$\lambda_t^\nu p_t = \lambda_t^\nu r_t^\nu f_{a^\nu}^\nu(x_t^\nu, a_t^\nu) \quad (36)$$

$$\psi^\nu = \lambda_t^\nu r_t^\nu[-f_{a^\nu}^\nu(x_t^\nu, a_t^\nu)], \quad (37)$$

where the values of Lagrangian unknowns λ_t^ν and $\lambda_t^\nu r_t^\nu$ are so chosen that feasibility conditions (29) and (30) are satisfied.

We multiply both sides of Equation (34) by c_t^ν and note the Euler identity for $u^\nu(c^\nu)$ to obtain

$$\varphi(V_t)u^\nu(c_t^\nu) = \lambda_t^\nu p_t c_t^\nu. \quad (38)$$

Multiply both sides of Equation (35) by z_t^ν to obtain

$$\pi^\nu\varphi(V_t)\alpha_{z^\nu}^\nu(\varphi(V_t)z_t^\nu, K_t^\nu)z_t^\nu = \lambda_t^\nu p_t z_t^\nu. \quad (39)$$

By adding both sides of Equations (38) and (39), we obtain

$$\varphi(V_t)u^\nu(c_t^\nu) + \pi^\nu\varphi(V_t)\alpha_{z^\nu}^\nu(\varphi(V_t)z_t^\nu, K_t^\nu)z_t^\nu = \lambda_t^\nu[p_t c_t^\nu + p_t z_t^\nu],$$

which, by noting the balance-of-payments conditions (29), yields

$$\varphi(V_t)u^{\nu}(c_t^{\nu}) + \pi^{\nu}\varphi(V_t)\alpha_{z^{\nu}}^{\nu}(\varphi(V_t)z_t^{\nu}, K_t^{\nu})z_t^{\nu} = \lambda_t^{\nu} p_t x_t^{\nu} = \lambda_t^{\nu} y_t^{\nu}, \tag{40}$$

where $y_t^{\nu} = p_t x_t^{\nu}$ is the national income of country ν at time t measured in units of world prices.

By substituting (40) into (32), we obtain

$$\omega_t^{\nu} = \lambda_t^{\nu}\tau(V_t)y_t^{\nu}, \tag{41}$$

where $\tau(V) = -\frac{\varphi'(V)}{\varphi(V)}$ is the impact coefficient of global warming.

Relation (41) in turn may be substituted into (33) to obtain

$$\psi^{\nu} = \lambda_t^{\nu}\frac{\tau(V_t)}{\delta + \mu}y_t^{\nu}. \tag{42}$$

Let us now introduce the new variable θ_t^{ν} by

$$\theta_t^{\nu} = \frac{\psi_t^{\nu}}{\lambda_t^{\nu}}, \tag{43}$$

which may be regarded as the imputed price of atmospheric concentrations of CO_2 for country ν at time t measured in units of the output.

In view of (43), relation (42) may now be written as

$$\theta_t^{\nu} = \frac{\tau(V_t)}{\delta + \mu}y_t^{\nu}. \tag{44}$$

Similarly, marginality conditions (36) and (37) are now written as

$$p_t = r_t^{\nu} f_{a^{\nu}}^{\nu}(x_t^{\nu}, a_t^{\nu}) \tag{45}$$

$$\theta_t^{\nu} = r_t^{\nu}[-f_{a^{\nu}}^{\nu}(x_t^{\nu}, a_t^{\nu})]. \tag{46}$$

Relations (45) and (46) imply that the optimum (x_t^{ν}, a_t^{ν}) is obtained by maximizing net profits

$$p_t^{\nu}x_t^{\nu} - \theta_t^{\nu}a_t^{\nu}, \quad (x_t^{\nu}, a_t^{\nu}) \in T^{\nu}.$$

The discussion above may be summarized in the following proposition.

Proposition 3. *Consider the world economy consisting of n countries, where produced goods are freely traded between countries, but, once the goods are invested as productive capital, no trade will take place between the countries. Each country has an economic structure as specified in Chapter 4.*

If the time-path of production, CO_2 emissions, consumption, and investment for each country ν, $(x_t^\nu, a_t^\nu, c_t^\nu, z_t^\nu)$, *is sustainable, then the combination of production and CO_2 emissions for each country* ν *at time* t, (x_t^ν, a_t^ν), *precisely coincides with the optimum combination that maximizes net profits*

$$p_t^\nu x_t^\nu - \theta_t^\nu a_t^\nu, \quad (x_t^\nu, a_t^\nu) \in T^\nu,$$

where

$$\theta_t^\nu = \frac{\tau(V_t)}{\delta + \mu} y_t^\nu, \quad \tau(V) = -\frac{\varphi'(V)}{\varphi(V)}.$$

6. SOCIAL OVERHEAD CAPITAL AND SUSTAINABILITY

The concept of sustainability, as introduced in the previous sections, may easily be extended to the case in which social overhead capital influences the level of welfare of the country in consideration.

Our discussion is carried out within the framework of the simple dynamic model of capital accumulation as posited in the previous sections except for the stock of social overhead capital as another component of the stock of capital in general. We denote by V_t the stock of social overhead capital existing in the society at time t, and the stock of private capital is denoted by K_t. Output $f(K_t)$ at each time t is divided between consumption c_t, investment in private capital z_t, and investment in social overhead capital w_t:

$$c_t + z_t + w_t = f(K_t),$$

where the production function $f(K_t)$ satisfies all the neoclassical conditions postulated in the previous sections.

The rate of increase in the stock of private capital, $\dot{K}_t$, is determined in terms of the Penrose function $\alpha(z, K)$:

$$\dot{K}_t = \alpha(z_t, K_t).$$

The Penrose function $\alpha(z, K)$ concerning the accumulation of private capital is assumed to satisfy the following conditions.

The function $\alpha(z, K)$ is defined for all $z \geqq 0$, $K > 0$, and is continuous, continuously twice-differentiable, concave, and strictly quasi-concave with respect to (z, K); that is,

$$\alpha_{zz} < 0, \quad \alpha_{KK} < 0, \quad \alpha_{zz}\alpha_{KK} - \alpha_{zK}^2 \geqq 0.$$

It is assumed that

$$\alpha_z(z, K) > 0, \quad \alpha_K(z, K) < 0.$$

We also assume that the effect of investment in social overhead capital is subject to the Penrose effect, and thus the rate of increase in the stock of social overhead capital, $\dot{V}_t$, is determined in terms of the Penrose function $\beta(w, V)$:

$$\dot{V}_t = \beta(w_t, V_t).$$

The Penrose function $\beta(w, V)$ concerning the accumulation of social overhead capital is also assumed to satisfy the concavity conditions.

The function $\beta(w, V)$ is defined for all $w \geqq 0$, $V > 0$, and is continuous, continuously twice-differentiable, concave, and strictly quasi-concave with respect to (w, V); that is,

$$\beta_{ww} < 0, \quad \beta_{VV} < 0, \quad \beta_{ww}\beta_{VV} - \beta_{wV}^2 \geqq 0.$$

It is assumed that

$$\beta_w(w, V) > 0, \quad \beta_V(w, V) < 0.$$

Note that, for the case of global warming, the stock V represents the difference of the critical level and the current level of the accumulation of atmospheric carbon dioxide.

We assume that the utility u_t at each time t is a function of the vector of consumption c_t and the stock of environmental capital V_t,

$$u_t = u(c_t, V_t),$$

where utility function $u(c, V)$ is assumed to be defined for all $(x, V) \geqq (0, 0)$, positive valued with positive marginal utilities, continuously twice-differentiable, and concave and strictly quasi-concave with respect to (c, V):

$$u(c, V) > 0, \quad u_c(c, V), \quad u_V(c, V) > 0$$
$$u_{cc}, u_{VV} > 0, \; u_{cc}u_{VV} - u_{cV}^2 \geqq 0, \quad \text{for all } (c, V) \geqq (0, 0).$$

The sustainable time-path of consumption and capital accumulation is obtained in terms of the imputed prices of private capital and social overhead capital. As with the case of private capital, the imputed price ψ_t of social overhead capital at time t is the discounted present value of the marginal increases in the outputs in the future due to the marginal increase in the level of investment in social overhead capital at time t; that is,

$$\psi_t = \int_t^\infty n_\tau e^{-\delta(\tau - t)} d\tau,$$

where $n_\tau = n(c_\tau, w_\tau, V_\tau)$ is the marginal efficiency of investment in social overhead capital at time τ.

The marginal efficiency of investment in social overhead capital $n = n(c, w, V)$ is given by

$$n = n(c, w, V) = s\beta_w(w, V) + \beta_V(w, V), \quad s = s(c, V) = \frac{u_V(c, V)}{u_c(c, V)}.$$

Note that $\beta_w(w, V)$ is the marginal product of investment in social overhead capital, whereas $s = \frac{u_V}{u_x}$ is the marginal rate of substitution between consumption and social overhead capital.

We now obtain the following Euler–Lagrange differential equations for the imputed prices of private capital and social overhead capital, π_t, ψ_t:

$$\frac{\dot{\pi}_t}{\pi_t} = \delta - m_t, \quad m_t = m(z_t, K_t) \tag{47}$$

$$\frac{\dot{\psi}_t}{\psi_t} = \delta - n_t, \quad n_t = n(c_t, w_t, V_t). \tag{48}$$

The time-path $(c_t, z_t, w_t, K_t, V_t)$ is sustainable when the imputed prices of private capital and social overhead capital, π_t, ψ_t, are so adjusted that the following conditions are satisfied:

$$m(z_t, K_t) = n(c_t, w_t, V_t) = \delta.$$

The imputed real national income at time t is given by

$$H_t = u(c_t, V_t) + \pi_t \alpha(z_t, K_t) + \psi_t \beta(w_t, V_t).$$

The optimum levels of consumption and investment in private capital and social overhead capital at each time t, (c_t, z_t, w_t), is obtained when the imputed real national income H_t is maximized subject to the constraints

$$c_t + z_t + w_t = f(K_t).$$

Let us denote by p_t the imputed price of output at time t. Then we obtain the following marginality conditions:

$$u_c(c_t, V_t) = p_t$$

$$\pi_t \alpha_z(z_t, K_t) = p_t$$

$$\psi_t \beta_w(w_t, V_t) = p_t.$$

For any given stock of private capital and social overhead capital, K, V $(K, V > 0)$, the levels of consumption and investment in private capital and in social overhead capital at the sustainable time-path, (c, z, w), are uniquely determined.

This is seen from the following relations:

$$c + z + w = f(K)$$

$$m(z, K) = \delta$$

$$n(c, w, V) = \delta.$$

By taking a differential of both sides of these equations, we obtain

$$\begin{pmatrix} 1 & 1 & 1 \\ 0 & m_z & 0 \\ n_c & 0 & n_w \end{pmatrix} \begin{pmatrix} dc \\ dz \\ dw \end{pmatrix} = \begin{pmatrix} r & 0 & 0 \\ -m_K & 0 & 1 \\ 0 & -n_V & 1 \end{pmatrix} \begin{pmatrix} dK \\ dV \\ d\delta \end{pmatrix}$$

$$\begin{pmatrix} dc \\ dz \\ dw \end{pmatrix} = \begin{pmatrix} 1 & 1 & 1 \\ 0 & m_z & 0 \\ n_c & 0 & n_w \end{pmatrix}^{-1} \begin{pmatrix} r & 0 & 0 \\ -m_K & 0 & 1 \\ 0 & -n_V & 1 \end{pmatrix} \begin{pmatrix} dK \\ dV \\ d\delta \end{pmatrix}$$

$$= \frac{1}{\Delta} \begin{pmatrix} 1 & -\frac{1}{m_z} & -\frac{1}{n_w} \\ 0 & \frac{1}{m_z}\left(1 - \frac{n_c}{n_w}\right) & 0 \\ -\frac{n_c}{n_w} & \frac{1}{m_z}\frac{n_c}{n_w} & \frac{1}{n_w} \end{pmatrix} \begin{pmatrix} r & 0 & 0 \\ -m_K & 0 & 1 \\ 0 & -n_V & 1 \end{pmatrix} \begin{pmatrix} dk \\ dV \\ d\delta \end{pmatrix}$$

$$= \frac{1}{\Delta} \begin{pmatrix} r + \frac{m_K}{m_z} & \frac{n_V}{n_w} & -\frac{1}{m_z} - \frac{1}{n_w} \\ -\frac{m_K}{m_z}\left(1 - \frac{n_c}{n_w}\right) & 0 & \frac{1}{m_z}\left(1 - \frac{n_c}{n_w}\right) \\ -\left(r + \frac{m_K}{m_z}\right)\frac{n_c}{n_V} & -\frac{n_V}{n_w} & \frac{1}{m_z}\frac{n_V}{n_w} + \frac{1}{n_w} \end{pmatrix} \begin{pmatrix} dK \\ dV \\ d\delta \end{pmatrix},$$

where

$$\Delta = 1 - \frac{n_c}{n_w} > 0, \quad m_z, m_K < 0, \quad n_w, n_V < 0, \quad n_c > 0$$

$$\begin{pmatrix} dc \\ dz \\ dw \end{pmatrix} = \begin{pmatrix} + & + & + \\ - & 0 & - \\ + & - & - \end{pmatrix} \begin{pmatrix} dK \\ dV \\ d\delta \end{pmatrix}.$$

On the other hand,

$$\begin{pmatrix} d\dot{K} \\ d\dot{V} \end{pmatrix} = \begin{pmatrix} d\alpha \\ d\beta \end{pmatrix}$$

$$= \begin{pmatrix} \alpha_K - \frac{\alpha_z}{\Delta}\frac{m_k}{m_z}\left(1 - \frac{n_c}{n_w}\right) & 0 \\ -\frac{\beta_w}{\Delta}\left(r + \frac{m_K}{m_z}\right)\frac{n_c}{n_V} & \beta_V - \frac{\beta_w}{\Delta}\left(\frac{1}{m_z}\frac{n_V}{n_w} + \frac{1}{n_w}\right) \end{pmatrix} \begin{pmatrix} dk \\ dV \end{pmatrix},$$

where

$$\alpha_K - \frac{\alpha_z}{\Delta}\frac{m_K}{m_z}\left(1 - \frac{n_c}{n_w}\right) < 0, \quad \beta_V - \frac{\beta_w}{\Delta}\left(\frac{1}{m_z}\frac{n_V}{n_w} + \frac{1}{n_w}\right) < 0.$$

Hence, the system of differential equations (47) and (48) is globally stable. We have thus established the following proposition.

Proposition 4. *For any given stock of private capital and social overhead capital, K, V, $(K, V > 0)$, the levels of consumption and investment in private capital and social overhead capital at the sustainable time-path, (c, z, w), are always uniquely determined.*

The larger the stock of private capital K, the higher are the consumption and investment in social overhead capital along the sustainable time-path, but the lower is investment in private capital. On the other hand, the larger the stock of social overhead capital V, the higher is the consumption in private capital along the sustainable time-path, but the lower is the investment in social overhead capital. The lower the rate of discount δ, the lower is the consumption along the sustainable time-path, whereas investments in private capital and social overhead capital both increase.

The sustainable time-path of consumption and investment in private capital and social overhead capital, (c, z, w), approaches the long-run stationary state as t goes to infinity.

6

Global Warming and Forests

1. INTRODUCTION

In this chapter, we further develop the economic analysis of global warming, focusing our attention on the role played by terrestrial forests in moderating processes of global warming, on the one hand, and in affecting the level of the welfare of people in the society by providing a decent and cultured environment, on the other. As in the previous chapters, we are primarily concerned with examining those time patterns of economic development that are either dynamically optimum or sustainable with respect to both the atmospheric environment and the market economy. The analysis we have developed so far is already complicated enough that the introduction of another factor would make the problems extremely difficult to handle. Therefore, we would like to keep our discussion simple enough to derive relevant theoretical conclusions and policy proposals while still reflecting the crucial characteristics of global warming. To make the discussion as self-contained and heuristic as possible, we would like, at the risk of repetition, to describe the premises of the model in full detail and to explain each deductive step thoroughly.

The analysis of the simple, dynamic model of global warming introduced in this chapter leads us to those institutional arrangements and policy measures that are effective in stabilizing the atmospheric concentration of greenhouse gases with minimal governmental intervention into private economic activities. Our analysis will guarantee that the allocation of scarce resources, including the global atmosphere and terrestrial forests, will be sustainable in the sense precisely defined in Chapter 5 without unduly hindering economic progress in the developing countries.

As in previous chapters, the institutional arrangements and policy measures proposed in this chapter are carbon tax schemes, in conjunction with the markets for tradable emission permits, in which the levels of carbon taxes to be levied on the emission of carbon dioxide and other greenhouse gases are determined based on the magnitude of the imputed price. The concept of the imputed price of greenhouse gas was introduced to measure the extent of damage likely to be felt by all future generations of the entire society due to the marginal increase in the level of the atmospheric concentrations of the greenhouse gas today.

The way in which the imputed price of each greenhouse gas is utilized is twofold. First, if a charge is levied on the emission of the greenhouse gas evaluated at the imputed price, the static efficiency is guaranteed provided that markets for private goods and services are perfectly competitive. Second, if the charges are levied on the emission of all greenhouse gases evaluated at their imputed prices at each time, the resulting pattern of resource allocation over time will correspond to those levels of atmospheric greenhouse gases that are sustainable with reference to the intertemporal preference ordering prevailing in the society. Thus, the optimum balance between global warming and economic growth will be sustained in the long-run.

It must be emphasized that the actual implementation of the carbon tax schemes and markets for tradable emission permits, as introduced in the previous chapters and also in this chapter, preclude the active intervention of the government. The role of the government is restricted to administrating the working of carbon tax schemes and markets for tradable emission permits.

The nature of the analysis developed herein may be illustrated in a simplified form by the following proposition. Under certain qualifying assumptions concerning the welfare effect of global warming, it is possible to derive simple formulas for calculating the level of the imputed price of each greenhouse gas. Let us consider a particular case of atmospheric carbon dioxide. The imputed price θ_t of atmospheric carbon dioxide at each time t is proportional to the national income

y_t of the country where carbon dioxide is emitted. That is,

$$\theta_t = \tau(V_t) y_t,$$

where $\tau(V_t)$ is the impact coefficient of global warming at time t to be given by

$$\tau(V_t) = \frac{\beta}{\delta + \mu} \frac{N_t}{\hat{V} - V_t},$$

where δ is the social rate of discount (usually on the order of 5%), μ is the rate at which atmospheric carbon dioxide in excess of the pre-Industrial Revolution level is absorbed into the surface ocean (normally estimated around 2–4%), β is the intensity at which the effect of global warming is felt by the society, and $\hat{V}$ is the critical level of atmospheric carbon dioxide beyond which climatic changes brought about by global warming are feared to exert serious, irrevocable damage on human life and the biosphere on the earth ($\hat{V}$ is usually taken to be about 1,200 GtC, which is twice the amount supposed to have existed at the time of the Industrial Revolution). The above formula is obtained if one supposes that each individual is virtually in charge of $1/N_t$ of total carbon dioxide accumulations V_t at each time t.

The imputed prices of terrestrial forests may be similarly calculated. They express the extent to which the society evaluates the contributions made by marginal increases in the acreage of land forests toward the decrease in the atmospheric level of carbon dioxide. If we consider a simple case in which the acreages of terrestrial forests do not have any influence on the welfare of the people, then the imputed price of a hectare of a particular forest, to be denoted by η_t, may be expressed by the following formula:

$$\eta_t = \frac{\gamma}{\delta} \theta_t,$$

where γ is the amount of atmospheric carbon dioxide annually absorbed by the terrestrial forests per hectare ($\gamma = 5$ tC/ha/yr for temperate forests, $\gamma = 15$ tC/ha/yr for tropical rain forests).

When several countries are involved, the formulas for the imputed prices of carbon dioxide and terrestrial forests above may be applied, where the impact coefficient $\tau(V)$ and the absorption coefficient γ may be assumed to be identical for all countries involved. Tables 3 and 4 show an illustrative calculation made to evaluate the imputed prices of carbon dioxide and land forests for major countries in the world.

Table 3. *Imputed Prices of Greenhouse Gases*

Country	Population 1999 (Millions)	National Income 1999 (Billion Dollars)	Per-Capita National Income 1999 (Dollars)	Gross Annual Atmospheric Increase In CO_2 1998 (Million Tons Carbon)	Per-Capita (Tons Carbon)	Imputed Price (Dollars Per Ton Carbon)	Assessment: Total (Million Dollars)	Assessment: Per-Capita (Dollars)
United States	278.2	8,880	31,910	1,487	5.3	319	474,438	1,700
Canada	30.5	614	20,140	128	4.2	201	25,682	840
Denmark	5.3	171	32,050	15	2.7	321	4,667	880
France	58.6	1,453	24,170	101	1.7	242	24,400	420
Germany	82.1	2,104	25,620	239	2.9	256	61,241	750
Italy	57.6	1,163	20,170	113	2.0	202	22,840	400
Netherlands	15.8	397	25,140	45	2.8	251	11,241	710
Sweden	8.9	237	26,750	13	1.5	268	3,550	400
United Kingdom	59.5	1,404	23,590	148	2.5	236	34,916	590
Indonesia	207.0	125	600	64	0.3	6	383	2
Japan	126.6	4,055	32,030	309	2.4	320	99,086	780
South Korea	46.9	398	8,490	99	2.1	85	8,427	180
Malaysia	22.7	77	3,390	33	1.4	34	1,115	50
Philippines	74.3	78	1,050	21	0.3	11	218	3
Singapore	4.0	95	24,150	22	5.6	242	5,424	1,360
Thailand	60.2	121	2,010	53	0.9	20	1,056	18
Australia	19.0	397	20,950	90	4.8	210	18,953	1,000
New Zealand	3.8	53	13,990	8	2.2	140	1,147	300

Sources: Oak Ridge National Laboratory; World Bank, "World Development Indicators, 2001."

Table 4. *Imputed Prices of Reforestation*

Country	Forest and Woodlands (Million ha)	Net Annual Reforestation (1000 ha)	Imputed Price (Per ha)	Assessment	
				Total (Million Dollars)	Per Capita (Dollars)
United States	296	1,616	31,910	51,567	185.4
Canada	436	720	20,140	14,501	475.4
Denmark	0.5	—	—	—	—
France	15	51	24,170	1,233	21.0
Germany	10	62	25,620	1,588	19.3
Italy	8	15	20,170	303	5.3
Netherlands	0.4	2	25,140	50	3.2
Sweden	28	207	26,750	5,537	622.2
United Kingdom	2	40	23,590	944	15.9
Indonesia	117	–756	1,800	–1,361	–6.6
Japan	25	240	32,030	7,687	60.7
South Korea	5	84	8,490	713	15.2
Malaysia	21	–230	10,170	–2,339	–103.0
Philippines	10	–80	3,150	–252	–3.4
Singapore	—	—	—	—	—
Thailand	16	–366	6,030	–2,207	–36.7
Australia	107	62	20,950	1,299	68.4
New Zealand	10	43	13,990	602	158.3

Sources: World Resources Institute, "World Resources 1990–91," Table 19.1. World Bank, "World Development Indicators, 2001."

We assume that the society is not particularly sensitive to global warming, say $\beta = 0.06$, and thus the imputation coefficients are given by

$$\frac{\theta_t}{y_t} = 0.01$$
$$\frac{\eta_t}{y_t} = 1.0, \text{ for temperate forests}$$
$$\frac{\eta_t}{y_t} = 3.0, \text{ for tropical rain forests}$$

Then the hypothetical values for imputed prices may be as follows:

- The imputed price of carbon dioxide is approximately \$319/tC for the United States and \$320/tC for Japan, whereas it is \$6 for Indonesia and \$11 for the Philippines. The carbon taxes on the per capita basis will therefore be \$1,700 for the United States and \$780 for Japan but \$2 and \$3, respectively, for Indonesia and the Philippines.
- The imputed prices of land forests are approximately \$32,000 for the United States and Japan, \$1,800 for Indonesia, and \$3,150 for the Philippines, all per hectare.

Similar calculations may be made for other greenhouse gases. One has simply to take into account the relative effect on global warming and the rate at which each greenhouse gas is depleted from the atmosphere.

2. THE MODEL OF GLOBAL WARMING AND FORESTS

In the simple, dynamic analysis of global warming introduced in the previous chapters, we have assumed that the combustion of fossil fuels is the only cause for atmospheric instability and that the surface ocean is the only reservoir of carbon on the earth's surface that exchanges carbon with the atmosphere. In this chapter, we consider the role of terrestrial forests, particularly of tropical rain forests, in stabilizing the processes of atmospheric equilibrium.

We introduce a new variable, the total acreage R^ν of forests existing in each country ν, into our dynamic model of global warming. We assume that the amount of atmospheric carbon dioxide annually absorbed by living terrestrial plants is determined by the total acreage of forests in country ν. The capacity of terrestrial forests to absorb atmospheric carbon dioxide through the processes of photosynthesis varies according to the types of trees constituting the forests as well as climate and other conditions. We consider the situation in which various types of terrestrial forests exist with respect to absorbing capacity. We particularly take note of the significant difference in absorbing capacity that exists between tropical rains forests and temperate forests. Hence, the variable R^ν is not a scalar but an F-dimensional vector $R^\nu = (R^\nu_f)$, where f generically refers to the type of forests. It is assumed that $R^\nu_f \geqq 0$, for all f.

Terrestrial forests are regarded as social overhead capital and managed by social institutions with an organizational structure similar to that of private enterprise except for the manner in which prices of the forests themselves and products from the forests are determined. We assume that the amount of atmospheric carbon dioxide absorbed by each type of terrestrial forest f per hectare is a certain constant on the average to be denoted by $\gamma_f > 0$, and $\gamma = (\gamma_f)$ is the vector of absorption coefficients. Then the basic dynamic equation concerning the change in the atmospheric concentrations of carbon dioxide V may be modified to take into account the amount of atmospheric carbon dioxide absorbed by terrestrial forests, γR^ν. We have

$$\dot{V} = a - \mu V - \gamma R, \tag{1}$$

where a is total CO_2 emissions in the world, R is the aggregate sum of the acreages of forests R^ν of all countries in the world,

$$a = \sum_\nu a^\nu, \quad R = \sum_\nu R^\nu,$$

and μ is the rate at which atmospheric carbon dioxide absorbed is absorbed by the oceans.

Numerous studies have been made to estimate the carbon sequester rates for various terrestrial forests. According to Dyson and Marland (1979), the carbon sequester rate for temperate forests is estimated at around 7.5 tC/ha/yr. For tropical rain forests, it is estimated at 9.6–10.0 tC/ha/yr according to Marland (1988) and Myers (1988). Our analysis is carried out on the assumed rate of 5 tC/ha/yr for temperate forests and 15 tC/ha/yr for tropical rain forests.

The change in the acreages of various types of terrestrial forests R^ν is determined first by the levels of afforestation activities and second by various economic activities carried out in country ν during the year in question – particularly by agricultural and lumber industries and by processes of urbanization. We denote by $w^\nu = (w_f^\nu)$ the vector of acreages of various types of terrestrial forests annually afforested and by $b^\nu = (b_f^\nu)$ the vector of acreages of various types of terrestrial forests annually lost due to economic activities. Then the vector of the acreages of various types of terrestrial forests R^ν in country ν is subject to the following system of dynamic equations:

$$\dot{R}^\nu = w^\nu - b^\nu \qquad (\nu = 1, \ldots, n). \tag{2}$$

The analysis of forests within the context of global warming, or rather in the context of global environmental issues, has been extensively developed in several contributions. We would like to cite only those that have implications pertinent to the discussion developed here: Dyson and Marland (1979), Dasgupta and Heal (1974, 1979), Dasgupta (1982a,b), Dickinson (1986), Myers (1988), Marland (1988), Conway et al. (1988), Detweiler and Hall (1988), and IPCC (2000).

Specifications for Utility Functions

Our discussion will be carried out on the premises similar to those introduced in Chapter 4. They will be briefly described before we proceed with the dynamic analysis of global warming involving for forests.

There exist n countries in the world. Each country is generically denoted by ν, $(\nu = 1, \ldots, n)$. We are concerned with the processes by which various relevant economic variables are determined at a particular moment in time t, although all variables are occasionally denoted without explicit reference to time t.

We assume that the utility level u^ν of each country ν is influenced by the vector of the acreages of various types of terrestrial forests, $R^\nu = (R_f^\nu)$, in addition to the atmospheric concentrations of CO_2, V. That is, the utility function for each country ν is expressed in the following manner:

$$u^\nu = u^\nu(c^\nu, R^\nu, V),$$

where $c^\nu = (c_j^\nu)$ is the vector of goods consumed in country ν, $R^\nu = (R_f^\nu)$ is the vector of the acreages of various types of terrestrial forests in country ν, and V is the atmospheric concentrations of CO_2 accumulated in the atmosphere, all at time t.

As in Chapter 1, for each country ν, we assume that utility function $u^\nu(c^\nu, R^\nu, V)$ is strongly separable with respect to (C^ν, R^ν) and

V in the sense originally introduced by Goldman and Uzawa (1964), as postulated in Chapter 1; that is,

$$u^\nu(c^\nu, R^\nu, V) = \varphi(V)u^\nu(c^\nu, R^\nu).$$

As in the static case, the function $\varphi(V)$ expresses the extent to which people are adversely affected by global warming, which is referred to as the impact index of global warming.

We assume that the impact index $\varphi(V)$ of global warming is identical for all countries and satisfies the following conditions:

$$\varphi(V) > 0, \quad \varphi'(V) < 0, \quad \varphi''(V) < 0, \quad (0 < V < \hat{V}),$$

where $\hat{V}$ is the critical level of the atmospheric accumulations of CO_2, which is the level beyond which drastic changes in climatic conditions would ensue and irrevocable damage would be incurred on the global environment.

As in Chapters 1 and 4, the impact index function $\varphi(V)$ of the following form is often postulated:

$$\varphi(V) = (\hat{V} - V)^\beta, \quad 0 < V < \hat{V},$$

where β is the sensitivity parameter, $0 < \beta < 1$.

The impact coefficient of global warming is defined by

$$\tau(V) = -\frac{\varphi'(V)}{\varphi(V)}.$$

The impact coefficient $\tau(V)$ satisfies the following conditions:

$$\tau(V) > 0, \quad \tau'(V) - [\tau(V)]^2 > 0.$$

For the impact index function $\varphi(V)$ specified above, the impact coefficient $\tau(V)$ is given by

$$\tau(V) = \frac{\beta}{\hat{V} - V}.$$

As in Chapter 4, we assume that, for each country ν, the utility function $u^\nu(c^\nu, R^\nu)$ satisfies the following neoclassical conditions:

(U1) $u^\nu(c^\nu, R^\nu)$ is defined, positive-valued, continuous, and continuously twice-differentiable, for all $(c^\nu, R^\nu) \geqq (0, 0)$.

(U2) Marginal utilities of the vector c^ν of the consumption of private goods and the vector R^ν of acreages of various types of terrestrial forests in country ν are always positive:

$$u^{\nu}_{c^{\nu}}(c^{\nu}, R^{\nu}) > 0, \quad u^{\nu}_{R^{\nu}}(c^{\nu}, R^{\nu}) > 0, \quad \text{for all } c^{\nu} \geqq 0, \quad \text{for any given } R^{\nu} > 0.$$

(U3) $u^{\nu}(c^{\nu}, R^{\nu})$ is strictly quasi-concave with respect to $c^{\nu} \geqq 0$ for any given $R^{\nu} > 0$; that is, for any given $R^{\nu} > 0$, for any pair of vectors of consumption c^{ν}_0 and c^{ν}_1 such that $c^{\nu}_0 \neq c^{\nu}_1$ and $u^{\nu}(c^{\nu}_0, R^{\nu}) = u^{\nu}(c^{\nu}_1, R^{\nu})$,

$$u^{\nu}((1-t)c^{\nu}_0 + tc^{\nu}_1, R^{\nu}) < (1-t)u^{\nu}(c^{\nu}_0, R^{\nu}) + tu^{\nu}(c^{\nu}_1, R^{\nu}), \quad \text{for all } 0 < t < 1.$$

(U4) $u^{\nu}(c^{\nu}, R^{\nu})$ is homogeneous of order 1 with respect to $c^{\nu} \geqq 0$, for any given $R^{\nu} > 0$:

$$u^{\nu}(tc^{\nu}, R^{\nu}) = tu^{\nu}(c^{\nu}, R^{\nu}), \quad \text{for all } t \geqq 0, c^{\nu} \geqq 0, \quad \text{for any given } R^{\nu} > 0.$$

From the homogeneity conditions (U4), we have the Euler identity:

$$u^{\nu}(c^{\nu}, R^{\nu}) = u^{\nu}_{c^{\nu}}(c^{\nu}, R^{\nu})c^{\nu}, \quad \text{for all } c^{\nu} \geqq 0, \quad \text{for any given } R^{\nu} > 0.$$

Specifications for Production Possibility Sets

The conditions concerning the production of goods in each country ν are specified by the production possibility set T^{ν} in exactly the same manner as in Chapter 4. We briefly recapitulate the discussion concerning the production possibility set T^{ν}.

Those factors of production that are essential in the production of goods are generically denoted by ℓ ($\ell = 1, \ldots, L$). The endowments of factors of production available in each country ν are expressed by an L-dimensional vector $K^{\nu} = (K^{\nu}_1, \ldots, K^{\nu}_L)$.

The endowments of factors of production available in each country ν are assumed to be exogenously given and to remain constant throughout the course of the discussion.

The conditions concerning the production of goods in each country ν are specified by the production possibility set T^{ν}, which summarizes the technological possibilities and organizational arrangements for country ν with the quantities of factors of production available in country ν.

In each country ν, the minimum quantities of factors of production needed to produce goods by the vector of production $x^\nu = (x_j^\nu)$ with the CO_2 emission at the level a^ν are specified by an L-dimensional vector-valued function

$$f^\nu(x^\nu, a^\nu) = \left(f_1^\nu(x^\nu, a^\nu), \ldots, f_L^\nu(x^\nu, a^\nu)\right).$$

Similarly, the minimum quantities of factors of production needed to engage in afforestation activities at the levels $w^\nu = (w_f^\nu)$ are specified by an L-dimensional vector-valued function

$$g^\nu(w^\nu) = \left(g_1^\nu(w^\nu), \ldots, g_L^\nu(w^\nu)\right).$$

We also assume that economic activities involve the depletion of terrestrial forests. Let us denote by b^ν the acreages of forests depleted in connection with the production of goods at the scale x^ν. Then we may assume that the following functional relation exists:

$$b^\nu = b^\nu(x^\nu).$$

As discussed in the previous chapters, we assume that marginal rates of substitution between the production of goods, the depletion of forests, afforestation activities, and the emission of CO_2 are smooth and diminishing, trade-offs always exist between the production of goods and the emission of CO_2, and the conditions of constant returns to scale prevail. That is, we assume that

(T1) $f^\nu(x^\nu, a^\nu), b^\nu(x^\nu), g^\nu(w^\nu)$ are defined, positive-valued, continuous, and continuously twice-differentiable for all $(x^\nu, a^\nu) \geqq 0$, $x^\nu \geqq 0$, $w^\nu \geqq 0$, respectively;

(T2) $f_{x^\nu}^\nu(x^\nu, a^\nu) > 0$, $b_{x^\nu}^\nu(x^\nu) > 0$, $f_{a^\nu}^\nu(x^\nu, a^\nu) \leqq 0$, for all $(x^\nu, a^\nu) \geqq 0$, and $g_{w^\nu}^\nu(w^\nu) > 0$, for $w^\nu \geqq 0$;

(T3) $f^\nu(x^\nu, a^\nu), b^\nu(x^\nu), g^\nu(w^\nu)$ are strictly quasi-convex with respect to (x^ν, a^ν), x^ν, w^ν, respectively;

(T4) $f^\nu(x^\nu, a^\nu), b^\nu(x^\nu), g^\nu(w^\nu)$ are homogeneous of order 1 with respect to (x^ν, a^ν), x^ν, w^ν, respectively; that is,

$$f^\nu(tx^\nu, ta^\nu) = tf^\nu(x^\nu, a^\nu), \quad \text{for all } t \geqq 0,\ (x^\nu, a^\nu) \geqq 0$$

$$b^\nu(tx^\nu) = tb^\nu(x^\nu), \quad \text{for all } t \geqq 0,\ x^\nu \geqq 0$$

$$g^\nu(tw^\nu) = tg^\nu(w^\nu), \quad \text{for all } t \geqq 0,\ w^\nu \geqq 0.$$

From the constant-returns-to-scale conditions (T4), we have the Euler identity

$$f^\nu(x^\nu, a^\nu) = f^\nu_{x^\nu}(x^\nu, a^\nu)x^\nu + f^\nu_{a^\nu}(x^\nu, a^\nu)a^\nu, \quad \text{for all } (x^\nu, a^\nu) \geqq 0$$

$$b^\nu(x^\nu) = b^\nu_{x^\nu}(x^\nu)x^\nu, \quad \text{for all } x^\nu \geqq 0$$

$$g^\nu(w^\nu) = g^\nu_{w^\nu}(w^\nu)w^\nu, \quad \text{for all } w^\nu \geqq 0.$$

The production possibility set T^ν is given by

$$T^\nu = \{(x^\nu, w^\nu, a^\nu): (x^\nu, w^\nu, a^\nu) \geqq 0,\ f^\nu(x^\nu, a^\nu) + g^\nu(w^\nu) \leqq K^\nu\}.$$

Postulates (T1–3), as specified in Chapter 1, imply that the production possibility set T^ν is a closed, convex set of $J + 1$-dimensional vectors (x^ν, a^ν).

The Producer Optimum

Suppose that prices of goods and terrestrial forests are given, respectively, by J-dimensional vectors $p = (p_j)$ and by F-dimensional vectors $\pi = (\pi_f)$, and that carbon taxes at the rate of θ^ν are levied on the emission of CO_2 in country ν.

Forests are generally regarded as social overhead capital, and there are no markets on which either the ownership of forests or the entitlements for the products from forests are transacted. Hence, prices of forests are generally not market prices but imputed prices. The imputed price of the ownership of a particular forest is the discounted present value of the stream of the marginal utilities of the forests and the expected value of the entitlements for the products from forests in the future. Indeed, determining the imputed prices of forests is one of the central problems we would like to solve in terms of the dynamic analysis of forests to be developed in this chapter.

The producers in country ν would choose those combinations (x^ν, w^ν, a^ν) of vector of production x^ν, vector of afforestation w^ν and CO_2 emissions a^ν that maximize net profits

$$px^\nu + \pi^\nu(w^\nu - b^\nu) - \theta^\nu a^\nu$$

over $(x^\nu, w^\nu, a^\nu) \in T^\nu$; that is, subject to the constraints

$$f^\nu(x^\nu, a^\nu) + g^\nu(w^\nu) \leqq K^\nu, \quad b^\nu = b^\nu(x^\nu).$$

Marginality conditions for the producer optimum are

$$p \leqq r^{\nu} f^{\nu}_{x^{\nu}}(x^{\nu}, a^{\nu}) + \pi^{\nu} b^{\nu}_{x^{\nu}}(x^{\nu}) \qquad (\text{mod. } x^{\nu}) \qquad (3)$$

$$\theta^{\nu} \geqq r^{\nu}[-f^{\nu}_{a^{\nu}}(x^{\nu}, a^{\nu})] \qquad (\text{mod. } a^{\nu}) \qquad (4)$$

$$\pi^{\nu} \leqq r^{\nu} g^{\nu}_{w^{\nu}}(w^{\nu}) \qquad (\text{mod. } w^{\nu}) \qquad (5)$$

$$f^{\nu}(x^{\nu}, a^{\nu}) + g^{\nu}(w^{\nu}) \leqq K^{\nu} \qquad (\text{mod. } r^{\nu}), \qquad (6)$$

where $r^{\nu} = (r^{\nu}_{\ell})$, $[r^{\nu}_{\ell} \geqq 0]$ denotes the vector of rental prices of factors of production.

As was true for the static case explained in Chapter 1, the meaning of these conditions is simple. Condition (3) means that

$$p_j = \sum_{\ell} r^{\nu}_{\ell} f^{\nu}_{\ell x^{\nu}_j}(x^{\nu}, a^{\nu}) + \sum_{f} \pi^{\nu}_f b^{\nu}_{f x^{\nu}_j}(x^{\nu}) \ \text{(with equality when } x^{\nu}_j > 0\text{)},$$

which expresses the familiar principle that the choice of production technologies and the levels of production are so adjusted as to equate marginal factor costs with output prices.

Condition (4) similarly means that CO_2 emissions are so determined that the marginal loss due to the marginal increase in CO_2 emissions is equal to carbon tax rate θ^{ν} when $a^{\nu} > 0$ and is not larger than θ^{ν} when $a^{\nu} = 0$.

Condition (5) means that the levels of afforestation are so determined that the marginal factors costs are equal to π^{ν}.

Condition (6) means that the employment of factors of production does not exceed the endowments and that the conditions of full employment are satisfied whenever rental price r^{ν}_{ℓ} is positive.

As in Chapter 4, all marginality and feasibility conditions are assumed to be satisfied with equality.

We have assumed that the technologies are subject to constant returns to scale (T4), and thus, in view of the Euler identity, conditions (3)–(6) imply that

$$\begin{aligned}
&px^{\nu} + \pi^{\nu}(w^{\nu} - b^{\nu}) - \theta^{\nu} a^{\nu} \\
&\quad = [r^{\nu} f^{\nu}_{x^{\nu}}(x^{\nu}, a^{\nu})x^{\nu} + \pi^{\nu} b^{\nu}_{x^{\nu}}(x^{\nu})x^{\nu}] + [r^{\nu} g^{\nu}_{w^{\nu}}(w^{\nu})w^{\nu} - \pi^{\nu} b^{\nu}] \\
&\qquad - r^{\nu}[-f^{\nu}_{a^{\nu}}(x^{\nu}, a^{\nu})a^{\nu}] \\
&\quad = r^{\nu}[f^{\nu}_{x^{\nu}}(x^{\nu}, a^{\nu})x^{\nu} + f^{\nu}_{a^{\nu}}(x^{\nu}, a^{\nu})a^{\nu} + g^{\nu}_{w^{\nu}}(w^{\nu})w^{\nu}] \\
&\qquad + \pi^{\nu}[b^{\nu}_{x^{\nu}}(x^{\nu})x^{\nu} - b^{\nu}] \\
&\quad = r^{\nu}[f^{\nu}(x^{\nu}, a^{\nu}) + g^{\nu}(w^{\nu})] + \pi^{\nu}[b^{\nu}(x^{\nu}) - b^{\nu}] \\
&\quad = r^{\nu} K^{\nu}.
\end{aligned}$$

That is, the net evaluation of output is equal to the sum of the rental payments to all factors of production.

Suppose all factors of production are owned by individual members of the country ν; then, national income y^ν of country ν is equal to the sum of the rental payments $r^\nu K^\nu$ and the tax payments $\theta^\nu a^\nu$ made by the producers for the emission of CO_2 in country ν subtracted by the imputed value of the net revenues of the social institution in charge of the management of forests in country ν, $\pi^\nu(w^\nu - b^\nu)$; that is,

$$\begin{aligned} y^\nu &= r^\nu K^\nu + \theta^\nu a^\nu - \pi^\nu(w^\nu - b^\nu) \\ &= [px^\nu + \pi^\nu(w^\nu - b^\nu) - \theta^\nu a^\nu] + \theta^\nu a^\nu - \pi^\nu(w^\nu - b^\nu). \end{aligned}$$

Hence,

$$y^\nu = px^\nu,$$

which is again in conformity with the standard practice in national income accounting.

3. FORESTS AND DEFERENTIAL EQUILIBRIUM

Exactly as in Chapters 1 and 4, deferential equilibrium is obtained if, when the producers in each country choose the levels of production and afforestation activities today, they take into account the impact on the future levels of the country's utilities brought about by CO_2 emissions of that country as well as the afforestation activities carried out today.

Imputed Prices of Atmospheric Concentrations of CO_2 and Forests

Consider the situation in which a combination (x^ν, w^ν, a^ν) of vector of production x^ν, vector of afforestation activities w^ν, and CO_2 emissions a^ν is chosen in country ν. Imputed prices of atmospheric concentrations of CO_2 and forests are defined as follows.

Suppose CO_2 emissions in country ν, a^ν, are increased by the marginal amount. This would induce the marginal increase in the aggregate amount of CO_2 emissions in the world, causing the marginal increase in the atmospheric level of CO_2. The resulting marginal increase in the degree of future global warming would cause the marginal decrease in country ν's utility.

The marginal decrease in country ν's utility due to the marginal increase in CO_2 emissions today in country ν is given by the partial derivative, with minus sign, of utility function $\varphi(V)u^{\nu}(c^{\nu}, R^{\nu})$ of country ν with respect to atmospheric accumulations of CO_2, V; that is,

$$-\frac{\partial u^{\nu}}{\partial V} = -\varphi'(V)u^{\nu}(c^{\nu}, R^{\nu}) = \tau(V)\varphi(V)u^{\nu}(c^{\nu}, R^{\nu}),$$

where $\tau(V)$ is the impact coefficient of global warming

$$\tau(V) = -\frac{\varphi'(V)}{\varphi(V)}.$$

We assume that future utilities of country ν are discounted at a certain constant rate δ that is exogenously given. We also assume that the rate of utility discount δ is positive and identical for all countries in the world. We have assumed that the rate at which atmospheric carbon dioxide is annually absorbed by the oceans is a certain constant μ, which is taken to have a value of around 4 percent. Hence, for each country ν, the imputed price ψ^{ν} of the atmospheric accumulations of CO_2, measured in units of the utility, is given by the discounted present value of the marginal decrease in country ν's utility due to the marginal increase in CO_2 emissions in country ν today:

$$\psi^{\nu} = \frac{1}{\delta + \mu}\tau(V)\varphi(V)u^{\nu}(c^{\nu}, R^{\nu}). \tag{7}$$

Similarly, the imputed prices of forests are defined as follows. Suppose the acreages of forests of type f in country ν, R^{ν}_f, are increased by the marginal amount. This would induce a marginal increase in the level of the utility of country ν, on the one hand, and the marginal increase in the utility of country ν in the future owing to the marginal decrease in the atmospheric level of CO_2 induced by the absorbing capacity of forests in country ν, on the other.

The marginal utility with respect to the acreages of forests of type f, R^{ν}_f, is given by

$$\frac{\partial u^{\nu}}{\partial R^{\nu}_f} = \varphi(V)u^{\nu}_{R^{\nu}_f}(c^{\nu}, R^{\nu}),$$

whereas the second component is given by

$$\gamma_f \psi^{\nu}.$$

Hence, the imputed price ξ_f^ν of forests of type f is given by

$$\xi_f^\nu = \frac{1}{\delta}[\varphi(V)u_{R_f^\nu}^\nu(c^\nu, R^\nu) + \gamma_f\psi^\nu]$$

or, in vector notation,

$$\xi^\nu = \frac{1}{\delta}[\varphi(V)u_{R^\nu}^\nu(c^\nu, R^\nu) + \gamma\psi^\nu]. \tag{8}$$

Forests and Deferential Equilibrium

Conditions for deferential equilibrium for each country ν are obtained in nearly the same way as those derived in Chapter 4 except for the introduction of the vector of acreages of forests in each country ν as a new variable.

We assume as given the atmospheric concentrations of CO_2, V, and the vector of acreages of forests in country ν, $R^\nu = (R_f^\nu)$, both at time t. Deferential behavioristic postulates for each country ν may be viewed as the optimum solution to the following maximum problem.

Find the combination $(c^\nu, x^\nu, w^\nu, a^\nu)$ of vector of consumption c^ν, vector of production x^ν, vector of afforestation activities w^ν, and CO_2 emissions a^ν that maximizes the net level of country ν's utility

$$\varphi(V)u^\nu(c^\nu, R^\nu) + \xi^\nu(w^\nu - b^\nu) - \psi^\nu a^\nu$$

subject to the constraints

$$pc^\nu = px^\nu, c^\nu \geqq 0 \tag{9}$$

$$f^\nu(x^\nu, a^\nu) + g^\nu(w^\nu) \leqq K^\nu, \tag{10}$$

where

$$b^\nu = b^\nu(x^\nu).$$

The ψ^ν and ξ^ν are, respectively, the imputed prices of atmospheric concentrations of CO_2 and forests as given by (7) and (8).

Deferential equilibrium for the world economy, then, is obtained if we find the prices of goods and services p at which total demand is equal to total supply:

$$\sum_\nu c^\nu = \sum_\nu x^\nu.$$

Total CO_2 emissions, a, are given by

$$a = \sum_{\nu} a^{\nu}.$$

The maximum problem for deferential equilibrium for country ν may be solved in terms of the Lagrangian form

$$L^{\nu}(c^{\nu}, x^{\nu}, w^{\nu}, a^{\nu}; \lambda^{\nu}, \lambda^{\nu} r^{\nu}) = \varphi(V) u^{\nu}(c^{\nu}, R^{\nu}) + \xi^{\nu}(w^{\nu} - b^{\nu}) - \psi^{\nu} a^{\nu}$$
$$+ \lambda^{\nu}(px^{\nu} - pc^{\nu}) + \lambda^{\nu} r^{\nu}[K^{\nu} - f^{\nu}(x^{\nu}, a^{\nu}) - g^{\nu}(w^{\nu})],$$

where V, ψ^{ν}, and ξ^{ν} are given. The variables $\lambda^{\nu}, \lambda^{\nu} r^{\nu}$ are the Lagrangian unknowns associated with constraints (9) and (10), respectively.

The marginality conditions at the optimum are

$$\varphi(V) u^{\nu}_{c^{\nu}}(c^{\nu}, R^{\nu}) = \lambda^{\nu} p$$
$$\lambda^{\nu} p = \lambda^{\nu} r^{\nu} f^{\nu}_{x^{\nu}}(x^{\nu}, a^{\nu}) + \xi^{\nu} b^{\nu}_{x^{\nu}}(x^{\nu})$$
$$\xi^{\nu} = \lambda^{\nu} r^{\nu} g^{\nu}_{w^{\nu}}(w^{\nu})$$
$$\psi^{\nu} = \lambda^{\nu} r^{\nu}[- f^{\nu}_{a^{\nu}}(x^{\nu}, a^{\nu})].$$

When expressed in units of market prices, the optimum conditions are

$$\alpha^{\nu} \varphi(V) u^{\nu}_{c^{\nu}}(c^{\nu}, R^{\nu}) = p \tag{12}$$
$$p = r^{\nu} f^{\nu}_{x^{\nu}}(x^{\nu}, a^{\nu}) + \pi^{\nu} b^{\nu}_{x^{\nu}}(x^{\nu}) \tag{13}$$
$$\pi^{\nu} = r^{\nu} g^{\nu}_{w^{\nu}}(w^{\nu}) \tag{14}$$
$$\theta^{\nu} = r^{\nu}[- f^{\nu}_{a^{\nu}}(x^{\nu}, a^{\nu})], \tag{15}$$

where

$$\alpha^{\nu} = \frac{1}{\lambda^{\nu}} > 0,$$

θ^{ν} and π^{ν} are, respectively, the imputed prices of atmospheric concentrations of CO_2 and forests, both measured in units of market prices:

$$\theta^{\nu} = \frac{\psi^{\nu}}{\lambda^{\nu}} = \frac{1}{\delta + \mu} \alpha^{\nu} \tau(V) \varphi(V) u^{\nu}(c^{\nu}, R^{\nu}) \tag{16}$$
$$\pi^{\nu} = \frac{\xi^{\nu}}{\lambda^{\nu}} = \frac{1}{\delta}\left[\alpha^{\nu} \varphi(V) u^{\nu}_{R^{\nu}}(c^{\nu}, R^{\nu}) + \gamma \theta^{\nu}\right]. \tag{17}$$

By multiplying both sides of relation (12) by c^{ν} and by noting the Euler identity for utility functions and the budgetary constraints (9), we obtain

$$\alpha^\nu \varphi(V) u^\nu(c^\nu, R^\nu) = pc^\nu = px^\nu = y^\nu,$$

which may be substituted into (16) to obtain

$$\theta^\nu = \frac{\tau(V)}{\delta + \mu} y^\nu.$$

Conditions (14) and (15) put together mean that the combination (x^ν, w^ν, a^ν) of vector of production x^ν, vector of afforestation activities w^ν, and CO_2 emissions a^ν maximizes net profits

$$px^\nu + \pi^\nu(w^\nu - b^\nu) - \theta^\nu a^\nu$$

over $(x^\nu, w^\nu, a^\nu) \in T^\nu$.

The discussion above may be summarized in the following proposition.

Proposition 1. *Deferential equilibrium corresponds precisely to the standard market equilibrium under the system of proportional carbon taxes, where, in each country* ν*, the carbon taxes are levied with the tax rate* θ^ν *that is proportional to the national income* y^ν *of country* ν *with the discounted present value* $\frac{\tau(V)}{\delta + \mu}$ *of the impact coefficient of global warming* $\tau(V)$ *as the coefficient of proportion, that is,*

$$\theta^\nu = \frac{\tau(V)}{\delta + \mu} y^\nu,$$

where δ *is the rate of utility discount and* μ *is the rate at which atmospheric carbon dioxide is annually absorbed by the oceans.*

4. UNIFORM CARBON TAXES AND SOCIAL OPTIMUM

In the previous section, we have seen that deferential equilibrium may be obtained as the standard market equilibrium provided the carbon tax rate θ^ν in each country ν is equal to

$$\theta^\nu = \frac{\tau(V)}{\delta + \mu} y^\nu,$$

where y^ν is the national income of country ν. Exactly as in Chapter 4, we examine the implications of market equilibrium when the uniform carbon taxes, with the rate θ, are levied:

$$\theta = \frac{\tau(V)}{\delta + \mu} y, \tag{18}$$

where y is the sum of all national incomes y^ν of all countries in the world expressed by

$$y = \sum_\nu y^\nu.$$

The conditions for market equilibrium under the uniform carbon tax scheme involving forests are obtained in exactly the same manner as discussed in Chapter 4.

The representative consumers and producers in each country ν have to solve the following maximization problems:

(i) Find the vector of consumption c^ν that maximizes country ν's utility

$$\varphi(V)u^\nu(c^\nu, R^\nu)$$

subject to budget constraints

$$pc^\nu = y^\nu, \quad c^\nu \geqq 0,$$

where y^ν is the national income of country ν:

$$y^\nu = px^\nu.$$

(ii) Find the combination (x^ν, w^ν, a^ν) of production vector x^ν, vector of afforestation w^ν, and CO_2 emissions a^ν that maximizes net profits

$$px^\nu + \pi^\nu(w^\nu - b^\nu) - \theta^\nu a^\nu$$

subject to the constraints

$$f^\nu(x^\nu, a^\nu) + g^\nu(w^\nu) \leqq K^\nu,$$

where

$$b^\nu = b^\nu(x^\nu),$$

and π^ν is the imputed price of forests in country ν, measured in units of market prices, to be defined by (18).

Market equilibrium for the world economy, then, is obtained if we find the prices of goods and services p at which total demand is equal to total supply:

$$\sum_\nu c^\nu = \sum_\nu x^\nu.$$

Total CO_2 emissions a are given by

$$a = \sum_\nu a^\nu.$$

When expressed in units of market prices, the optimum marginality conditions for country ν are

$$\alpha^\nu \varphi(V) u^\nu_{c^\nu}(c^\nu, R^\nu) = p \tag{19}$$

$$p = r^\nu f^\nu_{x^\nu}(x^\nu, a^\nu) + \pi^\nu b^\nu_{x^\nu}(x^\nu) \tag{20}$$

$$\pi^\nu = r^\nu g^\nu_{w^\nu}(w^\nu) \tag{21}$$

$$\theta = r^\nu[-f^\nu_{a^\nu}(x^\nu, a^\nu)]. \tag{22}$$

By multiplying both sides of relation (19) by c^ν and by noting the Euler identity for utility function $u^\nu(c^\nu, R^\nu)$, we obtain

$$\alpha^\nu \varphi(V) u^\nu(c^\nu, R^\nu) = pc^\nu = px^\nu.$$

Hence,

$$\alpha^\nu \varphi(V) u^\nu(c^\nu, R^\nu) = y^\nu. \tag{23}$$

We now define the world utility W by

$$W = \sum_\nu \alpha^\nu \varphi(V) u^\nu(c^\nu, R^\nu),$$

which, in view of (23), implies

$$W = \sum_\nu y^\nu = y.$$

If we take partial derivatives of W with respect to V, we obtain

$$\frac{\partial W}{\partial V} = \sum_\nu \alpha^\nu \varphi'(V) u^\nu(c^\nu, R^\nu) = -\tau(V) \sum_\nu \alpha^\nu \varphi(V) u^\nu(c^\nu, R^\nu).$$

By noting relations (23), we obtain

$$\frac{\partial W}{\partial V} = -\tau(V) \sum_\nu y^\nu = -\tau(V) y.$$

The imputed price ψ of the atmospheric concentrations of CO_2 with respect to the world utility W is defined by

$$\psi = \frac{1}{\delta + \mu}\left[-\frac{\partial W}{\partial V}\right] = \frac{\tau(V)}{\delta + \mu}y.$$

Hence,

$$\psi = \theta.$$

The imputed price ψ of the atmospheric concentrations of CO_2 with respect to the world utility W is equal to the uniform carbon tax rate θ that is initially given.

If we take into account the loss in the level of world utility W due to total CO_2 emissions a to be evaluated at the imputed price ψ of the atmospheric concentrations of CO_2 in addition to the gains due to the net increase in the acreages of forests in each country ν, the net level of world utility W' may be defined by

$$W' = \sum_\nu \alpha^\nu \varphi(V) u^\nu(c^\nu, R^\nu) + \sum_\nu \pi^\nu(w^\nu - b^\nu) - \psi a, \tag{24}$$

where π^ν is the imputed price of forests in country ν and ψ is the imputed price of the atmospheric concentrations of CO_2, respectively, given by

$$\pi^\nu = \frac{1}{\delta}\left[\alpha^\nu \varphi(V) u^\nu_{R^\nu}(c^\nu, R^\nu) + \gamma\theta\right] \tag{25}$$

$$\theta = \frac{\tau(V)}{\delta + \mu}\sum_\nu \alpha^\nu \varphi(V) u^\nu(c^\nu, R^\nu). \tag{26}$$

We consider the net level of world utility W' defined by (24), where π^ν is the imputed price of forests in country ν and ψ is the imputed price of atmospheric concentrations of CO_2, respectively, defined by (25) and (26).

Social Optimum in the Dynamic Context

Maximize the net level of world utility among all feasible patterns of allocation $(c^1, \dots, c^n, x^1, \dots, x^n, w^1, \dots, w^n, a^1, \dots, a^n, a)$:

$$\sum_\nu c^\nu = \sum_\nu x^\nu, \quad a = \sum_\nu a^\nu, \quad (x^\nu, w^\nu, a^\nu) \in T^\nu.$$

The social optimum may be obtained in terms of the Lagrangian form

$$L(c^1, \ldots, c^n, x^1, \ldots, x^n, w^1, \ldots, w^n, a^1, \ldots, a^n, a; p, r^1, \ldots, r^L, \theta)$$
$$= \left[\sum_\nu \alpha^\nu \varphi(V) u^\nu(c^\nu, R^\nu) + \sum_\nu \pi^\nu(w^\nu - b^\nu) - \psi a\right]$$
$$+ p\left[\sum_\nu x^\nu - \sum_\nu c^\nu\right] + \sum_\nu r^\nu [K^\nu - f^\nu(x^\nu, a^\nu) - g^\nu(w^\nu)]$$
$$+ \theta\left[a - \sum_\nu a^\nu\right],$$

where variables p^ν, r^ν, θ are the Lagrangian unknowns.

It is easily seen that

$$\theta = \psi,$$

and the Euler–Lagrange equations for this Lagrangian form are

$$\alpha^\nu \varphi(V) u^\nu_{c^\nu}(c^\nu, R^\nu) = p$$
$$p = r^\nu f^\nu_{x^\nu}(x^\nu, a^\nu) + \pi^\nu b^\nu_{x^\nu}(x^\nu)$$
$$\pi^\nu = r^\nu g^\nu_{w^\nu}(w^\nu)$$
$$\theta = r^\nu [-f^\nu_{a^\nu}(x^\nu, a^\nu)].$$

Thus, we have established the following proposition.

Proposition 2. *Consider the uniform carbon tax scheme with the same rate θ everywhere in the world, where the rate θ is proportional to the sum y of the national incomes of all countries in the world with the discounted present value $\frac{\tau(V)}{\delta + \mu}$ of the impact coefficient of global warming $\tau(V)$ as the coefficient of proportion:*

$$\theta = \frac{\tau(V)}{\delta + \mu} y,$$

where

$$y = \sum_\nu y^\nu.$$

Then the market equilibrium obtained under such a uniform carbon tax scheme is a social optimum in the sense that there exists a set of positive weights for the utilities of individual countries $(\alpha^1, \ldots, \alpha^n)$, $[\alpha^\nu > 0]$

such that the net level of world utility defined by

$$W' = \sum_\nu \alpha^\nu \varphi(V) u^\nu(c^\nu, R^\nu) + \sum_\nu \pi^\nu (w^\nu - b^\nu) - \psi a$$

is maximized among all feasible patterns of allocation $(c^1, \ldots, c^n, x^1, \ldots, x^n, a^1, \ldots, a^n, a)$:

$$\sum_\nu c^\nu = \sum_\nu x^\nu, \quad a = \sum_\nu a^\nu, \quad (x^\nu, w^\nu, a^\nu) \in T^\nu,$$

where π^ν *is the imputed price of forests in country* ν *and* ψ *is the imputed price of the atmospheric concentrations of* CO_2*, respectively, to be given by*

$$\theta = \frac{\tau(V)}{\delta + \mu} \sum_\nu \alpha^\nu \varphi(V) u^\nu(c^\nu, R^\nu)$$

$$\pi^\nu = \frac{1}{\delta} \left[\alpha^\nu \varphi(V) u^\nu_{R^\nu}(c^\nu, R^\nu) + \gamma\theta \right].$$

Then the imputed price ψ *of the atmospheric concentrations of* CO_2 *is equal to carbon tax rate* θ:

$$\psi = \theta.$$

NOTES. At the time when the uniform carbon tax rate

$$\theta = \frac{\tau(V)}{\delta + \mu} y$$

is announced, the level of world national income y is not exactly known. We may consider the adjustment process concerning the uniform carbon tax rate θ, as introduced in Chapter 4.

Suppose the uniform carbon tax rate is announced at an arbitrarily given level $\theta > 0$, and let the relevant variables at the market equilibrium under the carbon tax scheme with the rate θ be denoted by $p, c^\nu, x^\nu, w^\nu, a^\nu, y^\nu, y$. Then the imputed price ψ of atmospheric concentrations of CO_2 with respect to the world utility W is given by

$$\psi = \frac{\tau(V)}{\delta + \mu} y,$$

where

$$y = \sum_\nu y^\nu, \quad y^\nu = p x^\nu, \; \nu = 1, \ldots, n.$$

Then, we may consider the following adjustment process with respect to tax rate θ:

$$\frac{d\theta}{dt} = k(\psi - \theta),$$

where the speed of adjustment k is positive.

Contrary to the case discussed in Chapter 4, however, the global stability of the adjustment process is not easily proved.

Similarly, as in the static context, social optimum in the dynamic context may be defined for any arbitrarily given set of positive weights for the utilities of individual countries, $(\alpha^1, \ldots, \alpha^n)$, $[\alpha^\nu > 0]$. An allocation $(c^1, \ldots, c^n, x^1, \ldots, x^n, w^1, \ldots, w^n, a^1, \ldots, a^n, a)$ is a social optimum if the net level of world utility W', defined by (24), is maximized among all feasible patterns of allocation.

A social optimum in the dynamic context necessarily implies the existence of the uniform carbon tax scheme with the same rate $\theta = \tau(a)y$. However, the balance-of-payments requirements

$$pc^\nu = px^\nu$$

are generally not satisfied.

It is apparent that, if a social optimum satisfies the balance-of-payments requirements, then it corresponds to the market equilibrium under the uniform carbon tax scheme. The existence of such a social optimum is guaranteed by Proposition 3 below, which may be proved in exactly the same manner as Proposition 3 in Chapter 1.

Proposition 3. *There always exists a set of positive weights for the utilities of individual countries* $(\alpha^1, \ldots, \alpha^n)$, $[\alpha^\nu > 0]$ *such that the social optimum with respect to the world utility*

$$W' = \sum_\nu \alpha^\nu \varphi(V) u^\nu(c^\nu, R^\nu) + \sum_\nu \pi^\nu (w^\nu - b^\nu) - \psi a$$

satisfies the balance-of-payments requirements; that is,

$$pc^\nu = px^\nu.$$

Hence, the corresponding pattern of allocation $(c^1, \ldots, c^n, x^1, \ldots, x^n, w^1, \ldots, w^n, a^1, \ldots, a^n, a)$, *in conjunction with prices of goods* p *and the carbon tax scheme with the uniform rate* $\theta = \tau(a)y$, *constitutes a market equilibrium.*

7

Global Warming as a Cooperative Game[1]

We regard global warming as a cooperative game and examine the conditions under which the core of the global warming game is nonempty. It is carried out within the framework introduced in the previous chapters, where the economic welfare of each country may be expressed by the utility, which depends on the vector of goods consumed in that country and the total amount of carbon dioxide emitted by all the countries involved.

The players of the cooperative game of global warming are countries in the world. Each country may choose as a strategy a combination of the vector of goods to be consumed by that country and the amount of carbon dioxide to be emitted in that country from productive and other processes, and the payoff for each country is simply its utility.

A coalition for the global warming game is any group of countries, and the value of each coalition is the maximum of the sum of the utilities of the countries in the coalition on the assumption that those countries not belonging to the coalition form their own coalition and try to maximize the sum of their utilities.

The core of the global warming game consists of those allotments of the value of the game among individual countries that no coalition can block. The conditions under which the core of the global warming game with transferable utility is nonempty are examined. Then, an

[1] Reprinted, with permission of Springer–Verlag, from H. Uzawa. "Global Warming as a Cooperative Game," *Environmental Economics and Policy Studies*, 1999, Vol. 2, pp. 1–37.

alternative definition of the value of coalition for the global warming game with transferable utility is introduced, and we show that the core of the global warming game under the alternative definition is always nonempty.

Finally, our global warming game is regarded as a cooperative game with non-transferable utility, and we demonstrate that Lindahl equilibrium is always in the core of the game.

1. INTRODUCTION

One of the intrinsic difficulties involved with global warming is that the marginal private loss each country suffers from curtailing its atmospheric emission of carbon dioxide and other greenhouse gases is significantly greater than its own marginal welfare loss due to global warming, although the marginal social costs due to global warming borne either by other countries or by future generations are of a much larger magnitude. Accordingly, it is difficult to reach an international agreement on global warming that will substantially reduce the consumption of fossil fuels and the destruction of tropical rain forests to restore atmospheric equilibrium effectively. Global warming thus is a phenomenon to which the conceptual framework and analytical apparatuses of game theory may appropriately be applied. We regard global warming as a cooperative game and examine the conditions under which the core of the global warming game is nonempty.

The analysis of global warming in this chapter is carried out within the framework described in Chapters 1 and 2, where the economic welfare of each country may be expressed by the utility. Each country's utility depends on the vector of goods consumed in that country on the one hand and the total amount of carbon dioxide emitted by all the countries involved on the other. In the first part of this chapter, the utility is assumed to be cardinal and interpersonally comparable. The players of our cooperative game of global warming are countries in the world that may choose as a strategy a combination of the vector of goods to be consumed by that country and the amount of carbon dioxide to be emitted in that country from industrial production and other processes. The payoff for each country is simply its utility.

A coalition for the global warming game is any group of countries in the world, and the value of each coalition is the maximum of the sum of the utilities of the countries in the coalition on the assumption that those countries not belonging to the coalition form their own coalition and try to maximize the sum of their utilities. The value of a coalition S ($N \subset S$) is defined as the sum of the utilities of the countries in S when coalition S and the complementary coalition $N - S$ are in equilibrium.

The standard definition of the core in game theory is adopted. The core of the global warming game consists of those allotments of the value of the game among individual countries that no coalition can block. On the assumption that the standard neoclassical conditions for utility functions and production possibility sets are satisfied, the conditions under which the core of the global warming game is nonempty are examined in detail.

Then an alternative definition of the value of coalition for the global warming game with transferable utility is introduced, and it is shown that the core of the global warming game under the alternative definition is always nonempty.

Finally, we demonstrate that, if the global warming game is regarded as a cooperative game with nontransferable utility, Lindahl equilibrium is in the core of the game. Because the existence of Lindahl equilibrium is ensured by Mäler and Uzawa (1994), as described in Chapters 1 and 2, Theorem 3 serves as proof for the nonemptiness of the core for the global warming game with nontransferable utility as well.

Note that the concept of the core of the global warming game adopted in this chapter differs from that of Foley (1970) and those of virtually all game-theoretic contributions as described in the classic review article of Kurz (1994) on the game-theoretic approach to the problems of public goods, where all the articles referred to are formulated exactly in terms of Foley's specifications. In our formulation of the cooperative game associated with global warming, the sum of the utilities of the countries in coalitions S is defined as

$$\sum_{\nu \in S} u^{\nu}(c^{\nu}, a),$$

where, for each country ν, the utility is determined by the vectors c^{ν} of consumption goods and the aggregate quantity a of CO_2 emissions; that is,

$$a = a_S + a_{N-S},$$

where a_S and a_{N-S} denote, respectively, the quantities of CO_2 emission by the countries in coalition S and its complementary $N - S$. On the other hand, in Foley's model, the sum of the utilities of the countries in coalition S is given by

$$\sum_{\nu \in S} u^{\nu}(c^{\nu}, a_S),$$

where the relevant quantity of CO_2 emissions is the sum a_S of the CO_2 emission by the countries in coalition rather than the total quantity a emitted by all countries in the world. One of the difficulties involved with the analysis of the cooperative game associated with global warming, or with economies with public goods in the Samuelsonian sense in general, is that the value of each coalition S is influenced by the choice made by the players in the complementary coalition $N - S$. The somewhat tedious argument developed in this chapter is due to the intrinsic complications between the choices made by the two coalitions S and $N - S$.

Note that, although some countries may try to adopt less-CO_2-emitting technologies for domestic production while importing goods that are produced by more-CO_2-emitting technologies abroad, the very concept of the core of the cooperative game associated with global warming precludes such selfish behavior.

2. THE MODEL OF GLOBAL WARMING

The analysis of the cooperative game associated with global warming in this chapter is carried out within the conceptual framework introduced in Chapter 1, although the exact formulation of the model differs slightly.

We postulate, as in Chapters 1 and 2, that each greenhouse gas is so measured as to equate the greenhouse effect with that of carbon dioxide. Hence, the model is formulated so that carbon dioxide is the only chemical agent that has a greenhouse effect. We also postulate that the welfare effect of global warming is measured by the total quantity of CO_2 emitted annually into the atmosphere irrespective of the stock of carbon dioxide accumulated in the atmosphere. This is a valid hypothesis because we are concerned with the problems of global warming in the short-run, and thus the stock of CO_2 accumulation in the atmosphere may be assumed to remain constant, and the level of the utility of each country to be influenced only by the total amount of annual CO_2 emissions.

There exist n countries in the world. Each country is generically denoted by ν, and the set of all countries is denoted by $N = \{1, \ldots, n\}$. The economic welfare of each country ν is assumed to be represented by the utility function

$$u^\nu = u^\nu(c^\nu, a),$$

where $c^\nu = (c_j^\nu)$ is the vector of goods consumed in country ν, j generically refers to consumption goods ($j = 1, \ldots, J$), and a is the total amount of carbon dioxide annually emitted into the atmosphere. Thus, a may be written as

$$a = \sum_{\nu \in N} a^\nu,$$

where a^ν is the amount of carbon dioxide emitted into the atmosphere by country ν in relation to productive activities.

The specifications and postulates concerning the structural components of the model remain essentially identical with those of the models discussed in Chapters 1 and 2. However, they differ in certain crucial aspects. Because the analysis carried out in this chapter concerns extremely complicated and minute aspects of the phenomenon of global warming, detailed description of the model will, at the risk of repetition, be stated.

Postulates for Utility Functions

We assume that, for each country ν, the utility function $u^\nu(c^\nu, a)$ satisfies the following neoclassical conditions:

(U1) Function $u^\nu(c^\nu, a)$ is defined, continuous, and continuously twice-differentiable for all $(c^\nu, a) \geqq (0, 0)$.

(U2) Marginal utilities are positive for the consumption of private goods $c^\nu = (c_j^\nu)$, but the emission a of CO_2 has a negative marginal utility:

$$u_{c^\nu}^\nu(c^\nu, a) > 0, \quad u_a^\nu(c^\nu, a) < 0, \qquad \text{for all} \quad (c^\nu, a) \geqq (0, 0).$$

(U3) Function $u(c^\nu, a)$ is strictly quasi-concave with respect to (c^ν, a):

$$u^\nu((1-\theta)c_0^\nu + \theta c_1^\nu, (1-\theta)a_0 + \theta a_1) \\ > (1-\theta)u^\nu(c_0^\nu, a_0) + \theta u^\nu(c_1^\nu, a_1), \\ \text{for all } (c_0^\nu, a_0) \neq (c_1^\nu, a_1), u^\nu(c_0^\nu, a_0) = u^\nu(c_1^\nu, a_1), 0 < \theta < 1.$$

(U3)′ Function $u(c^\nu, a)$ is strictly concave with respect to (c^ν, a):

$$u^\nu((1-\theta)c_0^\nu + \theta c_1^\nu, (1-\theta)a_0 + \theta a_1) \\ > (1-\theta)u^\nu(c_0^\nu, a_0) + \theta u^\nu(c_1^\nu, a_1), \\ \text{for all } (c_0^\nu, a_0) \neq (c_1^\nu, a_1), 0 < \theta < 1.$$

In what follows, we occasionally need a slightly stronger form for the strict concavity of the utility function $u^\nu(c^\nu, a)$.

(U3)″ The matrix of second-order partial derivatives

$$\begin{pmatrix} u^\nu_{c^\nu c^\nu} & u^\nu_{c^\nu a} \\ u^\nu_{a c^\nu} & u^\nu_{aa} \end{pmatrix}$$

is negative definite for all $(c^\nu, a) \geqq (0, 0)$.

The strict concavity conditions as specified by (U3)″ may be reduced to the conditions that

(i) $(u^\nu_{c^\nu c^\nu})$ is negative definite, and
(ii) $u^\nu_{aa} - u^\nu_{ac^\nu}(u^\nu_{c^\nu c^\nu})^{-1}u^\nu_{c^\nu a} < 0$ for all $(c^\nu, a) \geqq (0, 0)$.

Conditions (i) and (ii) are easily derived in terms of the familiar identity for symmetrical matrices:

$$\begin{pmatrix} I & 0 \\ -b'A^{-1} & 1 \end{pmatrix}\begin{pmatrix} A & b \\ b' & c \end{pmatrix}\begin{pmatrix} I & -A^{-1}b \\ 0 & 1 \end{pmatrix} = \begin{pmatrix} A & 0 \\ 0 & c - b'A^{-1}b \end{pmatrix},$$

where $A = A'$.

In Chapters 1 and 2, the utility function $u^\nu(c^\nu, a)$ for each country ν is assumed to be homogeneous of order 1 with respect to c^ν for given a; hence, $u^\nu(c^\nu, a)$ cannot be strictly concave with respect to c^ν.

In our discussion of the game-theoretic approach to global warming, the following condition occasionally plays a crucial role:

(U4) $u^\nu_{c^\nu}(u^\nu_{c^\nu c^\nu})^{-1}u^\nu_{c^\nu a} > 0$, for all $(c^\nu, a) \geqq (0, 0)$.

The meaning of condition (U4) will be spelled out during the course of the following discussion. Condition (U4) is easily seen to be satisfied if utility functions $u^\nu(c^\nu, a)$ are strongly separable with respect to c^ν and a, and condition (i) is satisfied; that is,

$$u^\nu(c^\nu, a) = \varphi(a)u^\nu(c^\nu),$$

where

$$u^\nu(c^\nu) > 0,\ u^\nu_{c^\nu}(c^\nu) > 0,\ \left[u^\nu_{c^\nu c^\nu}(c^\nu)\right] \text{negative definite}$$
$$\varphi(a) > 0,\ \varphi'(a) < 0, \varphi''(a) < 0.$$

One may simply note the following relation:

$$u^\nu_{c^\nu}\left(u^\nu_{c^\nu c^\nu}\right)^{-1} u^\nu_{c^\nu a} = \varphi(a)u^\nu_{c^\nu}(c^\nu)\left[u^\nu_{c^\nu c^\nu}(c^\nu)\right]^{-1} u^\nu_{c^\nu}(c^\nu) > 0.$$

However, U(4) is not satisfied when $u^\nu(c^\nu, a)$ is homogeneous of order 1 with respect to c^ν. If $u^\nu(c^\nu, a)$ is homogeneous of order 1 with respect to c^ν, then

$$\det\left(u^\nu_{c^\nu c^\nu}\right) = 0.$$

Hence, the inverse matrix $(u^\nu_{c^\nu c^\nu})^{-1}$ does not exist.

The relations between the specifications of our model and those of Foley, as introduced in Foley (1970), may be noted. As mentioned in the introductory section, Foley's model presupposes that the utilities of the countries belonging to coalition S are given by $u^\nu(c^\nu, a_S)$, where a_S is the sum of the amounts of CO_2 emitted by those countries belonging to coalition S,

$$\sum_{\nu \in S} u^\nu(c^\nu, a_S) \quad \text{with} \quad a_S = \sum_{\nu \in S} a^\nu,$$

whereas, with respect to global warming, they should be given by

$$\sum_{\nu \in N} u^\nu(c^\nu, a),$$

where a is the sum of the amounts of CO_2 emitted by all the countries in the world:

$$a = \sum_{\nu \in N} a^\nu.$$

Indeed, Foley's model is concerned with the theory of clubs, where the utilities of the members belonging to club S are given by $u^\nu(c^\nu, a_S)$, where a_S is the sum of the amounts of public goods produced by those members belonging to club S:

$$a_S = \sum_{\nu \in S} a^\nu.$$

Postulates for Production Possibility Sets

The conditions concerning the production of goods and services in each country ν are specified by the production possibility set T^ν that summarizes the technological possibilities and organizational arrangements for country ν together with the endowments of factors of production available in country ν. The production possibility set T^ν is a nonempty set of $J+1$-dimensional vectors (x^ν, a^ν), where $x^\nu = (x_j^\nu)$ is the vector specifying the aggregate quantities x_j^ν of goods produced in country ν and a^ν denotes the quantity of CO_2 emitted into the atmosphere in country ν.

We assume that, for each country ν, the technological possibility set T^ν satisfies the following conditions:

(T1) Set T^ν is nonempty and closed. All vectors in T^ν are nonnegative:

$$(x^\nu, a^\nu) \geqq (0,0), \quad \text{for all} \quad (x^\nu, a^\nu) \in T^\nu, \quad \text{and } (0,0) \in T^\nu$$

(T2) Set T^ν is convex and monotone. That is,
(i) $(x_0^\nu, a_0^\nu), (x_1^\nu, a_1^\nu) \in T^\nu$ implies

$$((1-\theta)x_0^\nu + \theta x_1^\nu, (1-\theta)a_0^\nu + \theta a_1^\nu) \in T^\nu, \quad \text{for all } 0 \leqq \theta \leqq 1.$$

(ii) If $(x^\nu, a^\nu) \in T^\nu$, $x^{\nu\prime} \leqq x^\nu$, $a^{\nu\prime} \geqq a$, then $(x^{\nu\prime}, a^{\nu\prime}) \in T^\nu$.

(T3) For any nonnegative vector of prices $p = (p_j)$ and any positive value $q > 0$, the production plan (x^ν, a^ν) that maximizes

$$px^\nu - qa^\nu$$

among all vectors $(x^\nu, a^\nu) \in T^\nu$ always exists and is uniquely determined, to be denoted by $(x^\nu(p,q), a^\nu(p,q))$, which is assumed to be continuously twice-differentiable.

Conditions (T3) imply that the matrix of second-order partial derivatives

$$\begin{pmatrix} x_p^\nu & x_q^\nu \\ -a_p^\nu & -a_q^\nu \end{pmatrix}$$

is symmetrical and positive definite.

Value of Coalition

A pattern $(c^1, \ldots, c^n; a)$ of vectors of consumption goods $(c^1, \ldots, c^n)$ and the total emission of CO_2, a, are feasible if production plans $(x^\nu, a^\nu) \in T^\nu$, $(\nu \in N)$ exist such that

$$\sum_{\nu \in N} c^\nu \leqq \sum_{\nu \in N} x^\nu,$$

$$a = \sum_{\nu \in N} a^\nu.$$

A feasible pattern $(c_0^1, \ldots, c_0^n, a_0)$ is optimum if it maximizes the world utility

$$\sum_{\nu \in N} u^\nu(c^\nu, a)$$

among all feasible patterns $(c^1, \ldots, c^n; a)$.

A similar definition of optimality may be introduced for any coalition S of countries. A coalition S is simply any subset of $N = \{1, \ldots, n\}$, and a pattern $\{c^\nu(\nu \in S), a_S\}$ of consumption vectors $c^\nu(\nu \in S)$, and the total quantity a_S of the emission of CO_2 are feasible with respect to coalition S if production plans $(x^\nu, a^\nu) \in T^\nu(\nu \in S)$ exist such that

$$\sum_{\nu \in S} c^\nu \leqq \sum_{\nu \in S} x^\nu,$$

$$a_S = \sum_{\nu \in S} a^\nu.$$

A pattern of consumption vectors $c^{\nu 0}$ $(\nu \in S)$, and the quantity a_S^0 of the emission of CO_2 is optimum with respect to coalition S if it maximizes

$$\sum_{\nu \in S} u^\nu(c^\nu, a)$$

among all patterns $\{c^\nu(\nu \in S), a_S\}$ that are feasible with respect to coalition S, where

$$a = a_S + a_{N-S}$$

with given a_{N-S}.

The assumptions on utility functions and production possibility sets, as expressed by (U1–3) and (T1–3) above, ensure that, for any coalition S, the pattern of consumption vector c^ν, $(\nu \in S)$, and emission a_S of CO_2 that is optimum with respect to coalition S always exists and is uniquely determined for any given a_{N-S}. The pattern of the consumption vector and the emission of CO_2 that is optimum with respect to coalition S and the associated variables may be denoted as follows:

$$c^\nu(S, a_{N-S}),\ x^\nu(S, a_{N-S}),\ a^\nu(S, a_{N-S}), a_S(S, a_{N-S}),\ a(S, a_{N-S}),$$

where

$$\sum_{\nu \in S} c^\nu(S, a_{N-S}) = \sum_{\nu \in S} x^\nu(S, a_{N-S})$$
$$a_S(S, a_{N-S}) = \sum_{\nu \in S} a^\nu(S, a_{N-S})$$
$$a(S, a_{N-S}) = a_S(S, a_{N-S}) + a_{N-S}.$$

The maximum value of the sum of the utilities of the countries in coalition S may also be denoted by $v(S, a_{N-S})$ as follows:

$$v(S, a_{N-S}) = \sum_{\nu \in S} u^\nu(c^\nu(S, a_{N-S}), a(S, a_{N-S})).$$

The given quantity a_{N-S} represents the total quantity of CO_2 emitted by all the countries that do not belong to coalition S:

$$a_{N-S} = \sum_{\nu \in N-S} a^\nu.$$

We suppose that the countries that do not belong to the given coalition S form their own coalition $N - S$ and try to maximize the sum of their utilities

$$\sum_{\nu \in N-S} u^\nu(c^\nu, a),$$

where

$$a = \sum_{\nu \in N-S} a^\nu + a_S$$

with a_S given.

The relevant variables associated with the pattern of consumption vectors and the emission of carbon dioxide that is optimum with respect to coalition $N - S$ may be denoted in nearly the same way as those for coalition S. Then,

$$\sum_{\nu \in N-S} c^\nu(N - S, a_S) = \sum_{\nu \in N-S} x^\nu(N - S, a_S)$$
$$a_{N-S}(N - S, a_S) = \sum_{\nu \in N-S} a^\nu(N - S, a_S)$$
$$a(N - S, a_S) = a_{N-S}(N - S, a_S) + a_S.$$

The value $v(N - S, a_S)$ of coalition $N - S$ is also given by

$$v(N - S, a_S) = \sum_{\nu \in N-S} u^\nu(c^\nu(N - S, a_S), a(N - S, a_S)).$$

Equilibrium of Coalitions

Two coalitions, S and $N - S$, are in equilibrium if the total quantity a_{N-S} of the emission of carbon dioxide by the countries belonging to coalition $N - S$ that the countries belonging to coalition S take as given is exactly equal to the total quantity a_{N-S} of the emission of CO_2 actually emitted by the countries belonging to coalition $N - S$, and vice versa. That is, two coalitions, S and $N - S$, are in equilibrium if the total quantities of the emission of carbon dioxide, a_S and a_{N-S}, satisfy the following equations:

$$a_S = a_S(S, a_{N-S}), \quad a_{N-S} = a_{N-S}(N - S, a_S).$$

The value of coalition S may be defined as the value $v(S, a_{N-S})$ when two coalitions, S and $N - S$, are in equilibrium. It may simply be written as $v(S)$. Then we have

$$v(S) = \sum_{\nu \in S} u^\nu(c^\nu(S), a(S)),$$

where the values of the relevant variables at the equilibrium are written as $c^{\nu}(S), x^{\nu}(S), a^{\nu}(S), a_S(S)$, and $a(S)$. We also have

$$\sum_{\nu \in S} c^{\nu}(S) = \sum_{\nu \in S} x^{\nu}(S)$$
$$a_S(S) = \sum_{\nu \in S} a^{\nu}(S)$$
$$a(S) = a_S(S) + a_{N-S}(S).$$

We can also use similar notation for the complementary coalition $N - S$; that is,

$$c^{\nu}(N-S), x^{\nu}(N-S), a^{\nu}(N-S), a(N-S), v(N-S), \text{ and so on.}$$

It is apparent from the definition of the equilibrium for coalitions S and $N - S$ that

$$a(S) = a(N-S), a_S(S) = a_S(N-S),\ a_{N-S}(N-S) = a_{N-S}(S).$$

These relations have particularly pertinent implications for the nonemptiness of the core of the global warming game.

In following sections, we prove that the equilibrium for any pair of coalitions, S and $N - S$, always exists and is uniquely determined. Hence, the value of coalition S is uniquely determined, and our model of global warming may legitimately be regarded as a cooperative game in game theory. Before we proceed with our game-theoretic approach to global warming, however, it may be advisable to derive certain propositions concerning concave programming that are relevant to the following discussion but not readily available in the standard literature of cooperative games. The detailed proof will be given in mathematical notes at the end of this chapter.

3. PROPOSITIONS CONCERNING CONCAVE PROGRAMMING AND COOPERATIVE GAMES

In the definition of equilibrium for a pair of coalitions in the model of global warming, we consider two concave programming problems, one referring to the coalition S and another to the complementary coalition $N - S$.

MAXIMUM PROBLEM (S). Find the pattern $\{c^\nu, x^\nu, a^\nu(\nu \in S); a_S\}$ that maximizes

$$\sum_{\nu \in S} u^\nu(c^\nu, a)$$

subject to the constraints that

$$\sum_{\nu \in S} c^\nu \leqq \sum_{\nu \in S} x^\nu, \quad (x^\nu, a^\nu) \in T^\nu(\nu \in S)$$

$$a = a_S + a_{N-S}, \quad a_S = \sum_{\nu \in S} a^\nu$$

with a_{N-S} given.

MAXIMUM PROBLEM (N−S). Find the pattern $\{c^\nu, x^\nu, a^\nu(\nu \in N - S); a_{N-S}\}$ that maximizes

$$\sum_{\nu \in N-S} u^\nu(c^\nu, a)$$

subject to the constraints that

$$\sum_{\nu \in N-S} c^\nu \leqq \sum_{\nu \in N-S} x^\nu, \quad (x^\nu, a^\nu) \in T^\nu \quad (\nu \in N - S)$$

$$a = a_S + a_{N-S}, \qquad a_{N-S} = \sum_{\nu \in N-S} a^\nu$$

with a_S given .

The optimum amounts of CO_2 emissions in maximum problems (S) and (N−S) are uniquely determined by the given amounts of the complementary coalitions, a_{N-S} and a_S, respectively, and so we may denote them in the following functional form:

$$a_S = a_S(S, a_{N-S}), \quad a_{N-S} = a_{N-S}(N - S, a_S),$$

which is referred to as the response functions.

Proposition 1. *The response functions* $a_S = a_S(S, a_{N-S}), a_{N-S} = a_{N-S}(N - S, a_S)$ *both satisfy the following inequalities:*

$$-1 < a_S{}'(S, a_{N-S}) < 0, \quad \textit{for all } a_{N-S} > 0$$

$$-1 < a_{N-S}{}'(N - S, a_S) < 0, \quad \textit{for all } a_S > 0.$$

Two coalitions, S and N − S, are in equilibrium if, and only if, the following equations are simultaneously satisfied:

$$a_S = a_S(S, a_{N-S}), \quad a_{N-S} = a_{N-S}(N - S, a_S).$$

Proposition 2. *For any coalition S, the pair of* (a_S, a_{N-S}) *that satisfies equilibrium conditions always exists and is uniquely determined. Hence, for any coalition S, the value* $v(S)$ *always exists and is uniquely determined. They may simply be denoted by* $a_S(S),\ a_{N-S}(N-S)$.

We consider the adjustment process in (a_S, a_{N-S}) defined by the system of differential equations

$$\text{(A)} \qquad \begin{cases} \dot{a}_S = a_S(S, a_{N-S}) - a_S \\ \dot{a}_{N-S} = a_{N-S}(N-S, a_S) - a_{N-S}. \end{cases}$$

Proposition 3. *The adjustment process in* (a_S, a_{N-S}) *defined by the system of differential equations (A) is globally stable. That is, the solution path to the system of differential equations (A) with any initial conditions converges to the equilibrium point* $E = (w^0, z^0)$, *where*

$$w^0 = a_S(S), \quad z^0 = a_{N-S}(N-S) = a_{N-S}(S).$$

Proposition 4. *Let S be any coalition of the global warming game and* $v(S)$ *the value of coalition S. Then,*

$$a(S) \leqq a(N)$$
$$v(S) + v(N-S) \leqq v(N).$$

4. THE CORE OF THE GLOBAL WARMING GAME WITH TRANSFERABLE UTILITY

It may be recalled that an allotment of the total value $v(N)$ of a cooperative game $(N, v(S))$ with transferable utility is said to be in the core if no coalition of players can block that allotment. Formally, we have the following definition.

An allotment of the value $v(N)$ is a vector $x = (x^\nu)$ that satisfies the efficiency conditions

$$\sum_{\nu \in N} x^\nu = v(N). \tag{1}$$

An allotment $x = (x^\nu)$ is in the core if the following conditions are satisfied:

$$\sum_{\nu \in S} x^\nu \geqq v(S), \quad \text{for all coalitions } S \subset N. \tag{2}$$

The nonemptiness of the core for any cooperative game is addressed in a classic theorem attributed to Bondareva and Shapley.

BONDAREVA–SHAPLEY'S THEOREM. Let G be a cooperative game with characteristic function $v(S)$, $(S \subset N)$. The core of the game G is nonempty if, and only if, for any balancing weights (π_S), the following Bondareva–Shapley inequality holds:

$$\sum_S \pi_S \, v(S) \leqq v(N),$$

where Σ_S means the summation over all possible coalitions $S \subset N$.

A set of weights for all possible coalitions, (π_S), is simply any set of nonnegative numbers:

$$\pi_S \geqq 0, \quad \text{for all } S \subset N.$$

A set of weights, (π_S), is described as balancing if

$$\sum_{S \ni \nu} \pi_S = 1, \quad \text{for all } \nu \in N. \tag{3}$$

Bondareva–Shapley's theorem was originally proved by Bondareva (1962, 1963) and was later expounded by Shapley (1967). Further treatment of the Bondareva–Shapley theorem was provided by Aumann (1989), Kannai (1992), and others. The proof of Bondareva–Shapley's theorem will be given in mathematical notes at the end of this chapter.

Nonemptiness of the Core of n-person Cooperative Games with Transferable Utility

Bondareva–Shapley's theorem is generally applied to show the nonemptiness of the core of n-person cooperative games with transferable utility.

We first note the following fundamental inequalities concerning the optimum variables of our global warming game. For the whole coalition N, the value of the coalition and the optimum values of the relevant variables are denoted as introduced in detail in Section 2 by

$$c^\nu(N),\ x^\nu(N),\ a^\nu(N),\ a(N), \theta(N),\ \theta^\nu(N),\ p(N),$$

where the following relations are satisfied:

$$\nu(N) = \sum_{\nu \in N} u^{\nu}(c^{\nu}(N), a(N))$$
$$u^{\nu}_{c^{\nu}}(c^{\nu}(N), a(N)) = p(N), \quad \text{for all } \nu \in N$$
$$\sum_{\nu \in N} c^{\nu}(N) = \sum_{\nu \in N} x^{\nu}(N)$$
$$(x^{\nu}(N), a^{\nu}(N)) \in T^{\nu}, \quad \text{for all } \nu \in N$$
$$p(N)x^{\nu}(N) - \theta(N)a^{\nu}(N) \geqq p(N)x^{\nu} - \theta(N)a^{\nu}, \quad \text{for all } (x^{\nu}, a^{\nu}) \in T^{\nu}$$
$$\theta(N) = \sum_{\nu \in N} \theta^{\nu}(N), \; \theta^{\nu}(N) = -u^{\nu}_{a}(c^{\nu}(N), a(N)).$$

Similar relationships hold for the optimum values of the relevant variables for any coalition S:

$$c^{\nu}(S), x^{\nu}(S), a^{\nu}(S), a(S), v(S),$$

where

$$v(S) = \sum_{\nu \in S} u^{\nu}(c^{\nu}(S), a(S))$$
$$\sum_{\nu \in S} c^{\nu}(S) = \sum_{\nu \in S} x^{\nu}(S)$$
$$a(S) = \sum_{\nu \in N} a^{\nu}(S), (x^{\nu}(S), a^{\nu}(S)) \in T^{\nu}, \quad \text{for all } \nu \in N.$$

Thus,

$$a(S) = a_S(S) + a_{N-S}(S) = \sum_{\nu \in S} a^{\nu}(S) + \sum_{\nu \in N-S} a^{\nu}(S).$$

Because we have assumed that the utility functions $u^{\nu}(c^{\nu}, a)$ are concave with respect to (c^{ν}, a), we have the following fundamental inequalities:

$$\begin{aligned} &u^{\nu}(c^{\nu}(N), a(N)) - u^{\nu}(c^{\nu}(S), a(S)) \\ &\geqq u^{\nu}_{c^{\nu}}(c^{\nu}(N), a(N))(c^{\nu}(N) - c^{\nu}(S)) \\ &\quad + u^{\nu}_{a}(c^{\nu}(N), a(N))(a(N) - a(S), \end{aligned}$$

which imply

$$\begin{aligned} &u^{\nu}(c^{\nu}(N), a(N)) - u^{\nu}(c^{\nu}(S), a(S)) \\ &\geqq p(N)(c^{\nu}(N) - c^{\nu}(S)) - \theta^{\nu}(N)(a(N) - a(S)). \end{aligned} \tag{4}$$

Let (π_S) be any set of balancing weights; that is,

$$\pi_S \geqq 0, \quad \text{for all } S \subset N$$
$$\sum_{S \ni \nu} \pi_S = 1, \quad \text{for all } \nu \in N.$$

We define the new variables as follows:

$$c^\nu = \sum_{S \ni \nu} \pi_S c^\nu(S), \quad x^\nu = \sum_{S \ni \nu} \pi_S x^\nu(S), \quad a^\nu = \sum_{S \ni \nu} \pi_S a^\nu(S).$$

Then, we have

$$\begin{aligned} \sum_{\nu \in N} c^\nu &= \sum_{\nu \in N} \sum_{S \ni \nu} \pi_S c^\nu(S) = \sum_S \pi_S \sum_{\nu \in S} c^\nu(S) \\ &= \sum_S \pi_S \sum_{\nu \in S} x^\nu(S) = \sum_{\nu \in N} \sum_{S \ni \nu} \pi_S x^\nu(S) \\ &= \sum_{\nu \in N} x^\nu, (x^\nu, a^\nu) \in T^\nu, \quad \text{for all } \nu \in N. \end{aligned}$$

Now, both sides of the inequalities in (4) may be multiplied by π_S and summed over $\Sigma_{\nu \in N} \Sigma_{S \ni \nu}$ to obtain that

$$\begin{aligned} &\sum_{\nu \in N} u^\nu(c^\nu(N), a(N)) - \sum_{\nu \in N} \sum_{S\{\nu} \pi_S u^\nu(c^\nu(S), a(S)) \\ &\geqq p(N)\left[\sum_{\nu \in N} c^\nu(N) - \sum_{\nu \in N} c^\nu\right] - \theta(N)a(N) \\ &+ \sum_{\nu \in N} \theta^\nu(N) \sum_{S \ni \nu} \pi_S a(S). \end{aligned}$$

Therefore, we have

$$\begin{aligned} v(N) - \sum_S \pi_S v(S) &\geqq p(N)\left[\sum_{\nu \in N} x^\nu(N) - \sum_{\nu \in N} x^\nu\right] \\ &- \theta(N)a(N) + \sum_{\nu \in N} \theta^\nu(N) \sum_{S \ni \nu} \pi_S a(S). \end{aligned}$$

Let us note that

$$p(N)[x^\nu(N) - x^\nu] - \theta(N)[a^\nu(N) - a^\nu] \geqq 0.$$

Hence, the following inequality holds:

$$v(N) - \sum_S \pi_S v(S) \geqq \sum_S \pi_S[\theta_S(N)a(S) - \theta(N)a_S(S)]. \tag{5}$$

Suppose the following condition is satisfied:

$$\theta_S(N)a(S) = \theta(N)a_S(S), \quad \text{for all } S \subset N. \tag{6}$$

Then (5) implies the Bondareva–Shapley inequality

$$v_S(N) \geqq \sum_S \pi_S v(S) \quad \text{for all balancing weights } (\pi_S).$$

Hence, we have the following.

Proposition 5. *Let $G = (N, v(S))$ be the global warming game with transferable utility. Then the core of game $G = (N, v(S))$ is nonempty if condition (6) is satisfied.*

Condition (6) for the nonemptiness of the core of the global warming game $G = (N, v(S))$ with transferable utility as specified in Proposition 5 is so stringent that it may be satisfied only for an extremely limited class of global warming game. However, it plays an important role in the analysis of the global warming game with non-transferable utility, as is discussed in Section 6 below.

Before continuing this discussion, we examine the way by which the value of coalition is defined in our global warming game with transferable utility.

5. AN ALTERNATIVE DEFINITION OF COOPERATIVE GAME ASSOCIATED WITH GLOBAL WARMING

The discussion of the value of coalition for the global warming game with transferable utility, as developed in the previous sections, assumes the strictly game-theoretic circumstances concerning the outcome of the choice of the strategy for each coalition S and its complementary $N - S$. That is, the countries belonging to coalition S presuppose that the total quantity a of CO_2 emissions involving all countries in the world reflects the quantity a_S of CO_2 emission emitted by the countries of coalition S on the assumption that the emission a_{N-S} of the complementary coalition $N - S$ remains as it is now. Thus, when calculating the value of coalition S,

$$\sum_{\nu \in S} u^\nu(c^\nu, a^{(S)}),$$

it is assumed that

$$a^{(S)} = a_S + a_{N-S}$$

with a_{N-S} given.

Similarly, the value of coalition $N - S$ is given by

$$\sum_{\nu \in N-S} u^\nu(c^\nu, a^{(N-S)}),$$

where

$$a^{(N-S)} = a_{N-S} + a_S$$

with a_S given.

Two coalitions S and $N - S$ are in equilibrium if their respective CO_2 emissions, a_S and a_{N-S}, satisfy the equilibrium conditions

$$a = a_S + a_{N-S}$$

or

$$a = a^{(S)} = a^{(N-S)}.$$

Proposition 2 above states that, for any coalition S, the equilibrium for S and $N - S$ always exists and is uniquely determined. Thus, the global warming game with transferable utility is defined with the value of coalition S being the sum of the utilities of the countries of coalition S at the equilibrium.

In this section, we examine the implications of an alternative definition of the value of coalition for the global warming game with transferable utility. Let us denote by u_S and u_{N-S} the sums of the utilities of the countries in coalitions S and $N - S$, respectively, by

$$u_S = \sum_{\nu \in S} u^\nu(c^\nu, a), \quad u_{N-S} = \sum_{\nu \in N-S} u^\nu(c^\nu, a),$$

where $(c^\nu : \nu \in S, a_S)$ and $(c^\nu : \nu \in N - S, a_{N-S})$ are feasible with respect to coalitions S and $N - S$, respectively, with

$$a = a_S + a_{N-S}.$$

A pair of the utilities (u_S, u_{N-S}) is admissible if there is no pair (u'_S, u'_{N-S}) associated with allocations that are feasible with respect to coalitions S and $N - S$ such that

$$u_S \leqq u'_S, \quad u_{N-S} \leqq u'_{N-S}$$

with strict inequality for either S or $N - S$.

The global warming game may alternatively be conceived if the values of each coalition S and its complementary $N - S$ are defined by

$$v(S) = \sum_S u^\nu(c^\nu, a), \quad v(N - S) = \sum_{N-S} u^\nu(c^\nu, a),$$

for any allocations $(c^\nu : \nu \in S, a_S)$, $(c^\nu : \nu \in N - S, a_{N-S})$ that are admissible with respect to S and $N - S$.

It may easily be seen that if an allotment is in the core of the global warming game under the alternative definition, it is a fortiori in the core of the global warming game under the original definition. The alternative definition of the value of coalition thus defined, however, does not satisfy the standard condition required for the cooperative game with transferable utility, for admissible pairs (u_S, u_{N-S}) are not uniquely defined.

It is apparent, in terms of assumptions (U1–3) and (T1–3), that a pair of feasible allocations, $(c^\nu : \nu \in S, a_S)$ and $(c^\nu : \nu \in N - S, a_{N-S})$, is admissible if, and only if, a pair of positive weights $\beta = (\beta_S, \beta_{N-S}), (\beta_S, \beta_{N-S} > 0)$ exists such that $(c^\nu : \nu \in S, a_S)$ and $(c^\nu : \nu \in N - S, a_{N-S})$ maximize

$$\beta_S \sum_S u^\nu(c^\nu : \nu \in S, a_S) + \beta_{N-S} \sum_{N-S} u^\nu(c^\nu, a)$$

subject to the constrains

$$\sum_S c^\nu \leqq \sum_S x^\nu, \quad (x^\nu, a^\nu) \in T^\nu \quad (\nu \in S)$$

$$a_S = \sum_S a^\nu$$

$$\sum_{N-S} c^\nu \leqq \sum_{N-S} x^\nu, \quad (x^\nu, a^\nu) \in T^\nu \quad (\nu \in N - S)$$

$$a_{N-S} = \sum_{N-S} a^\nu$$

$$a = a_S + a_{N-S}.$$

The values of the relevant variables at the optimum for maximum problem(S), above are uniquely determined, and they may be denoted by

$$c^{\nu}(S, \beta), \; x^{\nu}(S, \beta), \; a^{\nu}(S, \beta), \; a_S(S, \beta), \; a(S, \beta), \text{ and so on.}$$

The values of the sums of the utilities for coalitions S and $N - S$ at the optimum may be denoted by $v(S, \beta)$, $v(N - S, \beta)$.

Then, for any pair $\beta = (\beta_S, \beta_{N-S})$ of positive weights β_S, β_{N-S}, the values thus defined, $v(S, \beta)$ and $v(N - S, \beta)$, are considered, respectively, as values of coalitions S and $N - S$ for the alternative global warming game with transferable utility.

"Balancedness" of Coalitions for the Global Warming Game

Proposition 5 prompts us to introduce the following concept of the "balancedness" of coalitions. A coalition S and its complementary $N - S$ are defined as being balanced if a pair of positive weights $\beta = (\beta_S, \beta_{N-S})$ exist such that

$$a_S(S, \beta) = t_S \, a(S, \beta), \quad a_{N-S}(S, \beta) = t_{N-S} \, a(S, \beta), \tag{7}$$

where

$$t_S = \frac{\theta_S(N)}{\theta(N)}, \; t_{N-S} = \frac{\theta_{N-S}(N)}{\theta(N)}, \; t_S, t_{N-S} > 0, \; t_S + t_{N-S} = 1,$$

and $\theta(N), \theta_S(N), \theta_{N-S}(N)$ are the imputed prices of CO_2 emission at the social optimum, as defined in Section 4 above.

The cooperative game associated with the general model of global warming introduced in this section is balanced if the value $\nu(S)$ of each coalition S is given by

$$v(S) = \sum_{\nu \in S} u^{\nu}(c^{\nu}(S, \beta), a(S, \beta)),$$

where $\beta = (\beta_S, \beta_{N-S})$ is the pair of positive weights with respect to which coalition S and $N - S$ are balanced.

We now have the following theorem, the proof of which will be described in detail in mathematical notes at the end of this chapter.

Theorem 1. *Let G be the cooperative game with transferable utility associated with the general model of global warming, where conditions (U1–3) and (T1–3) are assumed. Then, for any coalition S ($S \subset N$), there exists a pair of positive weights $\beta = (\beta_S, \beta_{N-S})$, $\beta_S, \beta_{N-S} > 0$ with* *respect to which coalition S and its complementary N − S are balanced, and the value v(S) of the cooperative game G is defined as the sum of the utilities of the countries belonging to coalition S when coalition S and its complementary N − S are balanced.*

Then the core of the cooperative game G associated with the general model of global warming is always nonempty.

6. LINDAHL EQUILIBRIUM AND THE CORE OF THE GLOBAL WARMING GAME WITH NONTRANSFERABLE UTILITY

In the previous sections, we have regarded global warming as a cooperative game with transferable utility. In this section, we consider the case in which the global warming game is played with nontransferable utility and examine the structure of the core of such a game.

Before we proceed with our discussion, we review the concept of the cooperative game with nontransferable utility with particular reference to the core of the global warming game as formulated in the previous sections.

Let us consider any given coalition S. Coalition S and its complementary $N-S$ are in equilibrium if allocations $(c^\nu : \nu \in S, a_S^0)$ and $(c_0^\nu : \nu \in N-S, a_{N-S}^0)$ exist that are feasible with respect to coalition S and $N-S$, respectively, and are admissible in the sense defined in Section 5 above; that is, there are no allocations $(c^{\nu\prime} : \nu \in S, a'_S)$ and $(c^{\nu\prime} : \nu \in N-S, a'_{N-S})$ that are feasible with respect to coalition S and $N-S$, respectively, and

$$u^\nu(c^\nu, a') \geqq u^\nu(c_0^\nu, a_0), \quad \text{for all } \nu \in S \quad \text{and} \quad N-S$$

with strict inequity for at least one $\nu \in S$ or $N-S$, where

$$a' = a'_S + a'_{N-S}, \quad a_0 = a_S^0 + a_{N-S}^0.$$

An allocation $(c_0^\nu : \nu \in N, a_0)$ is in the core of the global warming game with nontransferable utility when it is feasible with respect to the whole coalition N and there is no coalition S for which an allocation $(c^{\nu\prime} : \nu \in S, a'_S)$ exists that is feasible with respect to coalition S and

$$u^\nu(c^\nu, a') > u^\nu(c_0^\nu, a_0), \quad \text{for all } \nu \in S$$

with $a' = a'_S + a'_{N-S}$.

A pair of allocations, $(c_0^\nu : \nu \in S, a_S^0)$ and $(c_0^\nu : \nu \in N - S, a_{N-S}^0)$, which are feasible with respect to coalition S and $N - S$, respectively, is admissible for the global warming game with nontransferable utility if, and only if, a vector of positive weights $\alpha = (\alpha^1, \ldots, \alpha^N)$, $(\alpha^\nu > 0$, $\nu = 1, \ldots, N)$ exists such that it is admissible when the global warming game is regarded as a cooperative game with transferable utility where utility functions are given by

$$\alpha^\nu u^\nu(c^\nu, a), \quad (\nu \in N).$$

Hence, a feasible allocation $(c_0^\nu : \nu \in N, a_0)$ is in the core of the global warming game with nontransferable utility if, and only if, a vector of positive weights $\alpha_S = (\alpha_S^\nu)$ exists, assigned to every coalition S, such that

$$\sum_{\nu \in S} \alpha_S^\nu u^\nu(c_0^\nu, a_0) \geqq \sum_{\nu \in S} \alpha_S^\nu u^\nu(c^\nu, a)$$

for all allocations $(c^\nu : \nu \in S, a_S)$ feasible with respect to coalition S.

The discussion carried out in the previous section easily implies the following theorem.

Theorem 2. *For the cooperative game with nontransferable utility associated with the general model of global warming, the core is always nonempty.*

Proof. In view of Theorem 1, for any vector of positive weights $\alpha = (\alpha_1, \ldots, \alpha_n)$, there exists a pair of positive weights $\beta = (\beta_S, \beta_{N-S})$ associated with each coalition S such that coalitions S and $N - S$ are balanced; that is, condition (6) is satisfied. We may simply define

$$\alpha_S^\nu = \beta_S \alpha^\nu, \quad \text{for } \nu \in S$$
$$\alpha_{N-S}^\nu = \beta_{N-S} \alpha^\nu, \quad \text{for } \nu \in N - S. \qquad \text{Q. E. D.}$$

Lindahl Equilibrium Is in the Core of the Global Warming Game with Nontransferable Utility

With regard to n-person cooperative games with nontransferable utility, the concept of Lindahl equilibrium plays a central role when we seek those allotments of the value of the game among individual members that are optimum in a broad sense both from efficiency and equity points of view. In this section, we show that Lindahl equilibrium is always in the core of the global warming game with nontransferable utility. Because the existence of Lindahl equilibrium was established by Mäler and Uzawa (1994), as described in detail in Chapters 1 and 2 for the general model of global warming under the standard neoclassical assumptions on utility functions and production possibility sets, the nonemptiness of the core for our global warming game can be directly shown for the nontransferable case.

The existence of Lindahl equilibrium for the general model of global warming was proved by an analytical apparatus in welfare economics and later extended to a general case in which the economy involving public goods in the Samuelsonian sense is covered. It is based on the classic proposition that any Pareto-optimal allocation may be represented as the optimum allocation for the problem of maximizing the social welfare function of the type

$$\sum_{\nu \in N} \alpha^{\nu} u^{\nu}(c^{\nu}, a) \tag{8}$$

among all feasible allocations, where $\alpha = (\alpha^{\nu})$ is a nonnegative, nonzero vector of weights for individual members.

The optimum allocation $(c^1, \ldots, c^n, a)$ and the relevant variables x^{ν}, a^{ν} are all uniquely determined, as are the values of the Lagrangian unknowns $p = (p_j)$ and θ. They are denoted by $c^{\nu}(\alpha)$, $x^{\nu}(\alpha)$, $a^{\nu}(\alpha)$, $a(\alpha)$, $p(\alpha)$, and $\theta(\alpha)$. The following relations are satisfied:

$$\sum_{\nu \in N} c^{\nu}(\alpha) = \sum_{\nu \in N} x^{\nu}(\alpha)$$

$$a(\alpha) = \sum_{\nu \in N} a^{\nu}(\alpha)$$

$$(x^{\nu}(\alpha), a^{\nu}(\alpha)) \text{ maximizes } p(\alpha)x^{\nu} - \theta(\alpha)a^{\nu}$$

$$\text{over} \quad (x^{\nu}, a^{\nu}) \in T^{\nu}$$

$$\alpha^{\nu} u^{\nu}_{c^{\nu}}(c^{\nu}(\alpha), a(\alpha)) = p(\alpha)$$

$$-\sum_{\nu \in N} \alpha^{\nu} u^{\nu}_{a}(c^{\nu}(\alpha), a(\alpha)) = \theta(\alpha).$$

Then, under the assumptions concerning utility functions and production possibility sets postulated in Section 2, above, it can be shown that there exists a positive vector $\alpha = (\alpha^{\nu})$, $\alpha^{\nu} > 0\,(\nu \in N)$ such that the allocation $(c^1, \ldots, c^n, a)$ that maximizes the social welfare function (8) among all feasible allocations is a Lindahl equilibrium. That is, for each ν, $(c^\nu(\alpha), a(\alpha))$ maximizes the utility function $u^\nu(c^\nu, a^{(\nu)})$ subject to the budget constraint

$$p(\alpha)c^\nu - \theta^\nu(\alpha)a^{(\nu)} = p(\alpha)x^\nu(\alpha) - \theta(\alpha)\, a^\nu(\alpha), \qquad (9)$$

where

$$\theta^\nu(\alpha) = -\alpha^\nu u_a^\nu(c^\nu(\alpha), a(\alpha)) \quad (\nu \in N).$$

Note that

$$\theta(\alpha) = \sum_{\nu \in N} \theta^\nu(\alpha).$$

We now regard our global warming game as a cooperative one with transferable utility, where each country's cardinal utility is represented by $\alpha^\nu u^\nu(c^\nu, a)$. Then, for each coalition $S\,(S \subset N)$, the optimum allocation and the related variables with respect to coalition are denoted in the same manner as in the previous sections:

$$c^\nu(S), x^\nu(S), a^\nu(S), a(S), p(S), \theta(S), \theta^\nu(S).$$

The value $v(S)$ of coalition S is given by

$$v(S) = \sum_{\nu \in S} \alpha^\nu u^\nu(c^\nu(S), a(S)),$$

where

$$\sum_{\nu \in S} c^\nu(S) = \sum_{\nu \in S} x^\nu(S)$$
$$a(S) = \sum_{\nu \in S} a^\nu(S), (x^\nu(S), a^\nu(S)) \in T^\nu.$$

Note that $a(S)$ sums $a^\nu(S)$ over all $\nu \in N$, including those of the countries not in coalition S. In particular, for coalition N, we have

$$v(N) = \sum_{\nu \in N} \alpha^\nu u^\nu(c^\nu(N), a(N))$$
$$\sum_{\nu \in N} c^\nu(N) = \sum_{\nu \in N} x^\nu(N)$$
$$a(N) = \sum_{\nu \in N} a^\nu(N)$$
$$(x^\nu(N), a^\nu(N)) \in T^\nu \quad (\nu \in N).$$

Furthermore, we have

$$\alpha^\nu u^\nu_{c^\nu}(c^\nu(N), a(N)) = p(N) \quad (\nu \in N).$$
$$\theta(N) = \sum_{\nu \in N} \theta^\nu(N), \quad \theta^\nu(N) = -\alpha^\nu u^\nu_a(c^\nu(N), a(N)) \quad (\nu \in N),$$

and the Lindahl relations (9) may be written as

$$p(N)c^\nu(N) - \theta^\nu(N)a(N) = p(N)x^\nu(N) - \theta(N)a^\nu(N) \quad (\nu \in N).$$

Let us note the following inequality:

$$\begin{aligned}
&\alpha^\nu u^\nu(c^\nu(N), a(N)) - \alpha^\nu u^\nu(c^\nu(S), a(S)) \\
&\quad \geqq \alpha^\nu u^\nu_{c^\nu}(c^\nu(N), a(N))(c^\nu(N) - c^\nu(S)) \\
&\qquad + \alpha^\nu u^\nu_a(c^\nu(N), a(N))(a(N) - a(S)) \\
&\quad = p(N)(c^\nu(N) - c^\nu(S)) - \theta^\nu(N)(a(N) - a(S)) \\
&\quad = p(N)(x^\nu(N) - x^\nu(S)) - \theta(N)a^\nu(N) + \theta^\nu(N)a(S) \\
&\quad \geqq \theta^\nu(N)a(S) - \theta(N)a^\nu(S).
\end{aligned}$$

Thus, we obtain

$$\begin{aligned}
&\sum_{\nu \in S} \alpha^\nu u^\nu(c^\nu(N), a(N)) - \sum_{\nu \in S} \alpha^\nu u^\nu(c^\nu(S), a(S)) \\
&\quad \geqq \theta_S(N)a(S) - \theta(N)a_S(S),
\end{aligned} \tag{10}$$

where

$$\theta_S(N) = \sum_{\nu \in S} \theta^\nu(N), \quad a_S(S) = \sum_{\nu \in S} a^\nu(S).$$

We have shown that, for any coalition $S \subset N$, a pair of positive numbers $\beta = (\beta_S, \beta_{N-S})$ exists such that coalitions S and $N - S$ are balanced; that is, when the utilities of the countries in S and $N - S$ are given the weights $(\beta_S \alpha^\nu : \nu \in S)$ and $(\beta_{N-S} \alpha^\nu : \nu \in N - S)$, respectively, then the following conditions are satisfied:

$$\theta_S(N)a(S) = \theta(N)a_S(S), \quad \theta_{N-S}(N)a(S) = \theta(N)a_{N-S}(S), \tag{11}$$

where $a(S), a_S(S), a_{N-S}(S)$ are the values at the situation in which two countries in S and $N - S$ are at equilibrium.

We now substitute into relation (10) the values of the relevant variables at the optimum with respect to coalition S, where the utilities of countries are given the weights $\{\beta_S \alpha^\nu(\nu \in S), \beta_{N-S}\alpha^\nu(\nu \in N-S)\}$; we then obtain the following inequality:

$$\sum_{\nu \in S} \alpha^\nu u^\nu(c^\nu(N), a(N)) \geqq \sum_{\nu \in S} \alpha^\nu u^\nu(c^\nu(S), a(S)), \quad \text{for all } S. \tag{12}$$

Inequality (12) may be used to show that any Lindahl equilibrium $(c^1(N), \ldots, c^n(N), a(N))$ is in the core of the global warming game with nontransferable utility. This is simply shown when we note that, if $(c^1(N), \ldots, c^n(N), a(N))$ were not in the core, then a coalition S would exist such that, for some $(c^\nu(\nu \in S), a)$ that is feasible with respect to coalition S,

$$u^\nu(c^\nu(N), a(N)) < u^\nu(c^\nu, a) \quad \text{for all } \nu \in S,$$

contradicting (12).

We have now established the following theorem.

Theorem 3. *Let G be the global warming game with nontransferable utility, where the neoclassical assumptions concerning utility functions and production possibility sets as specified in Section 2 above are satisfied. Then, Lindahl equilibrium always exists, and the corresponding pattern $(c_0^1, \ldots, c_0^n, a_0)$ of private consumption $c_0^1, \ldots, c_0^n$ and the total amount a_0 of CO_2 emissions are in the core of the global warming game G with nontransferable utility.*

7. CONCLUDING REMARKS

We have established that, if global warming is regarded as a cooperative game with non-transferable utility, Lindahl equilibrium always exists and is in the core of such a game. The existence of the Lindahl equilibrium for the general model of global warming was proved by Mäler and Uzawa (1994), where Brouwer's fixed-point theorem was enlisted to show that a vector of positive weights exists for the levels of the utility indicators of the countries involved for which the social optimum is obtained in an allocation that satisfies the Lindahl conditions. Our global warming game is then regarded as a cooperative game with transferable utility in which the value of each coalition S is defined as the maximum of the sum of the utilities of the countries in coalition S among all feasible allocations with respect to coalition S with the vector of utility weights corresponding to the Lindahl equilibrium.

When defining the value of a coalition S in the global warming game with transferable utility, we have assumed that those countries that do not belong to the given coalition S form their own coalition $N - S$ and try to maximize the sum of the utilities of the countries in $N - S$, where the vector of utility weights corresponding to Lindahl equilibrium is also used for the complementary coalition $N - S$.

The patterns of allocation for coalition S and its complementary $N - S$ are in equilibrium if they are optimum with respect to coalitions S and $N - S$ and, at the same time, the total CO_2 emission stipulated at their respective optima is the same for two coalitions S and $N - S$. The value of coalition S then is defined as the maximized sum of the weighted utilities in coalition S when coalition S and its complementary $N - S$ are in equilibrium.

The uniqueness of the equilibrium for coalitions S and $N - S$ has been much more difficult to prove than originally anticipated, and certain constraint qualifications, in addition to standard neoclassical assumptions concerning utility functions and technological possibility sets, are required to ensure the uniqueness of the value of each coalition.

Having thus established that our global warming game is legitimately regarded as an n-person cooperative game, the question of whether the core is nonempty or not may be addressed. The standard technique in game theory concerning the nonemptiness of the core of an n-person cooperative game is to enlist the powerful Bondareva–Shapley theorem. In the present context of the global warming game, the Bondareva–Shapley inequality can be shown to be valid only under extremely stringent conditions primarily because CO_2 emission is a public good, or rather a public bad, exhibiting the externalities typically associated with Samuelsonian public goods.

An alternative definition of coalition value was then introduced. The core of the global warming game with nontransferable utility under the alternative definition of the value of coalition has been shown to be always nonempty.

When the value of coalition is defined in terms of the vector of utility weights that corresponds to Lindahl equilibrium, it is possible to show the nonemptiness of the core of the global warming game with nontransferable utility without recourse to the Bondareva–Shapley theorem. Indeed, we have proved that the pattern of allocation corresponding to Lindahl equilibrium is in the core. The proof of our main conclusion is simply to show that the sum of the weighted utilities of the countries in a given coalition S evaluated at the social optimum (i.e., the optimum allocation with respect to the coalition consisting of all countries in the world) is not less than the value $v(S)$ of coalition S. The proof critically depends on the Lindahl relations and finding a pair of relative weights for coalitions S and $N - S$ that results in the patterns of the respective optima for two coalitions S and $N - S$ that satisfy the stringent conditions needed to apply the Bondareva–Shapley theorem.

The method we have developed to prove the nonemptiness of the core of the global warming game, both with transferable and nontransferable utility, is general enough to be applied to obtain similar results for the cooperative games associated with the general model of public goods in the Samuelsonian sense, as discussed in detail in Uzawa (1997).

MATHEMATICAL NOTES

1. CONCAVE PROGRAMMING PROBLEMS ASSOCIATED WITH THE GLOBAL WARMING GAME

In the definition of equilibrium for a pair of coalitions in the model of global warming, we have considered two concave programming problems: Maximum Problem (S) and Maximum Problem ($N - S$) referring, respectively, to the coalition S and the complementary coalition $N - S$. To simplify the exposition, we use the standard notation in the theory of concave programming. We denote by $x = (x_j)$ the vector representing all the vectors of consumption goods for the countries in coalition S:

$$x = (c^\nu : \nu \in S).$$

The vector x should not be confused with the x^ν in the main part of this chapter. The sum of the utilities of all countries in coalition S may now be denoted by $f(x, a)$:

$$f(x, a) = \sum_{\nu \in S} u^\nu(c^\nu, a), \quad x = (c^\nu : \nu \in S).$$

For a given vector x, the minimum quantity of CO_2 emissions from all countries in coalition S required to produce goods by the amount x

is denoted by $\phi(x)$:

$$\phi(x) = \min \left\{ a_S = \sum_{\nu \in S} a^\nu : \sum_{\nu \in S} c^\nu \leqq \sum_{\nu \in S} x^\nu, (x^\nu, a^\nu) \in T^\nu(\nu \in S) \right\},$$

where $x = (c^\nu : \nu \in S)$.

Assumptions (T1–3) concerning production possibility sets T^ν imply that such a minimum always exists and the relevant variables are all uniquely determined.

The optimum value of coalition S is obtained as the solution to the following maximum problem:

Maximum Problem (S). Find (x^0, a^0) that maximizes $f(x, a)$ subject to the constraints

$$a = \phi(x) + z, \tag{1}$$

where $z = a_{N-S}$ is given.

Assumptions (U1–3) and (T1–3) imply that $f(x, a)$ is strictly concave with respect to (x, a) and $\phi(x)$ is strictly convex with respect to x. Because both functions $f(x, a)$ and $\phi(x)$ are continuously twice-differentiable in (x, a) and x, the following conditions are satisfied:

(a) $f_a(x, a) < 0$, for all $(x, a) \geqq (0, 0)$;
(b) $\phi_x(x) > 0$, for all $\geqq 0$;
(c) (f_{xx}) is negative definite, for all $x \geqq 0$;
(d) $f_{aa} - f_{ax}(f_{xx})^{-1} f_{xa} < 0$, for all $(x, a) \geqq (0, 0)$;
(e) (ϕ_{xx}) is positive definite, for all $x \geqq 0$.

The additional condition (U4) imposed on utility functions $u^\nu(c^\nu, a)$ may in the present notation system be expressed as

(f) $f_x(f_{xx})^{-1} f_{xa} > 0$, for all $(x, a) \geqq (0, 0)$.

Maximum Problem (S) now is a concave programming problem, and the Kuhn–Tucker theorem may be applied (see, e.g., Arrow et al. 1958). That is, (x^0, a^0) is an optimum solution to maximum problem (S) if, and only if, a nonnegative number λ^0 exists such that $(x^0, a^0; \lambda^0)$ is a nonnegative saddlepoint of the Lagrangian form

$$L(x, a; \lambda) = f(x, a) + \lambda(a - \phi(x) - z).$$

In what follows, we may without loss of generality assume that all relevant variables are positive at the optimum and the Kuhn–Tucker marginality conditions are satisfied with equality. That is,

$$f_x(x, a) = \lambda \phi_x(x) \tag{2}$$

$$f_a(x, a) = -\lambda \tag{3}$$

$$a = \phi(x) + z. \tag{4}$$

It is apparent that the optimum solution (x^0, a^0) for coalition S always exists and is uniquely determined. We now introduce an adjustment process of imputed price λ, which converges to the optimum regardless of the initial value assigned to λ.

Let us first consider the problem of maximizing imputed profit

$$f(x, a) - \lambda \phi(x)$$

with respect to unconstrained $x \geqq 0$.

The optimum x for such an unconstrained maximum problem always exists and is uniquely determined. The optimum x may be written as $x = x(\lambda, a)$. The optimum x is simply characterized by marginality condition (2). By taking differentials of both sides of (2), we obtain

$$(f_{xx} - \lambda \phi_{xx})\, dx = \phi_x\, d\lambda - f_{xa}\, da,$$

which in turn implies

$$dx = A^{-1}\phi_x\, d\lambda - A^{-1} f_{xa}\, da, \tag{5}$$

where

$$A = f_{xx} - \lambda \phi_{xx}.$$

The matrix A is negative definite, and so is the inverse A^{-1}.

Now we consider the total emission of carbon dioxide a that is determined as the level corresponding to the quantity emitted by the countries in coalition S; that is, constraint (1) is satisfied. Taking differentials of both sides of (1), we obtain

$$da = \phi_x\, dx, \tag{6}$$

which, by noting (2) and (5), yields

$$da = \frac{f_x A^{-1} f_x}{\lambda + f_x A^{-1} f_{xa}} \frac{d\lambda}{\lambda}. \tag{7}$$

Hence, we have

$$\frac{da}{d\lambda} < 0. \tag{8}$$

The relation in (8) means that, as the imputed price λ of CO_2 becomes higher, the CO_2 emissions $\phi(x)$ of the countries in coalition S decrease, as does the total CO_2 emission a.

We now define the marginal disutility θ of CO_2 emission by

$$\theta = -f_a(x, a),$$

through which, by taking differentials of both sides and noting (5), (6), and (8), we obtain the following relation:

$$d\theta = \left\{ \frac{-f_x A^{-1} f_x (f_{aa} - f_{ax} A^{-1} f_{xa})}{\lambda + f_x A^{-1} f_{xa}} - f_x A^{-1} f_{xa} \right\} \frac{d\lambda}{\lambda}.$$

Hence,

$$\frac{d\theta}{d\lambda} < 0. \tag{9}$$

The inequality (9) shows the validity of the intuitive observation that an increase in the imputed price λ of CO_2 emissions induces each country to reduce the scale of economic activities, resulting in a decrease in the CO_2 emissions a and the marginal disutility θ of CO_2 emissions.

We next consider the change in the sum $f(x, a)$ of the utilities of the countries in coalition S. We have

$$df = f_x\, dx + f_a\, da = \lambda \phi_x\, dx + f_a\, da,$$

which, together with (6), yields

$$\frac{df}{d\lambda} = (\lambda - \theta)\frac{da}{d\lambda}. \tag{10}$$

Relations (8) and (10) yield the following relations:

$$\frac{df}{d\lambda} \lesseqqgtr 0 \quad \text{according as} \quad \lambda \gtreqqless \theta. \tag{11}$$

As is easily seen from the Kuhn–Tucker marginality conditions, the optimum solution to the maximum problem for coalition S is obtained if, and only if, $\lambda = \theta$.

Stability of the Adjustment Process for the Optimum Solution

The preceding analysis suggests the following adjustment process for imputed price λ:

$$\text{(P)} \qquad \dot{\lambda} = k(\theta - \lambda)$$

with initial condition $\lambda_0 > 0$, where the speed of adjustment is a positive constant k.

STABILITY THEOREM. The adjustment process (P) of imputed price λ of CO_2 emissions is globally stable; that is, for any initial condition λ_0, the solution path $\lambda(t, \lambda_0)$ converges to the optimum level λ_* as t goes to infinity.

The convergence of the adjustment process (P) is monotone with respect to imputed price λ, total CO_2 emission a_S of coalition S, total utility $f = f(x, a)$, and disutility θ of CO_2 emission. In particular, if $\lambda_0 > \lambda_o$, then imputed price $\lambda(t, \lambda_0)$ and total disutility $\theta(t)$ both continue to decrease as t goes to infinity; and both total CO_2 emissions $a_S(t, \lambda_0)$ and total utility $f(t, \lambda_0)$ continue to increase to approach the optimum levels as t goes to infinity.

PROOF. One has only to note relations (8), (9), (10), and (11). Q.E.D.

Our next step is to examine how a change in the total emissions $z = a_{N-S}$ by the complementary coalition $N - S$ affects the optimum solution for coalition S. To see this, we take differentials of both sides of marginality conditions (2) and (3) to obtain the following system of equations:

$$\begin{pmatrix} f_{aa} - f_{ax}A^{-1}f_{xa} & \lambda + f_x A^{-1} f_{xa} \\ -(\lambda + f_x A^{-1} f_{xa}) & f_x A^{-1} f_x \end{pmatrix} \begin{pmatrix} da \\ \dfrac{d\lambda}{\lambda} \end{pmatrix} = \begin{pmatrix} 0 \\ -\lambda dz \end{pmatrix}. \qquad (12)$$

The determinant Δ of the system of equations (12) is

$$\Delta = (f_{aa} - f_{ax}A^{-1}f_{xa})(f_x A^{-1} f_x) + (\lambda + f_x A^{-1} f_{xa})^2 > 0.$$

The system of equations (12) may be solved to yield

$$\frac{da}{dz} = \frac{\lambda(\lambda + f_x A^{-1} f_{xa})}{\Delta}, \quad \frac{d\lambda}{dz} = \frac{-\lambda^2(f_{aa} - f_{ax}A^{-1}f_{xa})}{\Delta}.$$

Hence, we have

$$0 < \frac{da}{dz} < 1, \quad \frac{d\lambda}{dz} > 0. \tag{13}$$

Proposition 1. *Let the response function*

$$a_S = \alpha(a_{N-S})$$

represent the optimum CO_2 emissions a_S for coalition S in response to CO_2 emissions a_{N-S} of the complementary coalition $N - S$; that is

$$\alpha(a_{N-S}) = a_S(S, a_{N-S})$$

in terms of the terminology introduced in the previous section.

Then the following inequality holds:

$$-1 < \alpha'(a_{N-S}) < 0, \quad \textit{for all}\, a_{N-S} > 0. \tag{14}$$

Proof. One has simply to note relations (13) and $a_S = a - z$, $z = a_{N-S}$. Q.E.D.

The preceding discussion may be similarly applied to the complementary coalition $N - S$. In particular, we may introduce the response function

$$a_{N-S} = \beta(a_S),$$

which relates the optimum CO_2 emission for coalition $N - S$ in response to the CO_2 emission a_S of coalition S. That is,

$$\beta(a_S) = a_{N-S}(S, a_S).$$

Then, in view of Proposition 1, we have

$$-1 < \beta'(a_S) < 0, \quad \text{for all}\, a_S > 0. \tag{15}$$

Two coalitions, S and $N - S$, are in equilibrium if, and only if,

$$a_S = \alpha(a_{N-S}), \quad a_{N-S} = \beta(a_S), \tag{16}$$

where a_S and a_{N-S} are, respectively, the quantities of CO_2 emissions of coalitions S and $N - S$.

Proposition 2. *For any coalition S, the pair of* (a_S, a_{N-S}) *that satisfies equilibrium conditions always exists and is uniquely determined. Accordingly, the value* $v(S)$ *always exists and is uniquely determined for any coalition S.*

PROOF. To simplify the exposition, let us introduce the following notation:

$$w = a_S, \quad z = a_{N-S}.$$

Then equilibrium conditions (16) are written as

$$w = \alpha(z), \quad z = \beta(w),$$

where, in view of (14) and (15), functions $\alpha(z)$ and $\beta(w)$ satisfy the following conditions:

$$-1 < \alpha'(z), \quad \beta'(w) < 0, \quad \text{for all } z, w > 0. \tag{17}$$

Because both functions $\alpha(z)$ and $\beta(w)$ are continuous, relations (17) imply the unique existence of (w^0, z^0) for which equilibrium conditions (16) are satisfied. The unique determination of (w^0, z^0) is illustrated in Figure 7.1, where the abscissa measures $w = a_S$ and the ordinate $z = a_{N-S}$. The two curves $\alpha(z)$ and $\beta(w)$ always have a unique intersection $E = (w^0, z^0)$. Q. E. D.

It is possible to introduce an adjustment process with respect to $w = a_S$ and $z = a_{N-S}$ that is globally stable and always converges to the equilibrium pair (w^0, z^0). We define

$$\text{(A)} \qquad \begin{cases} \dot{w} = \alpha(z) - w \\ \dot{z} = \beta(w) - z \end{cases}$$

with initial condition $(w_0, z_0) > (0, 0)$.

The matrix ∇ of partial derivatives of the right-hand sides of the pair of differential equations (A) is given by

$$\nabla = \begin{pmatrix} -1 & \alpha'(z) \\ \beta'(w) & -1 \end{pmatrix}$$

$$\text{Tr}(\nabla) = -2 < 0, \quad 0 < \text{Det}(\nabla) = 1 - \alpha'(z)\beta'(w) < 1.$$

Hence, the characteristic roots of ∇ are both real and negative.

The solution paths for the system of differential equations (A) are illustrated by the arrowed curves in Figure 7.1, indicating that they

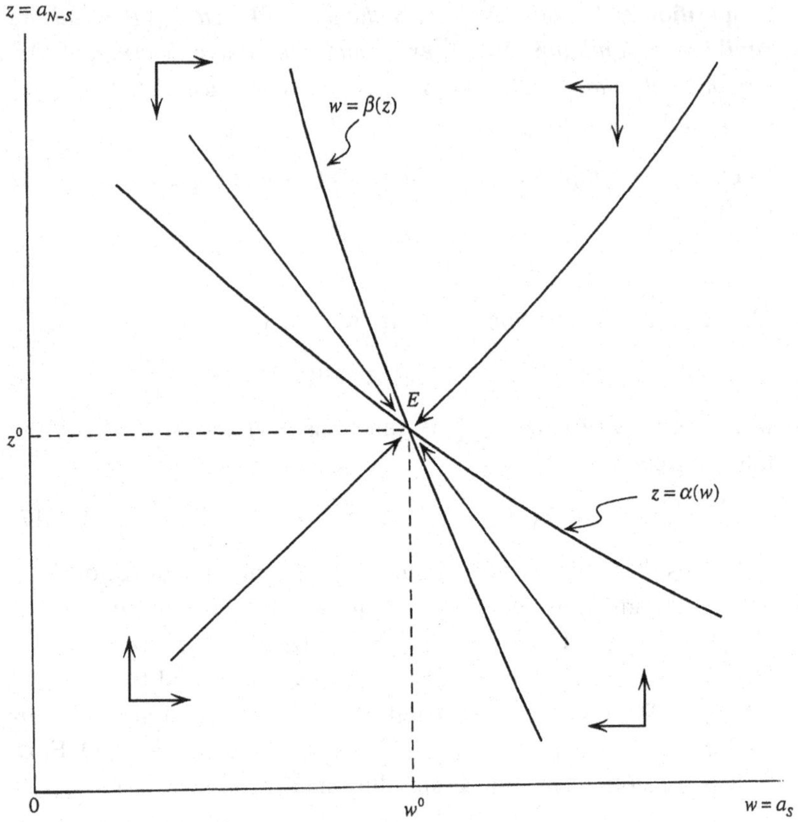

Figure 7.1. Determination of the Value of Coalition

converge to the equilibrium point $E = (w^0, z^0)$ regardless of the initial condition.

The preceding discussion may be summarized as the following proposition.

Proposition 3. *Let us consider the given coalition S and the complementary coalition $N - S$, and let $\alpha(z)$ and $\beta(w)$ be the optimum response functions, as defined in Proposition 2.*

Then the adjustment process in (a_S, a_{N-S}) as defined in terms of the system of differential equations

$$(A) \qquad \begin{cases} \dot{a}_S = a_S(S, a_{N-S}) - a_S \\ \dot{a}_{N-S} = a_{N-S}(N - S, a_S) - a_{N-S} \end{cases}$$

is globally stable.

The solution paths to the system of differential equations (A) with any initial conditions converge to the equilibrium point $E = (w^0, z^0)$, where

$$w^0 = a_S(S), \quad z^0 = a_{N-S}(N - S) = a_{N-S}(S).$$

2. FUNDAMENTAL PROPOSITIONS FOR COOPERATIVE GAMES

We are now in a position to derive a certain fundamental proposition concerning cooperative games that plays a crucial role in our game-theoretical approach to global warming.

We have formulated the processes of response taken by coalition S by the following concave programming problem:

(S) Find (x^0, a^0) that maximizes $f(x, a)$ subject to the constraint

$$a = \phi(x) + z,$$

where $z = a_{N-S}$ is given.

Let us recall that

$$f(x, a) = \sum_{\nu \in S} u^\nu(c^\nu, a), \quad x = (c^\nu : \nu \in S)$$

$$\phi(x) = \sum_{\nu \in S} a^\nu$$

$$\sum_{\nu \in S} c^\nu \leq \sum_{\nu \in S} x^\nu, \quad (x^\nu, a^\nu) \in T^\nu(\nu \in S).$$

The optimum solution to (S) always exists and is uniquely determined. The maximum value of $f(x^0, a^0)$ and the relevant variables at the optimum may be expressed in terms of the terminology of the global warming game, as introduced in Section 2, above; that is,

$$f(x^0, a^0) = v(S, a_{N-S})$$

$$\phi(x^0) = a_S(S, a_{N-S}) = \sum_{\nu \in S} a^\nu(S, a_{N-S})$$

$$a^0 = a_S(S, a_{N-S}) = \sum_{\nu \in S} a_S(S, a_{N-S}) + a_{N-S}.$$

A similar formulation may be made for the complementary coalition $N - S$. The processes of the optimum response taken by coalition $N - S$ may be formulated as the following concave programming problem:

(N – S) Find (y^0, a^0) that maximizes $g(y, a)$ subject to the constraints

$$a = \psi(y) + w,$$

where $w = a_S$ is given.

The relevant variables and functions are defined as follows:

$$g(y, a) = \sum_{\nu \in N-S} u^\nu(c^\nu, a), \quad y = (c^\nu; \nu \in N-S)$$

$$\psi(y) = \sum_{\nu \in N-S} a^\nu$$

$$\sum_{\nu \in N-S} c^\nu \leqq \sum_{\nu \in N-S} x^\nu, \quad (x^\nu, a^\nu) \in T^\nu \quad (\nu \in N-S).$$

The optimum solution to $(N-S)$ always exists and is uniquely determined. Note that, although the same notation a^0 is used for the optimum level of the total CO_2 emission both in (S) and $(N-S)$, the optimum value of a^0 in (S) may not coincide with the optimum value of a^0 in $(N-S)$. They coincide if, and only if, (a_S, a_{N-S}) is in equilibrium, where the maximum values of $f(x^0, a^0)$ and $g(y^0, a^0)$, respectively, correspond to the values of coalitions (S) and $(N-S)$; that is,

$$f(x^0, a^0) = v(S) = v_S(S, a_{N-S})$$

$$g(y^0, a^0) = v(N-S) = v_{N-S}(N-S, a_S)$$

$$a^0 = a(S) = a(N-S) = \sum_{\nu \in S} a^\nu(S) + \sum_{\nu \in N-S} a^\nu(N-S).$$

Let us now consider the coalition N. The maximum problem for coalition N is given by the following:

(N) Find $(\bar{x}, \bar{y}, \bar{a})$ that maximizes

$$f(x, a) + g(y, a)$$

subject to the constraint

$$a = \phi(x) + \psi(y).$$

The uniquely determined optimum solution $(\bar{x}, \bar{y}, \bar{a})$ may be written as

$$\bar{x} = x(N), \quad \bar{y} = x(N), \quad \bar{a} = x(N).$$

Recall that a positive imputed price $\bar{\lambda} = \lambda(N)$ exists such that

$(\overline{x}, \overline{y}, \overline{a}; \overline{\lambda})$ is a nonnegative saddlepoint of the Lagrangian form

$$L(x, y, a; \lambda) = f(x, a) + g(y, a) + \lambda(a - \phi(x) - \psi(y)).$$

The familiar Kuhn–Tucker conditions are expressed by the following marginality conditions:

$$f_x(\overline{x}, \overline{a}) = \overline{\lambda}\phi_x(\overline{x})$$
$$g_y(\overline{y}, \overline{a}) = \overline{\lambda}\psi_y(\overline{y})$$
$$-f_a(\overline{x}, \overline{a}) - g_a(\overline{y}, \overline{a}) = \overline{\lambda}$$
$$\overline{a} = \phi(\overline{x}) + \psi(\overline{y}).$$

The optimum solution $(\overline{x}, \overline{y}, \overline{a})$ to (N) and the associated imputed price $\overline{\lambda}$ satisfy

$$-f_a(\overline{x}, \overline{a}) < \overline{\lambda}. \tag{18}$$

This inequality means the following:

Whereas the marginal disutility of CO_2 emissions for the optimum problem involving the whole coalition (N) is nothing but the marginal social costs of CO_2,

$$\overline{\theta} = -f_a(\overline{x}, \overline{a}) - g_a(\overline{y}, \overline{a}),$$

the marginal disutility of CO_2 emission for coalition S is only part of $\overline{\theta}$, consisting of the sum of marginal disutilities of the countries in coalition S. Therefore, at the optimum for (N), the imputed price $\overline{\lambda}$, being equal to the marginal social costs of CO_2 emissions, is larger than the marginal disutility of CO_2 emissions for coalition S as expressed by θ_S:

$$\theta_S = -f_a(x, a). \tag{19}$$

We consider the adjustment process for the optimum problem (S) introduced in the stability theorem, presented earlier by

$$\text{(B)} \qquad \dot{\lambda}_S = k(\theta_S - \lambda_S),$$

where θ_S is the marginal disutility of CO_2 emission for coalitions S, as defined by (19), with the initial condition at the optimum level $\overline{\lambda}$ for (N).

Inequality (18) simply means that

$$\theta_S - \lambda_S < 0$$

at the initial condition $\overline{\lambda}$. Hence, in view of the stability theorem, the solution path $\lambda_S(t, \overline{\lambda})$ converges to the equilibrium value λ_S^0 for the dynamic process (B). We can also see from the stability theorem that $a_S(t, \overline{\lambda}) = \phi(x(t; \overline{\lambda}))$ converges to the equilibrium value a_S^0 to be given by

$$a_S^0 = a_S(S, \overline{a}_{N-S}),$$

where $\overline{a}_{N-S} = \psi(\overline{y}) = a_{N-S}(N)$.

The argument we have just presented may summarized in the following proposition.

Proposition 4. *Let S be any coalition of the global warming game and $v(S)$ the value of coalition S. Then,*

$$a(S) \geqq a(N)$$
$$v(S) + v(N - S) \leqq v(N).$$

3. PROOF OF BONDAREVA–SHAPLEY'S THEOREM

A set of weights for all possible coalitions (π_S) is simply any set of nonnegative numbers:

$$\pi_S \geqq 0, \quad \text{for all } S \subset N.$$

A set of weights (π_S) is balanced if

$$\sum_{S \ni \nu} \pi_S = 1, \quad \text{for all } \nu \in N.$$

If an allotment $x = (x^\nu)$ exists in the core, then conditions (1) and (2) in the main part of this chapter, are satisfied. For any balancing weights (π_S), we multiply both sides of (3) by π_S and sum over all S to obtain

$$\sum_S \pi_S v(S) \leqq \sum_S \pi_S \sum_{\nu \in S} x^\nu = \sum_{\nu \in N} \sum_{S\{\nu} \pi_S x^\nu = \sum_{\nu \in N} x^\nu = v(N),$$

thus proving the necessity part of the Bodareva–Shapley theorem.

To prove the sufficiency part of the Bondareva–Shapley theorem, let us make the following observation. The relationships between the concept of balancing weights and the definition of the core are easily seen if we consider the following linear programming problem (I) and its dual (II).

(I) Find $x = (x^\nu)$ that minimizes

$$\sum_{\nu \in N} x^\nu$$

subject to the constraints

$$\sum_{\nu \in N} \Lambda_S(\nu) x^\nu \geqq v(S), \quad \text{for all } S \subset N,$$

where $\Lambda_S(\nu) = 1$, if $\nu \in S$, and $\Lambda_S(\nu) = 0$, otherwise.

(II) Find $y = (y_S)$ that maximizes

$$\sum_S v(S) y_S$$

subject to the constraints

$$\sum_S \Lambda_S(\nu) y_S = 1, \quad \text{for all } \nu \in N$$

$$y_S \geqq 0, \quad \text{for all } S \subset N.$$

The duality theorem on linear programming ensures that the two linear programming problems (I) and (II) have the same value.

In view of the assumed conditions for any balancing weights, we know that the value of (II) is equal to $v(N)$. Hence, (I) also has the value $v(N)$, which implies the existence of $x = (x^\nu)$ such that the system of inequalities in (I) is satisfied, and

$$\sum_{\nu \in N} x^\nu = v(N).$$

Such an $x = (x^\nu)$ clearly belongs to the core of the game G. The Bondareva–Shapley theorem has thus been proved. Q. E. D.

4. PROOF OF THEOREM 1

We first show that any coalition S and its complementary $N - S$ are balanced, and the pair of positive numbers $\beta = (\beta_S, \beta_{N-S})$ at which coalitions S and $N - S$ are balanced is uniquely determined. To see this, let us first examine the structure of the optimum solution to maximum problem (S).

In view of assumptions (U1–3) and (T1–3), maximum problem (S) may be reduced to finding nonnegative saddlepoints of the Lagrangian:

$$\left[\beta_S \sum_S u^\nu(c^\nu, a) + \beta_{N-S} \sum_{N-S} u^\nu(c^\nu, a)\right] + \beta_S p_S \sum_S (x^\nu - c^\nu) + \beta_{N-S} p_{N-S} \sum_{N-S} (x^\nu - c^\nu) + q(a - a_S - a_{N-S}). \tag{20}$$

Finding nonnegative saddlepoints of Lagrangian (20) may in turn be reduced to solving the following two systems of equations:

$$u^\nu_{c^\nu} = p_S, \quad (\nu \in S) \tag{21}$$

$$\sum_S (x^\nu - c^\nu) = 0 \tag{22}$$

$$x^\nu = x^\nu(p_S, q_S), \quad a^\nu = a^\nu(p_S, q_S) \quad (\nu \in S) \tag{23}$$

$$a_S = \sum_S a^\nu \tag{24}$$

and similar equations for complementary coalition $N - S$, where

$$a = a_S + a_{N-S} \tag{25}$$

$$q_S = \frac{1}{\beta_S} q, \quad q_{N-S} = \frac{1}{\beta_{N-S}} q \tag{26}$$

$$q = -\beta_S \sum_S u^\nu_a - \beta_{N-S} \sum_{N-S} u^\nu_a. \tag{27}$$

We take differentials of both sides of Equations (21)–(24) to obtain the following system of liner equations:

$$dc^\nu = \left(u^\nu_{c^\nu c^\nu}\right)^{-1} (dp_S - u^\nu_{c^\nu a} da) \quad (\nu \in S) \tag{28}$$

$$\sum_S (dx^\nu - dc^\nu) = 0 \tag{29}$$

$$dx^\nu = x^\nu_p dp_S + x^\nu_q dq_S, \quad da^\nu = a^\nu_p dp_S + a^\nu_q dq_S \ (\nu \in S) \tag{30}$$

$$da_S - \sum_S da^\nu = 0. \tag{31}$$

Equations (28)–(31), when rearranged, may be written in the following matrix form:

$$\begin{pmatrix} A_S & 0 \\ b'_S & 1 \end{pmatrix} \begin{pmatrix} dq_S \\ da_S \end{pmatrix} = \begin{pmatrix} -b_S & -f_S \\ c_S & 0 \end{pmatrix} \begin{pmatrix} dq_S \\ da \end{pmatrix}, \tag{32}$$

where

$$A_S = \sum_S \left[x_p^\nu - (u_{c^\nu c^\nu}^\nu)^{-1}\right], \quad b_S = \sum_S x_p^\nu, \quad b_S' = -\sum_S a_p^\nu$$

$$f_S = \sum_S \left(u_{c^\nu c^\nu}^\nu\right)^{-1} u_{c^\nu a}^\nu, \quad c_S = \sum_S a_q^\nu.$$

Recall that $\begin{pmatrix} x_p^\nu & x_q^\nu \\ -a_p^\nu & -a_q^\nu \end{pmatrix}$ is symmetrical and positive definite. Hence, A_S is positive definite, and

$$R_S = -c_S - b_S' A_S^{-1} b_S > 0.$$

We multiply both sides of (32) by

$$\begin{pmatrix} A_S & 0 \\ b_S' & 1 \end{pmatrix}^{-1} = \begin{pmatrix} A_S^{-1} & 0 \\ -b_S' A_S^{-1} & 1 \end{pmatrix}$$

to obtain

$$\begin{pmatrix} dp_S \\ da_S \end{pmatrix} = \begin{pmatrix} -A_S^{-1} b_S & -A_S^{-1} f_S \\ -R_S & \nu_S \end{pmatrix} \begin{pmatrix} dq_S \\ da \end{pmatrix}, \tag{33}$$

where it may be assumed that

$$\nu_S = b_S' A_S^{-1} f_S < 0.$$

Hence,

$$da_S = -R_S dq_S + \nu_S da, \tag{34}$$

and similar relation holds for the relevant variables with respect to complementary coalition $N - S$.

Differentiating both sides of relations (26), we obtain

$$dq_S = \frac{1}{\beta_S} dq - q_S \frac{d\beta_S}{\beta_S}, \tag{35}$$

and similarly for coalition $N - S$.

Substituting (35) into (34), we obtain

$$da_S = -\frac{R_S}{\beta_S} dq + \nu_S da + R_S q_S \frac{d\beta_S}{\beta_S}, \tag{36}$$

and similarly for coalition $N - S$.

Differentiating both sides of (25) and substituting into (36), we obtain

$$\left(\frac{R_S}{\beta_S} + \frac{R_{N-S}}{\beta_{N-S}}\right) dq + (1 - \nu_S - \nu_{N-S})da$$
$$= R_S q_S \frac{d\beta_S}{\beta_S} + R_{N-S} q_{N-S} \frac{d\beta_{N-S}}{\beta_{N-S}}. \tag{37}$$

On the other hand, let us define marginal costs of CO_2 emissions with respect to coalition S by

$$\theta_S = -\sum_S u_a^\nu \tag{38}$$

and by θ_{N-S} for coalition $N - S$.

Differentiating both sides of (38) and substituting (28), we obtain,

$$d\theta_S = -\sum_S u_{ac^\nu}^\nu \left(u_{c^\nu c^\nu}^\nu\right)^{-1} dp_S - \sum_S \left\{u_{aa}^\nu - u_{ac^\nu}^\nu \left(u_{c^\nu c^\nu}^\nu\right)^{-1} u_{c^\nu a}^\nu\right\} da,$$

which may be written in matrix form

$$d\theta_S = -f'_S dp_S - e_S da, \tag{39}$$

where

$$e_S = \sum_S \left[u_{aa}^\nu - u_{ac^\nu}^\nu \left(u_{c^\nu c^\nu}^\nu\right)^{-1} u_{c^\nu a}^\nu\right].$$

The matrix

$$\begin{pmatrix} u_{c^\nu c^\nu}^\nu & u_{c^\nu a^\nu}^\nu \\ u_{ac^\nu}^\nu & u_{aa}^\nu \end{pmatrix}$$

is negative definite; therefore, we have

$$e_S = \sum_S \left\{u_{aa}^\nu - u_{ac^\nu}^\nu \left(u_{c^\nu c^\nu}^\nu\right)^{-1} u_{c^\nu a}^\nu\right\} < 0.$$

Substituting (33) into (39), we obtain

$$d\theta_S = -f'_S A_S^{-1} b_S dq_S + \left(f'_S A_S^{-1} f_S - e_S\right) da,$$

which may be written as

$$d\theta_S = \nu_S\, dq_S + \Delta_S\, da, \tag{40}$$

where

$$\Delta_S = f'_S a_S^{-1} f_S - e_S > 0.$$

Substituting (35) into (40), we obtain

$$d\theta_S = \frac{1}{\beta_S} \nu_S dq + \Delta_S \, da - \nu_S q_S \frac{d\beta_S}{\beta_S} \tag{41}$$

and similarly for marginal private costs for coalition $N - S$.

Marginal social costs θ of CO_2 emission are defined by

$$\theta = \beta_S \theta_S + \beta_{N-S} \theta_{N-S}. \tag{42}$$

We differentiate both sides of (42) and take note of (41) to obtain

$$\begin{aligned} d\theta &= (\nu_S + \nu_{N-S}) dq + (\beta_S \Delta_S + \beta_{N-S} \Delta_{N-S}) \, da \\ &\quad + (\beta_S \theta_S - \nu_S q) \frac{d\beta_S}{\beta_S} + (\beta_{N-S} \theta_{N-S} - \nu_{N-S} q) \frac{d\beta_{N-S}}{\beta_{N-S}}. \end{aligned} \tag{43}$$

The relation (27) may be written as

$$q = \theta = \beta_S \theta_S + \beta_{N-S} \theta_{N-S},$$

both sides of which may be differentiated and substituted by (43) to obtain

$$\begin{aligned} &-(\beta_S \Delta_S + \beta_{N-S} \Delta_{N-S}) \, da + (1 - \nu_S - \nu_{N-S}) \, dq \\ &\quad = (\beta_S \theta_S - \nu_S q) \frac{d\beta_S}{\beta_S} + (\beta_{N-S} \theta_{N-S} - \nu_{N-S} q) \frac{d\beta_{N-S}}{\beta_{N-S}}. \end{aligned} \tag{44}$$

Equations (37) and (44) may be written in matrix form as follows:

$$\begin{pmatrix} -\Delta & \gamma \\ \gamma & R \end{pmatrix} \begin{pmatrix} da \\ dq \end{pmatrix} = \begin{pmatrix} \beta_S \theta_S - \nu_S q & \beta_{N-S} \theta_{N-S} - \nu_{N-S} q \\ \dfrac{R_S}{\beta_S} q & \dfrac{R_{N-S}}{\beta_{N-S}} q \end{pmatrix} \begin{pmatrix} \dfrac{d\beta_S}{\beta_S} \\ \dfrac{d\beta_{N-S}}{\beta_{N-S}} \end{pmatrix} \tag{45}$$

$$\begin{aligned} \Delta &= \beta_S \Delta_S + \beta_{N-S} \Delta_{N-S} > 0 \\ R &= \frac{R_S}{\beta_S} + \frac{R_{N-S}}{\beta_{N-S}} > 0 \\ \gamma &= 1 - \nu_S - \nu_{N-S} > 0. \end{aligned}$$

The determinant of the system (45) of linear equations is given by

$$\begin{vmatrix} -\Delta & \gamma \\ \gamma & R \end{vmatrix} = -\Delta R - \gamma^2 < 0.$$

Hence, total quantity a of CO_2 emission and imputed price q of CO_2 emissions are uniquely determined for any given pair of positive weights $\beta = (\beta_S, \beta_{N-S})$.

We define

$$\tau_S(\beta) = \frac{a_S(S, \beta)}{a(S, \beta)}, \quad \tau_{N-S}(\beta) = \frac{a_{N-S}(S, \beta)}{a(S, \beta)}, \quad \beta = (\beta_S, \beta_{N-S}).$$

Then,

$$\tau_S(\beta) + \tau_{N-S}(\beta) = 1, \quad \tau(\beta),\ \tau_{N-S}(\beta) > 0.$$

Theorem 1 will be proved if we can show that, for any given pair of positive numbers (t_S, t_{N-S}) such that

$$t_S + t_{N-S} = 1, \quad t_S, t_{N-S} > 0$$

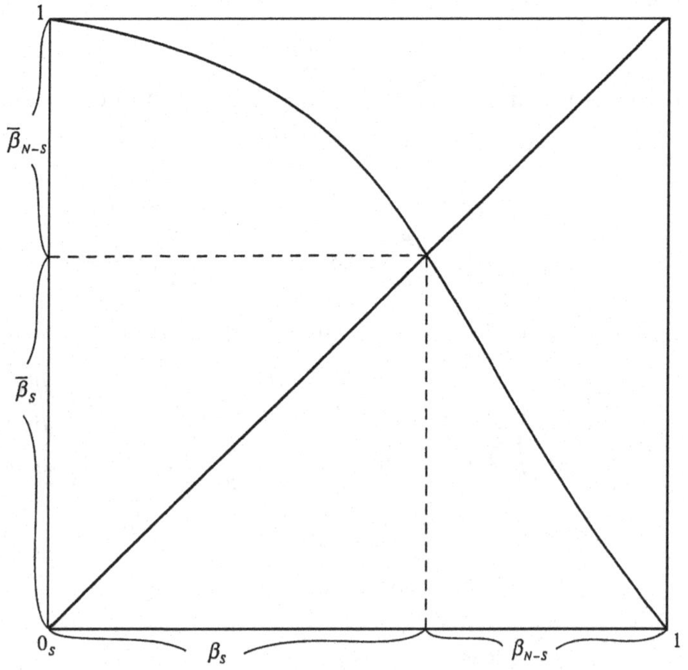

Figure 7.2. Determination of Weights (β_S, β_{N-S}) for Coalitions S, $N - S$

there exists a $\beta = (\beta_S,\ \beta_{N-S})$ that satisfies

$$\tau_S(\beta) = t_S, \quad \tau_{N-S}(\beta) = t_{N-S}. \tag{46}$$

To obtain the existence of a β satisfying (46), let us first note that, for any given $\beta^0_{N-S} > 0$,

$$\lim_{\beta_S \to 0} \tau_S\left(\beta_S, \beta^0_{N-S}\right) = 0, \quad \lim_{\beta_S \to +\infty} \tau_S(\beta_S, \beta^0_{N-S}) = 1.$$

Because $\tau(\beta_S, \beta^0_{N-S})$ is a continuous function of β_S, a β^0_S exists such that

$$\tau_S\left(\beta^0_S, \beta^0_{N-S}\right) = t_S,$$

and a fortiori

$$\tau_{N-S}\left(\beta^0_S, \beta^0_{N-S}\right) = t_{N-S}.$$

Thus, as is easily seen from Figure 7.2, for any coalition S, a pair of positive weights $\beta = (\beta_S, \beta_{N-S})$ exists such that coalition S and its complementary $N - S$ are balanced. Theorem 1 has thus been proved. Q. E. D.

Summary and Concluding Notes

STATIC ANALYSIS OF GLOBAL WARMING

In the static context with which Chapters 1, 2, and 3 are concerned, we have postulated that the welfare effect of global warming is measured in relation to the total quantity of CO_2 emitted annually into the atmosphere, where the dependency on the stock of CO_2 accumulated in the atmosphere is not explicitly brought out. Each greenhouse gas is so measured as to equate the greenhouse effect with the activity of carbon dioxide, and our model is formulated so that carbon dioxide is the only chemical agent that has a greenhouse effect. The behavior of individual countries is expressed in the aggregate by two representative economic agents: the consumers who are concerned with the choice of economic activities related to consumption and the producers who are in charge of the choice of technologies and scale of productive activities.

The economic welfare of each country ν is represented by the utility function

$$u^{\nu} = u^{\nu}(c^{\nu}, a),$$

where c^{ν} is the vector of goods consumed in country ν and a is the aggregate of CO_2 emissions a^{ν} of individual countries ν in the world:

$$a = \sum_{\nu} a^{\nu}.$$

For each country ν, marginal rates of substitution between any pair of consumption goods are diminishing, the utility function is homogeneous of order 1 with respect to the vector of goods consumed in country ν and it is strongly separable with respect to consumption vector c^ν and total CO_2 emissions a; hence,

$$u^\nu(c^\nu, a) = \varphi^\nu(a)u^\nu(c^\nu),$$

where $\varphi^\nu(a)$ is the impact index of global warming that expresses the extent to which the people of country ν are adversely affected by global warming. The higher the total CO_2 emissions a, the lower is the impact index of global warming $\varphi^\nu(a)$. The impact coefficient $\tau^\nu(a)$ of global warming is the relative rate of the marginal change in the impact index due to the marginal increase in the atmospheric emission of CO_2:

$$\tau^\nu(a) = -\frac{\varphi^{\nu\prime}(a)}{\varphi^\nu(a)}.$$

We have assumed that the impact coefficient of global warming $\tau^\nu(a)$ is identical for all countries, that is,

$$\tau^\nu(a) = \tau(a).$$

The conditions concerning the production of goods in each country ν are specified by the production possibility set T^ν that summarizes the technological possibilities and organizational arrangements for country ν with the endowments of factors of production available in country ν given. Marginal rates of substitution between the production of goods x^ν and CO_2 emissions a^ν in each country ν are smooth and diminishing, trade-offs always exist between the production of goods and CO_2 emissions, and the conditions of constant returns to scale prevail.

Deferential equilibrium is obtained if, when each country decides the levels of production activities, it takes into account the negative impact upon its own utility level brought about by its CO_2 emissions. The concept of deferential equilibrium precisely corresponds to that of the Nash solution in game theory.

Proposition. *Deferential equilibrium precisely coincides with the standard market equilibrium under proportional carbon taxes, when, in each country ν, carbon taxes are levied where the tax rate θ^ν is proportional to national income y^ν, with the impact coefficient of global warming $\tau(a)$*

as the coefficient of proportion

$$\theta^\nu = \tau(a) y^\nu.$$

Proposition. *Consider the uniform carbon tax scheme with the same rate θ for all countries in the world, where the tax rate θ is proportional to the aggregate national income y of the whole world with the impact coefficient of global warming $\tau(a)$ as the coefficient of proportion:*

$$\theta = \tau(a) y.$$

Then market equilibrium obtained under such a uniform carbon tax scheme is a social optimum in the sense that there exists a set of positive weights for the utilities of individual countries $(\alpha^1, \ldots, \alpha^n)$, $[\alpha^\nu > 0]$ such that the world utility

$$W = \sum_\nu \alpha^\nu \varphi^\nu(a) u^\nu(c^\nu)$$

is maximized among all feasible patterns of allocation.

Social optimum necessarily implies the existence of the uniform carbon tax scheme with the universal rate $\theta = \tau(a)y$. However, the balance-of-payments conditions are generally not satisfied. When a social optimum satisfies the balance-of-payments conditions, then it coincides with the market equilibrium under the uniform carbon tax scheme. The existence of such a social optimum is guaranteed by the following proposition.

Proposition. *There always exists a set of positive weights for the utilities of individual countries $(\alpha^1, \ldots, \alpha^n)$, $[\alpha^\nu > 0]$ such that the social optimum with respect to the world utility*

$$W = \sum_\nu \alpha^\nu \varphi(a) u^\nu(c^\nu)$$

satisfies the balance-of-payments conditions

$$pc^\nu = px^\nu,$$

and, accordingly, the corresponding pattern of allocation, in conjunction with prices of goods p and the uniform carbon tax scheme with the rate $\theta = \tau(a)y$ constitutes a market equilibrium.

In the context of global warming, the concept of Lindahl equilibrium corresponds to the situation in which, in each country ν, the present level a of total CO_2 emissions is exactly equal to the level that would be chosen by each country ν when it would be free to choose the level that is most desirable on the assumption that the price it would be paid would be equal to its own marginal disutility. The existence of Lindahl equilibrium is always assured.

Markets for Tradable Emission Permits

Let us suppose that there is an international market in which permits to emit CO_2 are freely traded between the countries involved. We denote by b^ν the amount of emission permits initially allotted to each country ν and by b the total amount of emission permits initially allotted to all countries:

$$b = \sum_\nu b^\nu.$$

When the amount of CO_2 emissions in country ν is a^ν, then country ν has to purchase emission permits by the amount $a^\nu - b^\nu$ or to sell them by the amount $b^\nu - a^\nu$.

Produced goods are assumed to be internationally traded on competitive markets. The balance-of-payments condition for country ν is expressed by

$$pc^\nu = px^\nu - q(a^\nu - b^\nu) = y^\nu,$$

where $p = (p_j)$ is the vector of prices of produced goods, q is the price of emission permits on the international market, and y^ν is national income of country ν.

Proposition. *The equilibrium of the market for tradable emission permits, with the total amount of the initial allotment of emission permits, $b = \sum_\nu b^\nu$, is Pareto-optimal, if, and only if, the price q on the market for tradable emission permits is given by*

$$q = \tau(a)y.$$

The initial allotment of emission permits to individual countries (b^ν) is generally given in the form

$$b^\nu = \left[(1+\varepsilon)\frac{N^\nu}{N} - \varepsilon\frac{y^\nu}{y}\right]b,$$

where N^ν is the population of country ν, and N is the world population ($N = \sum_\nu N^\nu$).

The egalitarian index ε takes the value not less than -1: $\varepsilon \geqq -1$. The first coefficient $(1+\varepsilon)\frac{N^\nu}{N}$ expresses the basic principle of humanitarianism that all people on the earth are treated equally. The second coefficient $\varepsilon\frac{y^\nu}{y}$ has a minus sign because the atmospheric concentrations of CO_2 and other greenhouse gases today are the result of past industrial activities, and the stock of factors of production endowed in each country indicates the extent of the effect of past accumulation of greenhouse gases that remains today of which national income y^ν is a proxy variable.

The larger the egalitarian index ε, the more egalitarian is the outcome.

The neutral case is denoted by $\varepsilon = 0, \quad b^\nu = \dfrac{N^\nu}{N}b.$

The anti-egalitarian case is denoted by $\varepsilon = -1, \quad b^\nu = \dfrac{y^\nu}{y}b.$

The equilibrium of the market for tradable emission permits satisfying the Lindahl conditions corresponds precisely to the anti-egalitarian case.

Dynamic Analysis of Global Warming

The problems regarding the phenomenon of global warming are genuinely dynamic. We inherit an excess concentration of atmospheric carbon dioxide from past human activities, and the choices we make today concerning the use of fossil fuels and related activities exert significant influence on all future generations.

We denote by V_t the amount of carbon dioxide accumulated in the atmosphere at time t, where the stable pre-Industrial Revolution level of 600 GtC is adopted as the origin of the measurement. A certain portion of atmospheric concentrations of CO_2, roughly estimated at 50 percent, is absorbed by the oceans and to a lesser extent by living land plants. In the simple dynamic model postulated in Chapter 4, the exchange of carbon dioxide between the atmosphere and the terrestrial biosphere is not taken into consideration. We assume that the amount of atmospheric carbon dioxide annually absorbed by the oceans is given by μV_t, where V_t is the atmospheric concentrations of CO_2 measured in actual tons of CO_2, and the rate of absorption μ is a certain constant. We have assumed that $\mu = 0.04$.

In the simple dynamic model, we assume that the anthropogenic change in atmospheric carbon dioxide is exclusively due to the combustion of fossil fuels in connection with industrial, agricultural, and urban activities. We denote by a_t the annual rate of increase in the atmospheric level of CO_2 due to anthropogenic activities. The magnitude of a_t is currently estimated around 6 GtC per annum; that is, $a_t =$ 6 GtC.

The dynamic equation for the atmospheric level of CO_2 is given by

$$\dot{V}_t = a_t - \mu V_t.$$

The rate of anthropogenic change in the atmospheric level of CO_2, a_t, is primarily determined by the combustion of fossil fuels and is closely related to the levels of production and consumption activities during the year observed.

In the dynamic analysis of global warming, we have postulated that the level of the utility u^ν of each country ν depends on the amount of atmospheric concentrations of CO_2 at time t, V, rather than the amount of annual CO_2 emissions a, as was the case with the static analysis. That is, the utility level u_t^ν of each country ν at time t is expressed by

$$u_t^\nu = u^\nu(c_t^\nu, V_t),$$

where $c_t^\nu = (c_j^\nu)$ is the vector of goods consumed in country ν and V_t is the atmospheric concentrations of CO_2, both at time t.

As with the static case, for each country ν, marginal rates of substitution between any pair of consumption goods are diminishing, the utility function is homogeneous of order 1 with respect to the vector of goods consumed in country ν and it is strongly separable with respect to consumption vector c^ν and atmospheric concentrations of CO_2 at time t, V_t:

$$u_t^\nu = \varphi^\nu(V_t) u^\nu(c_t^\nu),$$

where $\varphi^\nu(V)$ is the impact index of global warming that expresses the extent to which the people of country ν are adversely affected by global warming. As CO_2 concentrations are increased, the impact index of global warming $\varphi^\nu(V)$ is decreased. As with the static situation, the impact coefficient of global warming is the relative rate of the marginal change in the impact index due to the marginal increase in the atmospheric emission of CO_2:

$$\tau^\nu(V) = -\frac{\varphi^{\nu\prime}(V)}{\varphi^\nu(V)}.$$

The impact coefficient of global warming $\tau^\nu(V)$ is assumed to be identical for all countries:

$$\tau^\nu(V) = \tau(V).$$

Deferential Equilibrium in the Dynamic Context

Deferential equilibrium in the dynamic context is obtained if this marginal decrease in country ν's utility in the future due to the marginal increase in CO_2 emissions today in country ν is taken into consideration in determining the levels of consumption, production, and CO_2 emissions today.

The marginal decrease in country ν's utility due to the marginal increase in CO_2 emissions today in country ν is given by the partial derivative, with minus sign, of utility function $u^\nu(c^\nu, V)$ of country ν with respect to CO_2 accumulations V.

We assume that future utilities of country ν are discounted at the rate of discount δ that is exogenously given. We also assume that the rate of utility discount δ is a positive constant and is identical for all countries in the world. The imputed price ψ^ν of the atmospheric accumulations of CO_2 for each country ν is given by the discounted present value of the marginal decrease in country ν's utility due to the marginal increase in CO_2 emissions at time t in country ν.

Proposition. *Deferential equilibrium corresponds precisely to the standard market equilibrium under the system of carbon taxes, where, in each country* ν*, the carbon taxes are levied with the tax rate* θ^ν *that is proportional to national income* y^ν *of each country* ν *with the discounted present value* $\frac{\tau(V)}{\delta + \mu}$ *of the impact coefficient of global warming* $\tau(V)$ *as* *the coefficient of proportion; that is,*

$$\theta^\nu = \frac{\tau(V)}{\delta+\mu} y^\nu,$$

where $\tau(V)$ *is the impact coefficient of global warming,* δ *is the rate of utility discount, and* μ *is the rate at which atmospheric carbon dioxide is annually absorbed by the oceans.*

Proposition. *Consider the uniform carbon tax scheme with the same rate* θ *for all countries in the world, where the rate* θ *is proportional to the aggregate national income* y *of the whole world with the impact coefficient of global warming* $\tau(\nu)$ *as the coefficient of proportion:*

$$\theta = \tau(\nu) y.$$

Then market equilibrium obtained under such a uniform carbon tax scheme is a social optimum in the sense that there exists a set of positive weights for the utilities of individual countries $(\alpha^1, \ldots, \alpha^n)$, $[\alpha^\nu > 0]$ *such that the world utility*

$$W = \sum_\nu \alpha^\nu \varphi^\nu(\nu) u^\nu(c^\nu)$$

is maximized among all feasible patterns of allocation.

Proposition. *Consider the uniform carbon tax scheme, where the rate* θ *is proportional to the aggregate income* y *of the world with the discounted present value* $\frac{\tau(V)}{\delta+\mu}$ *of the impact coefficient of global warming* $\tau(V)$ *as the coefficient of proportion:*

$$\theta = \frac{\tau(V)}{\delta+\mu} y.$$

Then the market equilibrium obtained under such a uniform carbon tax scheme is a social optimum in the sense that a set of positive weights $(\alpha^1, \ldots, \alpha^n)$, $[\alpha^\nu > 0]$ *exists for the utilities of individual countries such that the net level of the world utility*

$$W - \theta a = \sum_\nu \alpha^\nu \varphi(V) u^\nu(c^\nu) - \theta a.$$

is maximized among all feasible patterns of allocation.

Then the world utility W *is equal to the aggregate national income of the world* y,

$$W = y,$$

and the imputed price ψ of the atmospheric concentrations of CO_2 *is equal to carbon tax rate* θ.

Proposition. *There always exists a set of positive weights for the utilities of individual countries* $(\alpha^1, \ldots, \alpha^n)$, $[\alpha^\nu > 0]$ *such that the social optimum in the dynamic sense with respect to the world utility*

$$W - \psi a = \sum_\nu \alpha^\nu \varphi(V) u^\nu(c^\nu) - \psi a,$$

where ψ is the imputed price of the atmospheric concentrations of CO_2 *with respect to the world utility W satisfies the balance-of-payments requirements*

$$pc^\nu = px^\nu,$$

and accordingly the corresponding pattern of allocation, in conjunction with prices of goods p and the carbon tax scheme with the uniform rate $\theta = \tau(a)y$, *constitutes a market equilibrium for the world.*

Proposition. *There always exists a set of positive weights for the utilities of individual countries* $(\alpha^1, \ldots, \alpha^n)$, $[\alpha^\nu > 0]$ *such that the social optimum with respect to the world utility W satisfies the balance-of-payments conditions*

$$pc^\nu = px^\nu,$$

and accordingly the corresponding pattern of allocation $(c^1, \ldots, c^n, x^1, \ldots, x^n, a^1, \ldots, a^n, a)$, *in conjunction with prices of goods p and the uniform carbon tax scheme with the rate* $\theta = \tau(a)y$, *constitutes a market equilibrium.*

Proposition. *The process of the atmospheric accumulation of* CO_2 *under the uniform carbon tax scheme is dynamically stable. That is, solution paths for the dynamic equation*

$$\dot{V} = a - \mu V,$$

where a is the level of total emissions of CO_2 *at time t and* μ *is the rate at which atmospheric concentrations of* CO_2 *are annually absorbed by the oceans, always converge to the stationary level* V_* *to be given by the stationarity condition*

$$a_* = \mu V,$$

where a_* is the total CO_2 emissions at the market equilibrium under the uniform carbon tax scheme.

Dynamic Optimality and Sustainabililty

Global warming involves international and intergenerational equity and justice. Although global warming is largely caused by the emission of carbon dioxide and other greenhouse gases accompanied by economic activities mostly in developed countries (and to a lesser extent by the disruption of forests – particularly by destruction of tropical forests – again mostly in relation to the industrial activities of the developed countries) it is the people in developing countries who have to bear the burden. The current generation may enjoy the fruits from the economic activities that contribute to global warming, but it is the people in all future generations who will have to suffer a significant increase in atmospheric instability as a consequence.

To examine the problems of global warming and other global environmental issues, primarily from the viewpoint of international and intergenerational distribution of utility, we have introduced the concept of sustainability that may capture some aspects of international and intergenerational equity and may be used to derive the conditions under which processes of capital accumulation and changes in environmental quality over time are sustainable. In Chapter 5, the conceptual framework of the dynamic analysis of environmental quality, as was developed in previous chapters, is extended to deal with the problems relating to the irreversibility of processes of capital accumulation that occur because of the Penrose effect.

The analysis focuses on the formula concerning the system of imputed prices associated with the dynamically optimum time-path of consumption with respect to the intertemporal preference relation, where the presence of the Penrose effect implies the diminishing marginal rate of investment in private capital and social overhead capital on the rate at which capital is accumulated. The dynamically optimum time-path of consumption is characterized by the proportionality of two systems of imputed prices – one associated with the given intertemporal preference ordering and another with the processes of capital accumulation of private capital and social overhead capital.

A time-path of consumption and capital accumulation is sustainable when the imputed price of each kind of capital, either private or social overhead capital, remains identical over time. In other words, a time-path of consumption is sustainable if all future generations will face the same imputed prices of various kinds of capital as those faced by the current generation. The existence of the sustainable time-path of consumption and capital accumulation starting with an arbitrarily given stock of capital is ensured when the processes of accumulation of various kinds of capital are subject to the Penrose effect, which exhibits the law of diminishing marginal rates of investment.

Proposition. *Consider the world economy as consisting of n countries in which produced goods are freely traded, but once they are invested as productive capital no trade will take place.*

If the time-path of production, CO_2 *emissions, consumption, and investment for each country* ν, $(x_t^\nu, a_t^\nu, c_t^\nu, z_t^\nu)$, *is sustainable, then the combination of production and* CO_2 *emissions for each country* ν *at time t,* (x_t^ν, a_t^ν), *precisely coincides with the optimum combination that maximizes net profits*

$$p_t^\nu x_t^\nu - \theta_t^\nu a_t^\nu, \quad (x_t^\nu, a_t^\nu) \in T^\nu,$$

where

$$\theta^\nu = \frac{\tau(V_t)}{\delta + \mu} y_t^\nu, \quad \tau(V) = -\frac{\varphi\prime(V)}{\varphi(V)}.$$

Global Warming and Forests

In the simple, dynamic analysis of global warming introduced in the previous chapters, we have assumed that the combustion of fossil fuels is the only cause for atmospheric instability, and the surface ocean is the only reservoir of carbon on the earth's surface that exchanges carbon with the atmosphere. In Chapter 6, we extended the economic analysis of global warming, focusing our attention on the role played by the terrestrial forest in moderating processes of global warming, on the one hand, and in affecting the welfare level of people in the society by providing a decent and cultured environment, on the other. We are concerned with the allocation of scarce resources, including the global atmosphere and terrestrial forests, that is sustainable in precisely the sense just defined.

Under certain qualifying assumptions concerning the welfare effect of global warming, it is possible to derive simple formulas for calculating the level of the imputed price of each greenhouse gas. Let us consider a particular case of atmospheric carbon dioxide. The imputed price θ_t of atmospheric carbon dioxide at each time t is proportional to the national income y_t of the country in which carbon dioxide is emitted. That is,

$$\theta_t = \tau(V_t)y_t,$$

where $\tau(V_t)$ is the impact coefficient of global warming at time t to be given by

$$\tau(V_t) = \frac{\beta}{\delta + \mu}\frac{1}{\hat{V} - V_t},$$

where δ is the social rate of discount (usually 5%), μ is the rate at which atmospheric carbon dioxide in excess of the pre-Industrial Revolution level is absorbed into the surface ocean (normally estimated around 2–4%), β is the intensity at which the effect of global warming is felt by the society, and $\hat{V}$ is the critical level of atmospheric carbon dioxide beyond which climatic changes brought about by global warming are feared to exert serious, irrevocable damage on human life and the earth's biosphere. The value of $\hat{V}$ is usually taken to be 1,200 GtC, which is twice the level estimated to have existed during the Industrial Revolution.

The imputed prices of terrestrial forests may be calculated similarly. They express the extent to which the society evaluates the contributions made by marginal increases in the acreage of land forests towards the decrease in the atmospheric level of carbon dioxide. If we consider a simple case in which the acreages of terrestrial forests do not have any influence on the welfare of the people, then the imputed price of a hectare of a particular forest, to be denoted by η_t, may be expressed by the following formula:

$$\eta_t = \frac{\gamma}{\delta}\theta_t,$$

where γ is the amount of atmospheric carbon dioxide annually absorbed by the terrestrial forests per hectare ($\gamma = 5$ tC/ha/yr for temperate forests, $\gamma = 15$ tC/ha/yr for tropical rain forests).

When several countries are involved, the formulas for the imputed prices of carbon dioxide and terrestrial forests above may be applied, where the impact coefficient $\tau(V)$ and the absorption coefficient γ may be assumed to be identical for all countries involved. Table 3 shows an illustrative calculation made to evaluate the imputed prices of carbon dioxide for major countries in the world. We assume that the society is sensitive to global warming, say $\beta = 0.06$, so that the imputation coefficients are given by

$$\frac{\theta_t}{y_t} = 0.01$$

$$\frac{\eta_t}{y_t} = 1.0, \text{ for temperate forests}$$

$$\frac{\eta_t}{y_t} = 3.0, \text{ for tropical rain forests.}$$

Then the hypothetical values for the imputed price for of carbon dioxide are shown in Table 3.

The imputed price of carbon dioxide is approximately \$320/tC for the United States and for Japan, whereas it is \$6 for Indonesia and \$17 for the Philippines. The carbon taxes on a per capita basis are \$1,700 for the United States and \$780 for Japan as against \$2 and \$3, respectively, for Indonesia and the Philippines.

Similar calculations may be made for other greenhouse gases. One has simply to take into account the relative effect upon global warming and the rate at which each greenhouse gas is depreciated from the atmosphere.

The imputed prices for land forests are approximately \$32,000 for the United States, and for Japan, \$1,800 for Indonesia, and \$3,150 for the Philippines, all per hectare.

Global Warming as a Cooperative Game

In Chapter 7, we regard global warming as a cooperative game and examine the conditions under which the core of the global warming game is nonempty. It is carried out within the framework introduced in the previous chapters, where the economic welfare of each country is expressed by the utility, which depends on the vector of goods consumed in that country and the total amount of carbon dioxide emitted by all the countries involved.

The players of the cooperative game of global warming are the countries in the world, each of which may choose as the strategy a combination of the vector of goods to be consumed by that country and the amount of carbon dioxide to be emitted from productive and other processes, and the payoff for each country is simply its utility.

A coalition for the global warming game is any group of countries, and the value of each coalition is the maximum of the sum of the utilities of the countries in the coalition on the assumption that those countries that do not belong to the coalition form their own coalition and try to maximize the sum of their utilities.

The core of the global warming game consists of those allotments of the value of the game among individual countries that no coalition can block. The conditions under which the core of the global warming game with transferable utility is nonempty are examined. Then, an alternative definition of the value of coalition for the global warming game with transferable utility is introduced, and it is shown that the core of the global warming game under the alternative definition is always nonempty.

Finally, our global warming game is regarded as a cooperative game with nontransferable utility, and it is shown that Lindahl equilibrium is always in the core of the game.

Extensions and Qualifications

In the dynamic analysis of global warming we have developed in the preceding chapters, several simplifying assumptions have been postulated partly to elucidate the economic and environmental implications of our analysis and partly for the sake of analytic manageability. We would like to briefly discuss some of the more qualifying assumptions postulated in our analysis and the implications they have for the main theme of our conclusions.

We have postulated that carbon dioxide is the only chemical agent that has a greenhouse effect. The analysis is easily extended to cover the situation in which numerous greenhouse gases such as methane, nitrous oxide, and CFCs are present in addition to carbon dioxide. When we take the effect of these greenhouse gases into consideration, we have to modify the definition of V_t. The V_t is now defined as the aggregate of these greenhouse gases, where each greenhouse gas is properly measured so that the unit quantity of each chemical agent plays the same role as carbon dioxide in the phenomenon of global warming. According to the estimates made by Ramanathan et al. (1985) and others, the effects of greenhouse gases upon the increase in atmospheric temperature are of the following magnitudes in relation to carbon dioxide:

$$\text{methane} = 12, \quad \text{nitrous oxide} = 350$$
$$\text{CFC-11} = 25{,}000, \quad \text{CFC-12} = 28{,}000.$$

The case of changing population poses a rather difficult problem when we try to extend the dynamic analysis of global warming. However, in terms of the concept of sustainability, as defined in Chapter 5, the case of changing population may easily be addressed by substituting the effective rate of discount, $\delta - \sigma$ (σ being the rate of increase in population) for the original rate of discount δ.

Let us suppose the population size N_t is increasing at a certain constant rate σ, and let the welfare criterion be defined in terms of the utility integral of the aggregate levels of utilities:

$$U = \int_0^\infty N_t y_t e^{-\delta t} dt, \quad y_t = u(c_t)\phi(V_t).$$

The utility integral U may be simply rewritten as

$$U = N_0 \int_0^\infty y_t e^{-(\delta - \sigma)} dt.$$

Hence, the imputation coefficients θ_t and η_t are expressed as follows:

$$\theta_t = \frac{1}{\delta - \sigma + \mu} \frac{\beta}{\hat{V} - V_t} N_t$$

$$\eta_t = \frac{\gamma}{\delta}\theta_t = \frac{\gamma}{\delta(\delta - \sigma + \mu)} \frac{\beta}{\hat{V} - V_t} N_t,$$

where N_t is the size of world population at time t, whereas the rate of increase in population, σ, refers to the country involved.

The preceding formulas imply that, the higher the rate of population increase, the higher will be the imputation coefficients both for atmospheric carbon dioxide and land forests, thus, the lower will be the long-run stationary level of atmospheric carbon dioxide.

One of the more qualifying assumptions we have postulated in our analysis concerns the malleability of various scarce resources in the processes of production and consumption. We have assumed that various types of scarce resources may be shifted from one use to another without incurring any cost or requiring any time. Indeed, the malleability hypothesis is one of the more basic postulates in neoclassical economic theory; it is difficult to dispense with and is crucial in deriving the efficiency of the allocative mechanism in terms of market institutions.

The malleability hypothesis is particularly disquieting in the dynamic analysis of global warming. It is a distinct feature of modern technologies and engineering techniques that they are intrinsically embodied in equipment functioning directly or indirectly by the combustion of fossil fuels. Equipment is hardly malleable, nor are the organizational and institutional arrangements used to manage scarce productive and entrepreneurial resources. The introduction of the carbon tax system or similar policy measures to stabilize atmospheric greenhouse gases is indeed intended to alter the nature of equipment so that the social costs associated with atmospheric concentrations of greenhouse gases are explicitly taken into account prior to its installation and at the same time to restructure organizational and institutional arrangements gradually so as to be able to manage environmental issues effectively. In the analysis developed in the previous chapters, we have postulated that scarce resources are malleable to make them reallocatable in whatever manner is most efficient with respect to the price and market configurations associated with the carbon tax system. It would be desirable to note explicitly that scarce resources and productive apparatuses are largely nonmalleable and that production organizations have been set up without taking proper recognizance of environmental costs, properly modifying the concept of imputed prices of atmospheric greenhouse gases and land forests, and adjusting the actual calculation of the imputed prices accordingly. In Chapter 5, the problems of malleability are discussed in the context of the Penrose effect, as originally introduced in Uzawa (1968, 1969).

The second qualifying assumption in our analysis concerns the distribution of income among individuals in each country. To focus our attention on intergenerational and international distributions, we have postulated that all the goods and services produced in the economy are equally distributed among individuals in the country. This postulate implicitly presupposes the existence of a redistribution scheme whereby any inequality in the distribution of real income is effectively taken care of. In the absence of such an idealistic redistribution scheme, one has to modify the concept of imputed prices associated with the phenomenon of global warming.

The stabilization of the atmospheric disequilibrium may be attained efficiently through the device of the carbon tax system evaluated at the imputed prices of greenhouse gases and land forests, which at least in theory is subject to the qualifying constraints described herein.

In our approach, we have taken into consideration some aspects of the equity problems involved with the phenomenon of global warming – particularly by adopting the imputed prices measured in terms of the per capita level of national income in constant prices. However, our approach only partially takes into account the equity issues brought about by global warming.

The International Fund for Atmospheric Stabilization

The disparity in economic performance between developed countries and developing countries, however, has steadily widened in the last three decades, and various institutional and policy measures that have been devised internationally or bilaterally have not had much impact in narrowing the gap between these two groups of countries. The introduction of the proportional carbon tax system as envisioned here, in spite of the implicit recognition of the equity aspect in its design, may tend to worsen the relative position of developing countries – at least in the short run. It would be desirable, therefore, to supplement the carbon tax system with an international redistribution scheme that would have significant impact in narrowing the gap between the stages of economic development in the various countries involved.

The International Fund for Atmospheric Stabilization is an institutional framework in which it is possible to combine an international arrangement to stabilize atmospheric equilibrium with a redistribution scheme to help the developing countries accelerate processes of economic development.

The International Fund for Atmospheric Stabilization presupposes that each country adopts the proportional carbon tax system under which emissions of carbon dioxide and other greenhouse gases are charged a levy evaluated at the imputed prices proportional to the per capita level of national income, and a charge (or a subsidiary payment) is made for the depletion (or the afforestation) of land forests – again based on the evaluation at the imputed prices of land forests that are proportional to the per capita level of national income, as discussed in detail in Chapter 5.

The tax revenues from the proportional carbon tax system are principally put into the general revenue account of each government, preferably to be earmarked partly for restoration of the natural and ecological environments and to encourage private economic agents to develop the technological and institutional knowledge crucial to restoring equilibrium conditions in the global environment.

Each country then transfers a fixed portion, say 5 percent, of the net revenue from the carbon tax system to the International Fund for Atmospheric Stabilization. The total amount thus transferred would be allocated to developing countries according to a predetermined schedule that properly takes into account the per capita levels of national income and the size of the population. Developing countries may use the amounts transferred from the International Fund for Atmospheric Stabilization for the purposes they think appropriate – preferably to compensate those who would suffer from the phenomena of global environmental disequilibrium and incur hardship through the implementation of the carbon tax system, to restructure industrial organizations and social infrastructure, and to introduce alternative energy sources and energy-saving technologies.

It is unlikely that the International Fund for Atmospheric Stabilization or similar international arrangements on the global scale will be instituted in the immediate future. Whether such international arrangements may be implemented effectively or not depends to a significant extent on the degree of the general public's awareness of the enormous burden and costs future generations will have to suffer from the phenomena of global warming and other global environmental disequilibria.

The strenuous effort by several geoscientists, ecologists, and other scientists to clarify the mechanisms of global warming and to identify its specific implications and other environmental issues for ecological, biological, social, and cultural life on earth has had a significant impact on the consciousness of the general public and the national governments. The numerous conferences and symposia organized by various international organizations such as the 1992 Rio Conference and the Intergovernmental Panel on Climate Change – particularly the Kyoto Protocol of 1997 – have substantially altered the perception of the international community as regards the plausibility and danger of global warming and other atmospheric disequilibria.

All these activities help the national governments involved to search for those policy measures and institutional arrangements that will make the practical implementation of the International Fund for Atmospheric Stabilization or similar international agreements feasible economically, socially, and politically. It would not be too optimistic to expect to have the International Fund for Atmospheric Stabilization or a similar framework instituted in the foreseeable – if not the immediate – future.

References

Aghion, P., and Howitt, P. (1992). "A Model of Growth through Creative Destruction," *Econometrica*, **60**, 323–352.

Arrow, K. J. (1951). *Social Choice and Individual Values*, New York: John Wiley.

Arrow, K. J. (1962a). "Optimal Capital Adjustment," in K. J. Arrow, S. Karlin, and H. Scarf (eds.), *Studies in Applied Probability and Management Science*, Palo Alto, CA: Stanford University Press.

Arrow, K. J. (1962b). "The Economic Implications of Learning by Doing," *Review of Economic Studies*, **29**, 155–73.

Arrow, K. J. (1965). "Criteria for Social Investment," *Water Resources Research*, **1**, 1–8.

Arrow, K. J. (1968). "Optimal Capital Policy with Irreversible Investment," in J. N. Wolfe (ed.), *Value, Capital and Growth: Papèrs in Honour of Sir John Hicks*, Edinburgh: Edinburgh University Press.

Arrow, K. J. (1973). "Some Ordinalist-Utilitarian Notes on Rawls's Theory of Justice," *Journal of Philosophy*, **70**, 245–263.

Arrow, K. J. (1983). "A Difficulty in the Concept of Social Choice," in *Social Choice and Justice: Collected Papers of Kenneth J. Arrow*, Cambridge, MA: Harvard University Press.

Arrow, K. J., and Debreu, G. (1954). "On the Existence of an Equilibrium for Competitive Economy," *Econometrica*, **22**, 256–291.

Arrow, K. J., and Hurwicz, L. (1956). " Reduction of Constrained Maxima to Saddle-Point Problems," in J. Neyman (ed.), *Proceedings of the Third Berkeley Symposium on Mathematical Statistics and Probability*, Berkeley: University of California Press, **5**, 1–20.

Arrow, K. J., Hurwicz, L., and Uzawa, H. (1958). *Studies in Linear and Non-linear Programming*, Stanford: Stanford University Press.

Arrow, K. J., and Kurz, M. (1970). *Public Investment, Rate of Return, and Optimal Fiscal Policy*, Baltimore: Johns Hopkins University Press.

Atkinson, A. B. (1975). *The Economics of Inequality*, Oxford: Clarendon Press.

Aumann, R. J. (1989). *Lectures on Game Theory*, Boulder, CO: Westview Press.

Barrett, S. (1990). "The Problem of Global Environmental Protection," *Oxford Review of Economic Policy*, **6**, 68–79.

Barrett, S. (1994). "The Self-Enforcing International Environmental Agreements," *Oxford Economic Papers*, **46**, 878–894.

Barrett, S., Grubb, K., Roland, A., Sandor, R., and Tietenberg, T. (1992). *Combating Global Warming: A Global System of Tradeable Emission Entitlements*, Geneva, UNCTAD.

Barrett, S., and Taylor, M. S. (1995). "Trade and Transboudary Pollution," *American Economic Review*, **85**, 716–737.

Baumol, W., and Oates, W. (1988). *The Theory of Environmental Policy*, Second Edition, Cambridge, UK: Cambridge University Press.

Bergstrom, T., Blume, L., and Varian, H. (1986). "On the private provision of public goods," *Journal of Public Economics*, **29**, 25–49.

Berkes, F. (ed.) (1989). *Common Property Resources: Ecology and Community-Based Sustainable Development*, London: Balhaven Press.

Bertram, G. (1992). "Tradable Emission Permits and the Control of Greenhouse Gases," *Journal of Development Studies*, **23**, 423–446.

Bertram, I. G., Stephens, R. J., and Wallace, C. C. (1989). "Economic Instruments and the Greenhouse Effect," paper prepared from New Zealand Ministry for the Environment.

Bishop, R. C., and Woodward, R. T. (1995). "Evaluation of Environmental Quality under Certainty," in D. W. Bromley (ed.), *The Handbook of Environmental Economics*, Cambridge, MA: Blackwell, 543–567.

Bondareva, O. N. (1962). "The Theory of Core in an *n*-Person Game," *Bulletin of Leningrad University*, Mathematics, Mechanics, and Astronomy Series, No. 13, 141–142 .

Bondareva, O. N. (1963). "Some Applications of Linear Programming Methods to the Theory of Cooperative Games," *Problemy Kybernikiti*, **10**, 119–139.

Bovenberg, A. L., and Smulders, E. (1995). "Environmental Quality and Pollution-Argumenting Technological Change in a Two-Sector Endogenous Growth Model," *Journal of Public Economics*, **57**, 369–391.

Bradford, D. F. (1975). "Constraints on Government Investment Opportunities, and the Choice of Discount Rate," *American Economic Review*, **65**, 887–899.

Bromley, D. W. (ed.) (1995). *The Handbook of Environmental Economics*, Cambridge: Blackwell.

Cass, D. (1965). "Optimum Economic Growth in an Aggregative Model of Capital Accumulation," *Review of Economic Studies*, **32**, 233–240.

Chichilnisky, G., and Heal, G. (1994). "Who Should Abate Carbon Emissions?: An International Perspective," *Economics Letters*, **44**, 443–449.

Cicerone, R. J., and Oremland, R. S. (1988). "Biogeochemical Aspects of Atmospheric Methane," *Global Biogeochemical Cycles*, **2**, 299–327.

Clark, C. W. (1990). *Mathematical Bioeconomics: The Optimal Management of Renewable Resources*, Second Edition, New York: John Wiley.

Clark, C. W., and Munro, G. R. (1975). "The Economics of Fishing and Modern Capital Theory," *Journal of Environmental Economics and Management*, **2**, 92–106.

Cline, W. R. (1992a). "The Economic Benefits of Limiting Global Warming," in *The Economics of Global Warming*, Washington, DC: Institute for International Economics, 81–138.

Cline, W. R. (1992b). "Benefit–Cost Synthesis," in *The Economics of Global Warming*, Washington, DC, Institute for International Economics, 277–320.

Cline, W. R. (1992c). *The Economics of Global Warming*, Washington, DC: Institute for International Economics.

Cline, W. R. (1993). "Give Greenhouse Abatement a Fair Chance," *Finance and Development*, **30**, 3–5.

Coase, R. H. (1960). "The Problem of Social Cost," *Journal of Law and Economics*, **3**, 1–44.

Conway, T. J., Tans, P., Waterman, L. S., Thoning, K. W., Masarie, K. A., and Gammon, R. H. (1988). "Atmospheric Carbon Dioxide Measurements in the Remote Global Troposphere, 1981–1984," *Tellus*, **40**, 81–115.

Copeland, B. R., and Taylor, M. S. (1986). "North–South Trade and the Environment," *Quarterly Journal of Economics*, **109**, 755–787

Copeland, B. R., and Taylor, M. S. (1995). "Trade and Transboundary Pollution," *American Economic Review*, **85**, 716–737.

Cornes, R., and Sandler, T. (1983). "On Commons and Tradegies," *American Economic Review*, **73**, 787–792.

Cropper, M., and Portney, P (1992). *Discounting Human Lives*, Washington, DC: Resources for the Future.

Crutzen, P. J., Aselmann, I., and Seiler, W. (1986). "Methane Production by Domestic Animals, Wild Ruminants, Other Herbivorous Fauna, and Humans," *Tellus*, **38B**, 271–284.

Dales, J. H. (1968). *Pollution, Property, and Prices*, Toronto, University of Toronto Press.

d'Arge, R. C. (1971). "Essays on Economic Growth and Environmental Quality," *Swedish Journal of Economics*, **11**, 25–41.

d'Arge, R. C. (1989). "Ethical and Economic System for Managing the Global Commons," in *Changing the World Environment*, D. B. Botkin, F. Margriet, J. E. Caswell, J. E. Estes, and A. A. Orio (eds.), New York: Academic Press.

d'Arge, R. C., Schultze, W., and Brookshire, D. S. (1982). "Carbon Dioxide and Intergenerational Choice," *American Economic Review*, **72**, 251–256.

Dasgupta, P. (1982a). "Resource Depletion, R&D, and the Social Rate of Discount," in *Discounting for Time and Risk in Energy Policy*, R. C. Lind, K. J. Arrow, and G. R. Corey (eds.), Baltimore: Johns Hopkins University Press, 275–324.

Dasgupta, P. (1982b). *The Control of Resources*, Oxford, UK: Blackwell.

Dasgupta, P. (1993). *An Inquiry into Well-Being and Destitution*, Oxford, UK: Clarendon Press.

Dasgupta, P., and Heal, G. M. (1974). "The Optimal Depletion of Exhaustible Resources," *Review of Economic Studies*, **51**, 3–27.

Dasgupta, P., and Heal, G. M. (1979). *Economic Theory and Exhaustible Resources*, Cambridge, UK: Cambridge University Press.

Demsetz, H. (1967). "Toward a Theory of Property Rights," *American Economic Review*, **62**, 347–1359.

Detweiler, R. P., and Hall, C. A. (1988). "Tropical Forests and the Global Carbon Cycle," *Science*, **239**, 4247.

Dickinson, R. E. (1986). "The Climate System and Modeling of Future Climate," in B. Bolin, B. R. Doos, J. Jager, and R. A. Warrick (eds.), *The Greenhouse Effect, Climatic Change, and Ecosystems*, New York: John Wiley, 207–270.

Dyson, F., and Marland, G. (1979). "Technical Fixes for the Climatic Effects of CO_2," in W. P. Elliot and L. Machta (eds.), *Workshop on the Global Effects of Carbon Dioxide from Fossil Fuels*, Washington, DC, United States Department of Energy, 111–118.

Epstein, L. G. (1987). "A Simple Dynamic General Equilibrium Model," *Journal of Economic Theory*, **41**, 68–95.

Epstein, L. E., and Haynes, J. A. (1983). "The Rate of Time Preference and Dynamic Economic Analysis," *Journal of Political Economy*, **91**, 611–681.

Fabre-Sender, F. (1969). "Biens collectifs et biens équalité variable," CEPREMAP.

Fenchel, W. (1953). *Convex Cones, Sets, and Functions*, Princeton University, Department of Mathematics.

Foley. D. (1967). "Resource Allocation and the Public Sector," *Yale Economic Essays*, **7**, 43–98.

Foley. D. (1970). "Lindahl Solution and the Core of an Economy with Public Goods," *Econometrica*, **38**, 66–72.

Forster, B. A. (1973). "Optimal Capital Accumulation in a Polluted Environment," *Southern Economic Journal*, **39**, 544–547.

Fraser, P. J., Elliott, W. P., and Waterman, L. S. (1986). "Atmospheric CO_2 Record from Direct Chemical Measurements during the 19th Century," in J. R. Trabalka and D. E. Reichle (eds.), *The Changing Carbon Cycle: A Global Analysis*, New York: Springer-Verlag, 66–88.

From, L., and Keeling, C. D. (1986). "Reassessment of Late 19th Century Atmospheric Carbon Dioxide Variations in the Air of Western Europe and the British Isles Based on an Unpublished Analysis of Contemporary Air Masses by G. S. Calendar," *Tellus*, **38B**, 87–105.

Furubotn, E. H., and Pejovich, S. (1972). "Property Rights and Economic Theory: A Survey of Recent Literature," *Journal of Economic Literature*, **10**, 1137–1162.

Godwin, R. K., and Shepard, W. B. (1979). "Forcing Squares, Triangles, and Ellipses into a Circular Paradigm: The Use of the Commons Dilemma in Examining the Allocation of Common Resources," *Western Political Quarterly*, **32**(3), 265–277.

Goldman, S. M., and Uzawa, H. (1964). "On the Separability in Demand Analysis," *Econometrica*, **32**, 387–399.

Gordon, H. S. (1954). "The Economic Theory of a Common Property Resources: The Fishery," *Journal of Political Economy*, **62**, 124–142.

Gorman, W. M. (1959). "Separable Utility and Aggregation," *Econometrica*, **27**, 469–481.

Gornitz, V., Lebedeff, S., and Hansen, J. (1982). "Global Sea Level Trend in the Past Century," *Science*, **215**, 1611–1614.

Gradus, R., and Smulders, E. (1993). "The Trade-Off between Environmental Care and Long-Term Growth: Pollution in Three Prototype Growth Models," *Journal of Economics*, **58**, 25–51.

Grossman, G., and Helpman, E. (1991). *Innovation and Growth in the Global Economy*, Cambridge, MA: The MIT Press.

Grubb, M. J. (1989). *Greenhouse Effect: Negotiating Targets*, London: Royal Institute of International Affairs.

Grubb, M. J. (1990). "International Marketable Emission Permits: Key Issues," IPCC/OECD Workshop on Financial and Economic Measures as a Response to Climate Change, Paris.

Grubb, M. J., and Sibenius, J. K. (1992). "Participation, Allocation, and Adaptability in International Tradeable Permit System for Greenhouse Gas Control," in T. Jones and J. Corfee-Morlot (eds.), *Climate Change: Designing a Tradeable Permit System*, Paris: OECD, 185–227.

Hampicke, U. (1979). "Man's Impact on the Earth's Vegetation Cover and Its Effects on Carbon Cycle and Climate," in W. Bach, J. Pankrath, and W. Kellog (eds.), *Man's Impact on Climate*, Amsterdam: Elsevier, 139–159.

Hansen, J., Johnson, D., Lacis, A., Lebedeff, S., Lee, P., Rina, D., and Russell, G. (1981). "Climate Impact of Increasing Atmospheric Carbon Dioxide," *Science*, **213**, 957–966.

Hansen, J., and Lebedeff, S. (1987). "Global Trends of Measured Surface Air Temperature," *Journal of Geophysical Research*, **92**, 13345–13372.

Hansen, J., and Lebedeff, S. (1988). "Global Surface Air Temperature: Update through 1987," *Geophysical Research Letters*, **15**, 323–326.

Hardin, G. (1968). "The Tragedy of the Commons," *Science*, **162**, 1243–1248.

Hoel, M. (1991). "Efficient International Agreements for Reducing Emissions of CO_2," *The Energy Journal*, **12**, 93–107.

Hoel, M. (1992). "Carbon Taxes: An International Mix or Harmonized Domestic Taxes," *Oxford Review of Economic Policy*, **7**, 99–122.

Hoel, M. (1994). "Efficient Climate Policy in the Presence of Free Riders," *Journal of Environmental Economics and Management*, **27**, 259–274.

Hogan, W. W., and Jorgenson, D. W. (1991). "Productive Trend and the Costs of Reducing Carbon Emissions," *The Energy Journal*, **12**, 67–85.

Houghton, R. A., Boone, R. D., Fruci, J. R., Hobbie, J. E., Melillo, J. M., Palm, C. A., Peterson, B. J., Shaver, G. R., Woodwell, G. M., Moore, B., Skole, D. L., and Myers, N. (1987). "The Flux of Carbon from Terrestrial Ecosystems to the Atmosphere in 1980 due to Changes in Land Use: Geographic Distribution of the Global Flux," *Tellus*, **39B**, 122–139.

Houthhakker, H. S. (1960). "Additive Preferences," *Econometrica*, **28**, 244–257.

Howarth, R. B., and Monahan. P. A. (1992). *Economics, Ethics, and Climate Policy*, Lawrence Berkeley Library, LBL-33230.

Howarth, R. B., and Norgaard, R. B. (1990). "Intergenerational Resource Rights, Efficiency, and Social Optimally," *Land Economics*, **66**, 1–11.

Howarth, R. B., and Norgaard, R. B. (1992). "Environmental Valuation under Sustainable Development," *American Economic Review*, **82**, 473–477.

Howarth, R. B., and Norgaard, R. B. (1995). "Intergenerational Choices under Global Environmental Changes," in D. W. Bromley (ed.), *The Handbook of Environmental Economics*, Oxford, UK: Blackwell, 112–138.

Huan, C-H., and Cai. D. (1994). "Constant Returns Endogenous Growth with Pollution Control," *Environmental and Resource Economics*, **4**, 383–400.

Ingham, A., Maw, J., and Ulph, A. (1974). "Empirical Measures of Carbon Taxes," *Review of Economic Studies*, **51**, 3–27.

IPCC (1991a). *Scientific Assessment of Climate Change – Report of Working Group I*, Cambridge, UK: Cambridge University Press.

IPCC (1991b). *Impact Assessment of Climate Change – Report of Working Group II*, Cambridge, UK: Cambridge University Press.

IPCC (1991c). *Climate Change: IPCC Response Strategies – Report of Working Group III*, Cambridge, UK: Cambridge University Press.

IPCC (1991d). *Climate Change: IPCC Response Strategies – Report of Working Group III*, Cambridge, UK: Cambridge University Press.

IPCC (1992). *Supplementary Report to the IPCC Scientific Assessment*, edited by J. T. Houghton, B. A. Callander, and S. K. Varney, Cambridge, UK: Cambridge University Press.

IPCC (1996a). *Climate Change 1995: The Science of Climate*, Cambridge, UK: Cambridge University Press.

IPCC (1996b). *Climate Change 1995: Impacts, Adaptations and Mitigation of Climate Change: Scientific-Technical Analysis*, Cambridge, UK: Cambridge University Press.

IPCC (1996c). *Climate Change 1995: Economic and Social Dimensions of Climate Change*, Cambridge, UK: Cambridge University Press.

IPCC (2000). *Land Use, Land-Use Change, and Forestry*, Cambridge, UK: Cambridge University Press.

IPCC (2001a). *Climate Change 2001: The Scientific Basis*, Cambridge, UK: Cambridge University Press.

IPCC (2001b). *Climate Change 2001: Impacts, Adaptations and Vulnerability*, Cambridge, UK: Cambridge University Press.

IPCC (2001c). *Climate Change 2001: Mitigation*, Cambridge, UK: Cambridge University Press.

IPCC (2001d). *Climate Change 2001: Synthesis Report*, Cambridge, UK: Cambridge University Press.

Johansen, L. (1963). "Some Notes on the Lindahl Theory of Determination of Public Expenditures," *International Economic Review*, **4**, 346–358.

Johansson, P.-O., and Löfgren, K.-G. (1985). *The Economics of Forestry and Natural Resources*, Oxford: Basil Blackwell.

Jorgenson, D. W., and Wilcoxon P. J., (1990a). "Environmental Regulation and U.S. Economic Growth," *Rand Journal of Economics*, **21**, 314–340.

Jorgenson, D. W., and Wilcoxon, P. J. (1990b). "Intertemporal General Equilibrium Modelling of U.S. Environmental Regulation," *Journal of Policy Modelling*, **12**, 715–744.

Jorgenson, D. W., and Wilcoxon, P. J. (1992). "Reducing U.S. Carbon Dioxide Emissions: The Costs of Different Goals," in J. R. Morony (ed.), *Advances in the Economics of Energy and Natural Resources*, Greenwich, CT: JAI Press, **7**, 125–158.

Jorgenson, D. W., and Wilcoxon, P. J. (1993). "Reducing U.S. Carbon Emissions: An Econometric General Equilibrium Assessment," *Resources and Energy Economics*, **15**, 7–25.

Kaneko, M. (1977). "The Ratio Equilibrium and a Voting Game in a Public Goods Economy," *Journal of Economic Theory*, **16**, 123–136.

Kannai, Y. (1992). "The Core and Balancedness," in R. J. Aumann and S. Hart (eds.), *Handbook of Game Theory I*, Amsterdam: Elsevier Science, 355–395.

Keeler, E., Spence, M., and Zeckhauser, R. (1971). "The Optimal Control of Pollution," *Journal of Economic Theory*, **4**, 19–34.

Keeling, C. D. (1968). "Carbon Dioxide in Surface Ocean Waters, 4: Global Distribution," *Journal of Geophysical Research*, **73**, 4543–4553.

Keeling, C. D. (1983). "The Global Carbon Cycle: What We Know from Atmospheric, Bio-spheric, and Oceanic Observations," *Proceedings of Carbon Dioxide Research, Science and Consensus*, United States Department of Energy, Washington, DC, II, 3–62.

Keeling, C. D., Bacastow, R. B., Bainbridge, A. E., Ekdahl, Jr., C. A., Guenther, P. R., Waterman, L. S., and Chin, J. F. S. (1976). "Atmospheric Carbon Dioxide Variations at Mauna Loa Observatory, Hawaii," *Tellus*, **28**, 538–551.

Khalil, M. A. K., and Rasmussen, R. A. (1983). "Sources, Sinks, and Seasonal Cycles of Atmospheric Methane," *Journal of Geophysical Research*, **88**, 5131–5144.

Kneese, A. V., Ayres, R. U., and d'Arge, R. C. (1968). *Economics and the Environment: A Materials Balance Approach*, Washington, DC: Resources for the Future.

Komhyr, W. D., Gammon, R. H., Harris, T. B., Waterman, L. S., Conway, T. J., Taylor, W. R., and Thoning, K. W. (1985). "Global Atmospheric CO_2 Distribution and Variations from 1968 to 1982 NOAA/CMCC CO_2 Flask Sample Data," *Journal of Geophysical Research*, **90**, 5567–5596.

Koopmans, T. C. (1965). "On the Concept of Optimum Economic Growth," *Semaine d'Etude sur le Role de l'Analyse Econometrique dans la Formation de Plans de Development*, Pontificae Academemiae Scientiarium Seprita Varia, 225–287.

Krautkraemer, J. A. (1985). "Optimal Growth, Resource Amenities, and the Preservation of Natural Environments," *Review of Economic Studies*, **52**, 153–170.

Kuhn, H. W., and Tucker, A. W. (1951). "Nonlinear Programming," in J. Neyman (ed.), *Proceedings of the Second Berkeley Symposium on Mathematical Statistics and Probability*, Berkeley: University of California Press, 481–492.

Kurz, M. (1994). "Game Theory and Public Economics," in R. J. Aumann and S. Hart (eds.), *Handbook Game Theory* II, Amsterdam: Elsevier Science, 1153–1192.

Larsen, B., and Shah, A. (1992). "Global Tradable Carbon Permits, Participation Incentives, and Transfers," *Oxford Economic Papers*, **29**, 33–62.

Larsen, B., and Shah, A. (1994). "Combating the Greenhouse Effect," *Finance and Development*, **46**, 842–856.

Leggett, J. (ed.). (1990) *Global Warming: The Greenpeace Report*, Oxford, UK: Oxford University Press.

Leontief, W. W. (1947). "A Note on the Interrelation of Subsets of Independent Variables of a Continuous Function with Continuous First Derivatives," *Bulletin of the American Mathematical Society*, **53**, 343–350.

Lerner, J., Matthews, E., and Fung, I. (1988). "Methane Emissions from Animals: A Global High-Resolution Data Base," *Global Biogeochemical Cycles*, **2**, 139–156.

Lind, R. C. (1982a). "A Primer on Major Issues Relating to the Discount Rate for Evaluating National Energy Options," in R. C. Lind, K. J. Arrom, and G. R. Corey (eds.), *Discounting for Time and Risk in Energy Policy*, Baltimore: Johns Hopkins University Press, 275–324.

Lind, R. C. (1982b). "Intergenerational Equity, Discounting, and the Role of Cost–Benefit Analysis in Evaluating Global Climate Policy," *Energy Policy*, **23**, 379–389.

Lindahl, E. (1919). Positive Lösung, die Gerechtigkeit der Besteurung, Lund. Translated in R. A. Musgrave and A. T. Peacock (eds.), *Classics in the Theory of Public Finance*, 1958.

Lloyd, W. F. (1833). "On the Checks to Population," Reprinted in *Managing the Commons*, G. Hardin and J. Baden (eds.), San Francisco: W. H. Freeman, 1977, 8–15.

Lucas, R. E., Jr., and Stokey, N. L. (1984). "Optimal Growth with Many Consumers," *Journal of Economic Theory*, **32**, 139–171.

Mäler, K.-G. (1974). *Environmental Economics: A Theoretical Inquiry*, Baltimore: Johns Hopkins University Press.

Mäler, K.-G., and Uzawa, H. (1994). "Tradable Emission Permits, Pareto Optimality, and Lindahl Equilibrium," The Beijer Institute Discussion Paper Series.

Malinvaud, E. (1971). "A Planning Approach to the Public Goods Problem," *Swedish Journal of Economics*, **11**, 96–112.

Manne, A., Mendelsohm, R., and Richels, R. (1995). "MERGE: A Model for Evaluating Regional and Global Effects of GHG Reduction Policies," *Energy Policy*, **23**, 17–34.

Manne, A., and Richels, R. (1992). *Buying Greenhouse Insurance: The Economic Costs of CO_2 Emission Limits*, Cambridge, MA: MIT Press.

Markusen, J. R. (1975a). "International externalities and optimal tax structures," *Journal of International Economics*, **5**, 15–29.

Markusen, J. R. (1975b). "Cooperative control of international pollution and common property resources," *Quarterly Journal of Economics*, **89**, 618–632.

Marland, G. (1988). *The Prospect of Solving the CO_2 Problem through Global Reforestation*, United States Department of Energy, Washington, DC.

Mas-Colell, A. (1980). "Efficiency and Decentralization in the Pure Theory of Public Goods," *Quarterly Journal of Economics,* **94**, 625–641.

Mas-Colell, A. (1985). *The Theory of General Economic Equilibrium: A Differentiable Approach*, New York: Cambridge University Press.

McCay, B. J., and Acheson, J. M. (1987). *The Question of the Commons: The Culture and Economy of Communal Resources*, eds., Tucson: The University of Arizona Press.

McKenzie, G. W. (1983). *Managing Economic Welfare: New Methods*, New York: Cambridge University Press.

Mendelsohm, R., Nordhaus, W., and Shaw, D. (1994). "The Impact of Climate Change on Agriculture: A Ricardian Analysis," *American Economic Review*, **84**, 753–771.

Menger, C. (1871). *Grundsätze der Volkswirtschaftslehre*, Vienna: Wilhelm Barunmüller. Translated by J. Dingwell and B. Hoselitz, *Principles of Economics*, Glencoe IL: Free Press, 1950.

Mill, J. S. (1848). *Principles of Political Economy with Some of Their Applications to Social Philosophy*, New York, D. Appleton [5th edition, 1899].

Milleron, J.-C. (1972). "The Theory of Value with Public Goods: A Survey Article," *Journal of Economic Theory*, **5**, 419–477.

Musu, I. (1990). "A Note on Optimal Accumulation and the Control of Environmental Quality," *Revista Internationale di Scienze Economiche et Commerciali*, **37**, 193–202.

Musu, I. (1994). "On Sustainable Endogenous Growth," ENI Enrico Mattei Working Paper Series.

Myers, N. (1988). "Tropical Forests and Climate," referred to in United States Environmental Protection Agency, *Policy Options for Stabilizing Global Climate*, Washington, DC, 1989.

Neftel, A., Moor, E., Oeschger, H., and Stauffer, B. (1985). "Evidence from Polar Ice Cores for the Increase in Atmospheric CO_2 in the Past Two Centuries," *Nature*, **315**, 45–47.

Nordhaus, W. (1980). "Thinking about Carbon Dioxide: Theoretical and Empirical Aspects of Optimal Control Strategies," Yale University, Cowles Foundation Discussion Paper, No. 565.

Nordhaus, W. (1982). "How Fast Should We Graze the Global Commons?" *American Economic Review*, **72**, 242–246.

Nordhaus, W. (1993a). "Rolling the 'DICE': An Optimal Transition Path for Controlling Greenhouse Gases," *Resources and Energy Economics*, **15**, 27–50.

Nordhaus, W. D. (1993b). "Reflections on the Economics of Climate Change," *Journal of Economic Perspectives*, **7**, 11–25.

Norgaard, R. B. (1990a). "Economic Indicators of Resource Scarcity: A Critical Essay," *Journal of Environmental Economics and Management*, **19**, 19–25.

Norgaard, R. B. (1990b). Sustainability and the Economics of Assuring Assets for Future Generations, WPS 832, Washington, DC: World Bank.

Norton, B. G. (1989). "Intergenerational Equity and Environmental Decisions: A Model Using Rawls's Veil of Ignorance," *Ecological Economics*, **1**, 137–159.

Pearce, D. (1991). "The Role of a Carbon Tax in Adjusting to Global Warming," *Economic Journal*, **101**, 938–948.

Pearman, G. I., and Hyson, P. (1986). "Global Transport and Inter-Reservoir Exchange of Carbon Dioxide with Particular Reference to Stable Isotopic Distributions," *Journal of Atmospheric Chemistry*, **4**, 181–224.

Penrose, T. E. (1959). The Theory of the Growth of the Firm, Oxford, UK: Blackwell.

Pezzey, J. (1992). "Sustainability: An Interdisciplinary Guide," *Environmental Values*, **1**, 321–362.

Pigou, A. C. (1925). *The Economics of Welfare*, London: Macmillan.

Pearce, D. (1991). "The Role of a Carbon Tax in Adjusting to Global Warming," *Economic Journal*, **101**, 938–948.

Poterba, J. M. (1991). "Tax Policy to Combat Global Warming: On Designing a Carbon Tax," in R. Dornbusch and J. M. Poterba (eds.), *Global Warming: Economic Policy Responses*, Cambridge, MA: MIT Press, 71–98.

Ramanathan, V., Cicerone, R. J., Singh, H. B., and Kiehl, J. T. (1985). "Trace Gas Trends and Their Potential Role in Climate Change," *Journal of Geophysical Research*, **90**, 5547–5566.

Ramsey, F. P. (1928). "A Mathematical Theory of Saving," *Economic Journal*, **38**, 543–559.

Randall, A., and Stoll, J. R. (1983). "Existence Value in a Total Valuation Framework," in R. D. Rowe and L. G. Chestnut (eds.), *Managing Air Quality and Scenic Resources at National Parks and Wilderness Areas*, Boulder, CO: Westview Press.

Rawls, J. (1971). *A Theory of Justice*, Cambridge, MA: Harvard University Press.

Rebelo, S. T. (1993). "Transitional Dynamics and Economic Growth in the Neoclassical Model," *American Economic Review*, **83**, 903–931.

Roberts, D. J. (1974). "The Lindahl Solution for Economies with Public Goods," *Journal of Public Economics*, **3**, 23–42.

Roemer, P. M. (1986). "The Rate of Time Preference and Dynamic Economic Analysis," *Journal of Political Economy*, **91**, 611–681.

Rose, A., and Stevens, B. (1993). "The Efficiency and Equity of Marketable Permits for CO_2 Emissions," *Resources and Energy Economics*, **15**, 117–146.

Rosenberg, N. J., Easterling, W. E., Jr., Crosson, P. R., and Damsstadter, J. (eds.). (1989), *Global Warming: Abatement and Assessment*, Washington, DC: Resources for the Future.

Rosenzweig, C., and Parry, M. L. (1994). "The Potential Impact of Climate Change on World Food Supply," *Nature*, **367**, 133–138.

Rotty, R. M. (1987). "Estimates of Seasonal Variations in Fossil Fuel CO_2 Emissions," *Tellus*, **39B**, 184–202.

Samuelson, P. A. (1954). "The Pure Theory of Public Expenditures," *Review of Economics and Statistics*, **37**, 387–389.

Sen, A. K. (1973). *On Economic Inequality*, Oxford, UK: Clarendon Press.

Sen, A. K. (1982). "Approaches to the Choice of Discount Rate for Social Benefit–Cost Analysis," in R. C. Lind, K. J. Arrow, and G. R. Corey (eds.), *Discounting for Time and Risk in Energy Policy*, Baltimore: Johns Hopkins University Press, 325–353.

Sen, A. K., and Williams, B. (1982). *Utilitarianism and Beyond*, edited by B. Williams, Cambridge, UK: Cambridge University Press.

Shapley, L. S. (1967). "On Balanced Sets and Cores," *Naval Research Logistics Quarterly*, **14**, 453–460.

Slater, M. (1950). "Lagrange Multipliers Revisited: A Contribution to Non-Linear Programming," Cowles Commission Discussion Paper, Math. 403.

Smulders, S. (1995). "Entropy, Environment, and Endogenous Economic Growth," *Journal of International Tax and Public Finance*, **2**, 317–338.

Smulders, S., and Gradus, R. (1996). "Pollution Abatement and Long-Term Growth," *European Journal of Political Economy*, **12**, 505–532.

Solow, R. M. (1974a). "Intergenerational Equity and Exhaustible Resources," *Review of Economic Studies*, **41**, 29–45.

Solow, R. M. (1974b). "The Economics of Resources, or the Resources of Economics," *American Economic Review*, **64**, 1–14.

Srinivasan (1965). "Optimum Saving in a Two-Sector Growth Model," *Econometrica*, **32**, 358–373.

Stiglitz, J. E. (1982). "The Rate of Discount for Cost–Benefit Analysis and the Theory of Second Best," in R. C. Lind, K. J. Arrow, and G. R. Corey (eds.), *Discounting for Time and Risk in Energy Policy*, Baltimore: Johns Hopkins University Press, 151–204.

Stiglitz, J. E., and Dasgupta, P. (1971). "Differential Taxation, Public Goods, and Economic Efficiency," *Review of Economic Studies*, **37**, 151–174.

Stockfish, J. A. (1982). "Measuring the Social Rate of Return on Private Investment," in R. C. Lind, K. J. Arrow, and G. R. Corey (eds.), *Discounting for Time and Risk in Energy Policy*, Baltimore: Johns Hopkins University Press, 257–271.

Strotz, R. H. (1957). "The Empirical Implications of a Utility Tree," *Econometrica*, **25**, 269–280.

Tahvonen, O., and Kuuluvainen, J. (1993). "Economic Growth, Pollution, and Renewable Resources," *Journal of Environmental Economics and Management*, **24**, 101–118.

Takahashi, T., Broeker, W. S., Werner, S. R., and Bainbridge, A. E. (1980). "Carbonate Chemistry of the Surface Waters of the World Oceans," in E. Goldberg, Y. Horibe, and K. Saruhashi (eds.), *Isotope Marine Chemistry*, Tokyo: Uchida Rokkakubo, 291–326.

Tietenberg, T. (1985). *Emissions Trading: An Exercise in Reforming Pollution Policy*, Washington, DC: Resources for the Future.

Tietenberg, T. (1992). "Relevant Evidence with Tradable Entitlements," in R. Dornbusch and J. M. Poterba (eds.), *Combating Global Warming:Study on a Global System of Tradable Carbon Emission Entitlements*, Cambridge, MA: MIT Press, 233–263.

Uzawa, H. (1961). "On the Stability of Dynamic Processes," *Econometrica*, **29**, 617–631.

Uzawa, H. (1964). "Optimal Growth in a Two-Sector Model of Capital Accumulation," *Review of Economic Studies*, **31**, 1–24.

Uzawa, H. (1968). "The Penrose Effect and Optimum Growth," *Economic Studies Quarterly*, **19**, 1–14.

Uzawa, H. (1969). "Time Preference and the Penrose Effect in a Two-Class Model of Economic Growth," *Journal of Political Economy*, **77**, 628–652.

Uzawa, H. (1974a). "Sur la théorie économique de capital collectif social," *Cahier du Séminaire d' Économetrie*, 103–122. Translated in *Preference, Production, and Capital: Selected Papers of Hirofumi Uzawa*, New York: Cambridge University Press, 1988, 340–362.

Uzawa, H. (1974b). "The Optimum Management of Social Overhead Capital," in J. Rothenberg and I. G. Heggie (eds.), *The Management of Water Quality and the Environment*, London: Macmillan, 3–17.

Uzawa, H. (1974c). *Social Costs of the Automobile* (in Japanese), Tokyo, Iwanami Shoten.

Uzawa, H. (1975). "Optimum Investment in Social Overhead Capital," in E. S. Mills (ed.), *Economic Analysis of Environmental Problem*, New York: Columbia University Press, 9–26.

Uzawa, H. (1982). "Social Stability and Collective Public Consumption," in R. C. O. Matthews and G. B. Stafford (eds.), *The Grants Economy and Public Consumption*, London: Macmillan, 23–37.

Uzawa, H. (1991). "Global Warming Initiatives: The Pacific Rim," in R. Dornbusch and J. M. Poterba (eds.), *Global Warming: Economic Policy Responses*, Cambridge, MA: MIT Press, 275–324.

Uzawa, H. (1992a). "Imputed Prices of Greenhouse Gases and Land Forests," *Renewable Energy*, **3**, 499–511.

Uzawa, H. (1992b). "The Tragedy of the Commons and the Theory of Social Overhead Capital," *The Beijer Discussion Paper Series*.

Uzawa, H. (1993). "Equity and Evaluation of Environmental Degradation," in D. Ghai and D. Westendorff (eds.), *Monitoring Social Development in the 1990s: Data Constraint, Concerns, and Priorities*, Avebury, UK: Aldershot.

Uzawa, H. (1995). "Global Warming and the International Fund for Atmospheric Stabilization," in *Equity and Social Considerations Related to Climate Change, Proceedings of IPCC WG III Workshop*, Nairobi 1994, Nairobi: ICIPE Science Press, 49–54.

Uzawa, H. (1996). "An Endogenous Rate of Time Preference, the Penrose Effect, and Dynamic Optimality of Environmental Quality," *Proceedings of the National Academy of Sciences of the United States of America*, Vol. 93, June 1996, pp. 5770–5776.

Uzawa, H. (1997). "Lindahl Equilibrium and the Core of an Economy Involving Public Goods," The Beijer Institute Discussion Paper Series.
Uzawa, H. (1998). "Toward a General Theory of Social Overhead Capital," in G. Chichilnsky (ed.), *Markets, Information, and Uncertainty*, New York: Cambridge University Press, 253–304.
Uzawa, H. (1999). "Global Warming as a Cooperative Game," *Environmental Economics and Policy Studies*, **2**, 1–37.
Veblen, T. B. (1899). *The Theory of Leisure Class*, New York: Macmillan.
Victor, D. G. (1991). "Limits of Market-Based Strategies for Slowing Global Warming: The Case of Tradable Permits," *Policy Sciences*, **24**, 199–222.
Wallace, L. (1993). "Discounting Our Descendants," *Finance and Development*, **30**, 2.
Warr, P. G. (1983). "The Private Provision of a Public Good is Independent of the Distribution of Income," *Economics Letters*, **13**, 207–211.
Weitzman, M. L. (1993). "On the Environmental Discount Rate," *Journal of Environmental Economics and Management*, **26**, 200–209.
Weyant, J. P. (1993). "Costs of Reducing Global Carbon Emissions," *Journal of Economic Perspectives*, **7**, 27–46.
Whally, J., and Wigle, R. (1991). "The International Incidence of Global Warming," in R. Dornbusch and J. M. Poterba (eds.), *Global Warming: Economic Policy Responses*, Cambridge, MA: MIT Press, 233–263.
Woodwell, G. W., and Houghton, R. A. (1977). "Biotic Influences on the World Carbon Budget," in W. Stumn (ed.), *Global Chemical Cycles and Their Alternation by Man*, Berlin: Dahlern Konferenzen, 61–72.
World Bank. (1999). *World Development Indicators*, New York: Oxford University Press.
World Resources Institute. (1991). *World Resources 1990–91*, New York: Oxford University Press.
World Resources Institute. (1996). *World Resources 1996–97*, New York: Oxford University Press.

Index

Printed in the United States
by Baker & Taylor Publisher Services